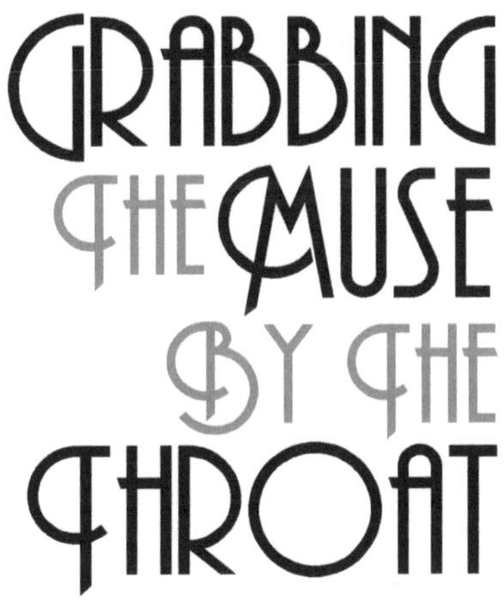

A Year of Creative Challenges

Wendy Barrett

Published by Banksia Lane Press
PO Box 2111
Marmion WA 6020
Australia
First published in Australia by Banksia Lane Press 2015

Author's Note: Some names have been changed
throughout this book

Cover illustration © Wendy Barrett
Cover typography and digital formatting: Sunbeam Books

National Library of Australia
Cataloguing-in-Publication entry:

Creator: Barrett, Wendy, author.

Title: Grabbing the muse by the throat : a year of creative challenges / Wendy Barrett.

ISBN: 9780994366009 (paperback)

Subjects: Barrett, Wendy.
Women artists–Western Australia–Perth–Biography
Inspiration–Creative ability–Painting–Writing
Self-realization–Obsessive-compulsive disorder

Dewey Number: 700.92

Ah, the muse! She is an enigmatic creature whose origins trace back to ancient Greek mythology where epic poems and stories told of nine muses. These sister goddesses; daughters of Zeus and Mnemosyne, embodied the arts and sciences and inspired the mortals within those fields.

The *muse* in modern usage has become the singular and is synonymous with inspiration in the form of a goddess or a mortal. Or, it can simply be another word for inspiration itself, speaking of its unfathomable profundity. Being that the very emotion, or act, of inspiration can appear to come from the divine itself, it is no wonder that we have personified the invocation of it in the form of a visiting goddess. So too, a person can be considered a muse by another who finds that person inspires them to great works. We often hear mention of famous artists whose friends or lovers personify the muse.

I rather like the idea that inspiration in its pure and inscrutable form comes on the wings of a fickle but benevolent goddess.

To Mum and Dad

*Thank you for engendering a creative spirit
in my heart from my very first breath*

CONTENTS

INTRODUCTION

"Then indecision brings its own delays and days are lost lamenting over lost days... What you can do or think you can do, begin it. For boldness has genius, power and magic in it."

Wolfgang von Goethe (John Anster's paraphrased translation from Faust)

December 2011

I was running around like a mad thing at the local shops buying groceries and Christmas crackers. It was a frenzy of people – all sharp elbows and hunted looks – scrabbling to get the Christmas fare before stocks ran out. I wondered what had possessed us to have friends over for dinner the night before Christmas. Having had a reprieve this year from hosting the big day, here I was anyway, in the thick of the stressful Christmas scrum.

As I flashed past the health food shop on my way back to the car, something made me grab one of their free magazines. Later that night, while flicking through it in bed, I happened upon an article about an art challenge. A school community in the outer suburbs was inviting artists to create 30 works of art in 30 days. The artists would each be provided with 30 small canvasses and were free to assign 30 consecutive days of their choosing to the project. Sales of the work would go towards raising funds for the school. Not for a nanosecond did I consider applying. It was years since I'd done any painting, and besides, who on earth would have time for such a commitment? I did find the concept quite intriguing though.

The next few days were spent in a haze of festive activity and overindulgence, so it was a surprise to discover that the art challenge idea continued to rattle around in the further reaches of my mind. Despite having no interest in participating, there was something about the concept that really caught my imagination. Maybe a challenge of some sort would be just the kick-start I needed to begin painting again. For years I'd wanted to get back into painting with acrylics, but somehow was never able to break through the barrier of inertia to make a start. I'd done the occasional painting over the years; experimenting with various media, but often four or five years would pass between each work. I'd been told that to become a successful painter you must meet just two criteria: have a distinctive style and be prolific. At the sluggish rate I was amassing my body of work I'd need to live for a *very* long time – a few more centuries at least for any chance of becoming a successful painter.

A few days on and with the festive melee behind us, I found myself hatching a plan while lying in bed one night. I decided I could modify the details of the challenge and use it as a tool to get painting again. Instead of 30 paintings in 30 days, I would do 10 paintings in 10 days with the weekend off in the middle. Not very impressive compared to the 30 day challenge maybe, but it felt doable. I started to see the possibilities of undertaking a whole series of challenges that would overhaul my entire creative life. There was no need to restrict them to painting, they could also include illustration and writing, and any other sort of challenge for that matter – the possibilities were endless.

Due to the incessant stream of rampaging ideas, and because of the overlarge slice of cheesecake I'd eaten just before bed, it was difficult to fall asleep. I tried to still my mind so I could drift off. I don't know if it was due to the stillness, or to the sugar rush, but suddenly an idea popped into my head: I would make these challenges span a whole year – and I would write a book about it.

It had been many years since I'd eagerly engaged in the optimistic ritual of writing out New Year's resolutions for the sparkling new year ahead. After too many instances of the resolutions going down the toilet by lunchtime on January 1, I'd become too world-weary to believe in the Resolution Fairy anymore. Now, with this challenge idea swizzling around in my head, there was a return of the puppy-like excitement of believing I might actually have it in me to make real changes in my life. I was ripe for a shift in the way I approached things. No longer would I always do what I'd always done and always get what I'd always got. I wanted to end the frustration I felt at never fully achieving the rich creative life I knew was inside me just trying to claw its way out.

To be fair to myself, there was more to my "failure to launch" over the years than simply a lack of willpower. From my early twenties onwards I'd been plagued with health issues that made life very hard at times. I had a long history of trying to climb the mountain of various endeavours only to be kicked in the head with bad health when I got within a handhold of the summit. After getting pushed off the mountain too many times, I got to a point when I didn't even bother to put on my hiking boots anymore. But now, here I was with peri-menopause upon me, ushering in some unlikely improvements both physically and mentally. My children were growing up and overall my health appeared to be improving. I could smell a paradigm shift in the air and felt that 2012 could prove to be the year of flowering to my full potential – becoming a fully realised artist/illustrator/writer – or at least somewhere in the vicinity of it. Maybe there was still a chance of reaching the summit after all.

Ever since my teenage years I'd dreamt of making a living from art and writing. I was just sixteen when I sent off my first children's story submission to a publisher. That first tilt at glory never did come to anything, but I did go on to have a few successes over the years. They were very intermittent though, and making a living from them was nowhere on the horizon – or even in the same hemisphere. If I structured this art challenge to my own strengths and weaknesses, it could be the perfect thing to help make my passion prove financially viable.

I was heartily sick of saying to myself – and to others – that one day I hoped to make a living from my art. Did I really want to look my sixteen year old self in the mind's eye and know that all that fire in her belly had come to so much less than her wildest dreams had anticipated? Or face my eighty year old self that could still take vengeance if I settled for my modest achievements to date? I'd always had a pact with my future octogenarian self that she would never have to look back on her life lamenting, "If only…!" left regretting that the potential she'd shown as a mere slip of a girl hadn't been fully explored.

With all these thoughts cavorting through my mind it was no wonder I was having a crisis about turning fifty – even though I still had several years to go. I could hear a little voice inside my head saying, "Wake up and smell the candles!" It felt like time was fast running out. I'd never been one to fear the increasing glare of ever more candles burning on my birthday cakes; the only reason I'd begun to worry about this particular milestone – and prematurely at that – was because I feared I was cutting it fine if I wanted to fit my grand creative career in this side of the grave. So with my salad days many buffet tables ago and the big FIVE OH looming large in my psyche, I resolved to seize the day.

I was going to grab the muse by the throat!

Chapter One

JANUARY

After all my grand intentions, 2012 didn't begin as auspiciously as hoped. A bad start was made by quaffing too many flutes of sparkling Shiraz on New Year's Eve. I'd only had a few glasses but I was a one-pot-screamer at the best of times. So on the first day of the shiny new year, I dragged myself out of bed parched of mouth and heavy of head – and that was the highlight of the day.

The plan was to make a start on getting to the bottom of a menacing pile of paperwork and a load of other jobs that were backlogged from the pre-Christmas madness. I'd hoped to end the day feeling cleansed and ready to initiate some heavy-duty creativity into the new year. That didn't happen, but at least I had resisted crawling back into bed.

It proved very difficult to shoe-horn much of anything creative into January because of all the activities we'd already had in our schedule for the school holidays. Early in the month we went on a beach holiday with friends, and a week or so later my two daughters and I went to Melbourne for eight days of nice, girly time together. The time in-between was taken up with all the packing and unpacking that accompanies holidays, as well as other various appointments and social outings.

All this was undertaken with limited resources as I'd become terribly weakened from anaemia and other issues at the beginning of the year. The anaemia had been diagnosed after a week of frightening heart symptoms that culminated in a trip to the emergency department one night. Owing to my depleted state, I feared that I wouldn't be well enough to go ahead with the trip to Melbourne that had been planned and booked weeks before. But thankfully, I managed to harness just enough energy, and the holiday went ahead.

Whilst holidaying in Melbourne, I was slowly building up a plan of how I would structure the year. Because of the two prearranged holidays, I'd known from the beginning that there wouldn't be time to complete the painting challenge in January. However, having declared it a *year* of challenges, I felt I must try to execute at least one small challenge before the month was over.

The first goal would be to try my hand at writing a travel article once we returned from Melbourne near the end of the month. It was something I'd never attempted before but I had been toying with the idea for some time. As an optional extra, I also intended to thoroughly spring-clean my art space in readiness for the challenges ahead – I am lucky enough to have a room of my own in which to write and paint.

Due to January unfolding at a frenetic pace, and with my dodgy state of health, I'd barely made a dent in the clutter in my art room. Having returned from Melbourne in the late afternoon of the 27th of January, it left just four days to find out if I was capable of squeezing an article out on time.

As the last few days of the month hove into view and with the fatigue all-consuming, I began to feel less optimistic about my big plans. I feared I'd be forced to concede defeat on the January challenge and start in February, which was a depressing thought. It would make for a shaky start to the project if I fell through on the very first commitment. But somehow on the evening of the 29th, no doubt fuelled in part by the fear of failing on the first challenge, I managed to rear up and make a start on the article.

CHALLENGE #1 – Write a travel article. Submit a 1,000 word article about Melbourne for publication. Publication not essential for the successful completion of the challenge.

Before embarking on our trip to Melbourne, I'd rung *The West Australian* to ask if they accepted freelance articles and if so what word count would be required. I was excited to find myself speaking to the travel editor himself and thankfully my travel writing credentials weren't questioned. Upon hearing the angle I intended to focus on, he said to call him on my return. He let me know that the paper didn't take a great deal of freelance work, but our conversation was encouraging nonetheless. It motivated me to take notes and to keep a wider audience in mind when taking photos while we were away.

Being entirely unfamiliar with the travel writing genre, I read through one of the newspaper's recent travel supplements to get a feel for the format and style of their articles before putting pen to paper. The next couple of days were spent constructing and honing my piece, and I finished it right on the knocker – the 31st January. When I rang the editor the following day he was just about to embark on a work-trip to some exotic location. He said to email it to him on the 13th Feb, as he'd be back at his desk by then and would have time to look at it.

Over the years, I'd had a long history of pitching creative ideas to various establishments only to be met with a brick wall from the earliest points of enquiry, so it was exciting to get this far so quickly. Trying to get work published in any arena was known to be notoriously difficult. Being aware of the difficulties is what stopped me from making publication necessary for fulfilling this particular challenge. Completing and submitting the article was within my control, but the outcome wasn't. It could be self-defeating to make the stakes too high right from the beginning

By completing the article, my first challenge was fulfilled. *If* the article went on to be published then that would be a bonus. It was fantastic to be off and running.

Chapter Two

FEBRUARY

By the 3rd of February I was becoming concerned that I had yet to make a start on my painting challenge. A lot had been happening over the last few days with my eldest daughter Olivia enrolling in her first year of university and my youngest daughter Lola starting back at high school. Still well entrenched in my regular habits of inefficiency, I continued to find it difficult to carve out time in the day to fit in my creative stuff. But that's what this year was all about: shaking myself into action by banishing the demons of procrastination and bad time-management – amongst other things.

Despite being a stay-at-home mum, there never seemed to be huge slabs of time at my disposal for doing the things I wanted to do. I knew there was more time hiding in the cracks of my life, I just had to improve my health and manage my time more efficiently to be able to access it. Hopefully, with my new approach to things, I would soon be joining the happy ranks of normal energy-levelled people. I really appreciated that my husband Kevin supported me in following my creative dream, but I didn't feel I could indulge these dreams forever unless they could generate an income. I intended to put my all into it.

February rattled along briskly while I struggled to get my act together, and the challenges waited patiently in the wings. Before making a start on the painting challenge, I was trying to manhandle some order into the house and get my art room tidied up; otherwise my mental state wouldn't be conducive to make the most of it. I always felt happier and was able to think more clearly when the house was humming with at least some vestige of efficiency.

For the first week of the month my schedule was jam packed with running the kids around and catching up on long languishing odd-jobs – as well as meeting up with family and friends. All the while I continued to contend with the hormonal difficulties that can accompany peri-menopause. With the relentless and dreadfully heavy toll on my iron stores, I began to fear I might need surgical intervention. However, through it all I managed to whittle away at the mess in my art room and spend time fine-tuning my plans for the challenges. My ideas twisted and turned and contradicted themselves, but the 10 day painting challenge remained intact and was to be the first off the blocks.

It was fitting that the first major challenge should be the 10 paintings in 10 days, owing to it being the idea that sparked off the whole enterprise in the first place. It would also be fitting to end the year with another 10 day painting challenge. Perhaps several painting stints could be scattered throughout the year in-between all the other challenges. The challenges could vary to include such things as trying a new recipe every day and even knocking off a to-do list of odd jobs that had long been neglected. The format could also be used for improving my health and fitness – the possibilities were endless. I decided that each challenge would have a two week duration, and in-between each challenge would be a free week whereby I could catch up with friends and family and attend to other jobs.

Finally the clouds parted, the sun shone, and the planets aligned. It was time to begin. There was still so much more I could have done in order to be more organised, but it was already nearly half way through the month and I had to draw the line somewhere.

A few weeks before, I had reread the article that first triggered the idea for my year of challenges and was surprised to note that the canvas size the participants were to paint upon was actually very small – only 20.5cms (8 inches) square. I had hoped to use up the neglected canvases that cluttered my art room, but they were rather large by comparison: one being 61cm x 91.5cm (2ft x 3ft). It just showed how removed I was from painting that I thought it would be possible to cover a canvas that size in one day, so I bought a few smaller ones in preparation.

On the weekend prior to beginning the challenge, I spent some time looking through art books and magazines for inspiration, and on Sunday night I spent hours trawling through all my digital photos looking for painting reference for the week ahead. Photos for the Melbourne article were also chosen and ready to be sent as attachments.

It had been around six years since my acrylic paints had last seen any action so I checked to see they hadn't become dried up and crusty from lack of use. Some were a little questionable as the medium had begun to separate from the pigment but mostly they were usable. They'd only ever been used for one painting which I had executed over a six month period, and mainly in class time. I had joined a painting class with the sole purpose of learning how to use acrylics. They proved harder to use than anticipated and I wasn't sure if I liked the medium or not. I reckoned that after I'd done ten paintings I would be in a good position to decide if I wanted to persevere with them or to try a different medium altogether.

I had loved working in oils, having done half a dozen paintings over the course of a few years two decades ago. The texture of the paint was luscious and opulent and I'd loved the way it dried slowly enough to blend easily with other colours. The acrylics seemed to dry as soon as they hit the canvas. But I was resigned to the knowledge that I was unlikely to ever use traditional oils again. Having developed the mental condition – obsessive compulsive disorder (OCD) some time ago, I had become terribly neurotic about chemicals of any sort. I feared that the tiniest trace of anything toxic had the potential to fell people in their tracks. Just the thought of using solvents for cleaning brushes had become untenable to my new and unbalanced way of thinking.

With getting everything in place ready for the big morning, I ended up getting to bed late and it was after 1am when I finally fell asleep. I awoke for the day prematurely at 6am, groggy from the poor night's sleep and still white around the gills from lack of iron. But nothing was going to get in my way today!

I made a fresh vegetable juice and a school lunch, got a load of washing on the line and emailed my travel article to the paper as previously arranged. At 10.30am I rolled up my sleeves and armed myself with a paintbrush. I had set the easel up the night before and chosen a photo to work from. After scouring every kilobyte of my computer's innards the night before and spending hours sifting through the photo files of every snap taken over the past eight years, I ended up choosing one that I'd just taken yesterday. It was a photo of a succulent growing in a pot in my backyard.

CHALLENGE #2 - Complete 10 paintings in 10 days. To be done in two 5 day-in-a-row components with the weekend off in-between. Challenge weeks must be kept free of social outings.

First week of painting challenge

On Monday 13th February, nearly a month and a half into the year and with only one little challenge under my belt, I felt a lot was riding on my ability to wipe the smirk off the blank canvas' face that challenged me from the easel. With the photo of the succulent displayed on the computer just to the right of me, I began by drawing the outline of the plant on to a 30cm x 23cm (12" x 9") stretched cotton canvas.

I misjudged things badly and instead of the plant covering the whole canvas as intended, I ended up with swathes of white background, having begun the drawing on too small a scale. It looked ridiculous, but I pushed on and being mindful of having to finish it in one day soon made a start with the paints.

It was as if I'd never painted before in my life. I'd forgotten everything I'd ever learnt about acrylics and found the going very difficult; particularly when it came to mixing colours. It had never been my forte even when in my most "prolific" era. As I squeezed out random blobs of paint onto my startled palette, recollections of stern words and severe looks from a previous teacher came to mind, "Every self-respecting artist must invest time in mixing up their *own* colour charts if they ever want to master colour." I wholeheartedly agreed with this in theory but had never quite pushed through my sloth to begin such an undertaking. I always just wanted to get straight to the exciting stuff and paint a painting.

I felt a little shame-faced that I'd never put in the hard yards, but rather than try to redeem myself now, I tried to cut corners instead. When shopping for some small canvasses a week or so earlier, I had spotted a book that contained hundreds of paint recipes. It showed which colour to mix with which for every shade imaginable, and into my basket it went. But it wasn't until now as I started on my first painting that it became apparent I had very few of the same tubes of colour the author had used. Well that would learn me! So after my initial feelings of ineptitude, I was rather surprised and thrilled when my concoctions of paint began to develop into colours ever so vaguely near what I was aspiring to.

My intention was to paint in an impressionist style, but that failed immediately. I soldiered on with what seemed like a lost cause, all the while fearing I'd end up with a canvas of unidentifiable splotches. That might have been okay if I'd planned an abstract piece, but I hadn't – and I already had witnesses that knew of my intentions. So pretending it was an abstract was now out of the question. It was only because of my plan to write about these challenges, maybe even accompanied by photographs, that I forced myself to persist past the point where I would normally have declared it a flop and walked away.

Eventually, I was able to wrangle some representational qualities out of it, but still felt embarrassed by the results, so imagine my surprise when Olivia walked in and said, "Wow! I like that!" Upon further reflection she decided it was just okay rather than wow. But that was fine because it also became my own final analysis. It was just passable as a painting. But the challenge for the day had been met, so I was fairly happy with my efforts; particularly after I'd had time to reconcile the actual painting with the one I'd had in my head before I started – and stopped comparing the two.

The remainder of the day was busy with the usual errands relating to kids and house. I stumbled into bed exhausted and got another late night.

On Tuesday I decided to try something simpler. I have always loved hydrangeas and for years had wanted to paint one in an impressionist style. But after yesterday's debacle I dispensed with my hopes of channelling Monet and instead decided to do a more stylised, decorative piece. An illustration of a hydrangea plucked from my art-reference file made for the perfect inspiration.

The painting took a couple of hours to complete and was leagues away from the painterly, Monet-esque hydrangea that had existed in my mind's eye for all those years, but nonetheless, I had met the brief. I was beginning to realise that the paintings would be limited because of having to complete them in just one day.

By Wednesday, I resorted to using my delicate water colour brushes in order to gain more control over the fineness of the work. Having decided to paint one of my favourite china patterns, I brought out a cup, saucer and a jug, set them up near the easel and drew them straight onto the canvas. It was a less exact drawing than I would usually do as the aim was to nail this loosening up style, and I was also trying for 1950s era colours.

It was shaping up well in both form and colour, and it seemed I had hit on a trendy sort of retro style. This was more like it! As the paintbrush flapped across the canvas, my imagination was having a lovely time of it. I pictured myself doing a whole series in the same relaxed style, using the images for a range of greeting cards that would top the greeting card bestseller list for weeks – if such a thing existed. However, as the work progressed, my premature dreams of glory shrivelled on the vine of my imagination. My natural bent had taken over and I kept adding more detail, losing the lovely spontaneous style that had been developing. If I'd had any inkling of what I'd finish up with, I would have done a more accurate drawing in the first place. In the end it was a very amateurish looking painting, but I was pleased with it overall in that the colours had come very close to what I had been aiming for. Every day I gained a little more understanding of the medium, but I still wasn't sure if I liked it.

It was exhilarating to be firmly and successfully entrenched into my week of painting and to finally make good on long held intentions. It was like a miracle of sorts after so many years of broken promises to myself. With my miserable track record, I had begun to think of myself as a one-day-I'm-gonna kind of girl. The constant failures to make good on my word in this department had eventually built up a barrier so impenetrable – so immune to my hollow promises – that I feared I'd never be able to break through it to paint again. And yet, here I was dancing on the grave of that impenetrable barrier, and it was only three days in!

Later in the afternoon an email came through from the travel editor. When I spotted it in my inbox, I had that familiar butterfly-with-a-sledge-hammer sensation that comes with knowing that only a millisecond from now, with a click of a button, I would find out if it was a yes or a no. My brain was busily plumping up the cushions to absorb the blow while simultaneously holding its breath in positive anticipation. In the meantime, my eyes just got on with it and read the email. It was a yes!

I was so thrilled to have it accepted and was amazed at how straight forward it had all been. It was outside my usual experiences of trying to get things published, which more times than not, were decidedly unsuccessful.

This was the first time I'd had validation of my non-fiction writing on a professional level and been offered money for it! The editor said it would be a while before it was published due to a backlog of articles waiting in the wings, and it would also need to be edited due to my overenthusiastic word count.

On Thursday I painted a cartoon style fox which was reminiscent of a 1950s style illustration. Due to it being a simple picture involving flat colours and no detail, I thought I'd have it done in a flash. But attempting fine edges with a thick medium was time-consuming and difficult. I had yet to understand that acrylics couldn't be treated like watercolours and so I'd begun adding water to the pigment in order to get a nice consistency. It diluted the paint to an unsustainable level which made a second coat necessary for a nice matt finish. All this fussing and fiddling made the time stretch out, and in the end the painting took four and a half hours to finish; the longest spent on a painting so far this week.

It had been done at Lola's request as she wanted a picture of a red fox to hang in her bedroom. She loved it, and I too was pleased with the outcome, but in reality, it was more an illustration than a painting. It would have looked better if I'd been able to get the flat colours truly flat.

The week had begun with a fairly set list of subjects that I wanted to tackle. It seemed practical to choose the reference material in the evenings for the following day's painting so I would be all organised and ready to go. But as the week progressed I found that it could end up being a waste of time. The choice of subject wouldn't necessarily resonate with me by morning, so I'd have to sift through my photos and art reference all over again to find something that appealed to me.

Friday was the hardest day to motivate myself. It took longer than usual to choose the subject matter but eventually I decided to sketch a novelty Easter eggcup from life. This time I made the effort to get the detail and perspective right which took about half an hour. The intention was to paint in a realistic manner rather than try for the elusive impressionistic style, but I ran out of steam before I even began working in paint. Instead, I just used flat colour and didn't bother with a background. It was all finished within one and a half hours. It was a poor outcome, but on the other hand, it was a triumph to attempt anything at all in the face of all-consuming exhaustion. I had successfully completed the first half of my challenge. Thank goodness I had allowed myself a break over the weekend!

It had been an exhausting week and the return of heart palpitations reminded me that the anaemia had yet to resolve itself. Adding several hours of intensive painting time to my usual commitments for the day was taking its toll physically – but certainly not mentally.

Since committing to the challenges it was as if I'd entered a rarefied realm where anything was possible. I was beginning to experience the genius, power and magic that Goethe spoke of when one is bold and commits to something. The excitement and the extraordinary atmosphere that had been brewing during the week had grown deeper once I discovered my article had been accepted.

That night in the glow of my success – and the computer screen – I thought I'd take a cruise around the internet to see if there were other people out there engaged in similar challenges, and if so, what approach they had taken. I Googled "30 day art challenges" and found thin offerings in the form of just a couple of blogs and sites. One person had done abstract pieces every day that to my eye spoke only of the destination rather than a journey of growth or discovery: each painting looked like it had been churned out in ten minutes flat. It reiterated to me what I wanted to avoid. I didn't find much to inspire me in that little sortie into cyberspace.

Even though I'd only been painting for five days, I was becoming a tad more accustomed to the vagaries of the medium and was really pleased that I'd had the discipline to complete the first half of my goal. To be painting at all felt astonishing, let alone five days in a row. But I'd be careful this coming week to avoid a similar pattern to the last whereby it had declined into pumping something out for the sake of it. I didn't want to end up with more half-hearted pieces like today's eggcup – with no real merit other than to be able to say I'd done one a day. Although of course, doing one a day was critical to the whole concept of the challenge, but at the same time, I wanted to stretch myself as an artist in both skills and productivity. The whole idea behind the challenge was to initiate lasting improvements in my creative life.

It seemed clearer now as to exactly what it was I was trying to achieve in the ten days of painting. So I decided to devote the second half of the challenge to doing what I'd originally envisaged. I'd paint the subjects that had been rattling around in my head for years and be careful to avoid straying into illustration.

Illustration was something that I hadn't lost touch with over the decades so it didn't need quite the same attention in the motivation department. Later in the year I hoped to do some illustration challenges using watercolour and ink which were my usual choice of medium. I didn't want this painting challenge to be a case of doing similar subject matter to my illustrations but simply changing the medium and the materials.

I dearly wanted to be an accomplished painter and to learn to loosen my style. I wanted to emulate the impressionists. I wanted to be amazing! In the weekend leading up to the first week of challenges, I had spent ages reading up about painting techniques and styles and felt I was imbibing helpful knowledge that would simply pour forth upon my canvas once setting paintbrush to paint. Ha! That didn't happen!

The main difficulty of the week had been pushing through the fatigue, but my emotional state was a very different matter; I was on a creative high. It had been a magically thrilling week.

Weekend off

Over the weekend there wasn't much rest to be had due to all the usual running around and domestic obligations. On Sunday, I began preparing for the week ahead and decided to revisit the hydrangea idea, but this time I would steer clear of stylising it. I Googled images of painted hydrangeas to get some insight into how others had approached the subject. It was while doing this that I happened upon a website called *dailypaintworks.com*

It was boggling to discover a whole world of artists out there who were painting *every* day – or if not every day, then most days. These paintings were of an excellent quality and I was in awe. It made my 10 day challenge look rather pathetic by comparison, but it gave me far greater insight into what I could be trying to achieve. It was fascinating to see that many of the daily painters were using very small canvasses of around 15 centimetres (6 inches) square. I felt like Alice falling through the looking glass: as if I'd happened upon an alternate reality. I guess I had in a way, being that it was in cyberspace.

In the end I skipped the hydrangea as I didn't have a pink one among my reference photos, and trying to translate it from my blue hydrangea photo seemed too difficult. Inspiration was proving to be a skittish beast: it didn't take much to spook it away from a subject that had initially felt promising. Yet again I trawled through my photos for inspiration and found the perfect subject. It was a photo of Olivia eating a gelato while looking over the streets of Venice from our hotel room window where we had stayed in 2010. The photo had been a disappointment at the time, having come out blurry due to the poor light, but I had always loved the composition.

Some time back, I noticed that I sometimes felt a bit hollow after painting faithfully from photos that were already beautiful in themselves. A great photo is already a work of art so why have two works of art identical to each other? Not that they *would* be identical of course, the painting would always be the inferior version of the two with me behind the paintbrush. I found I enjoyed working from photos that hadn't quite turned out right; as in being a little blurry like the Venetian one, or perhaps poorly composed. This allowed me to improve upon rather than fruitlessly try to compete with a photo. Of course, if I was ever able to master a lovely loose, painterly style, my painting would be different enough to justify using the most superior breed of photo as art reference.

On the other hand, if a photo was taken *solely* for the purpose of using as art reference, as many of mine were, it didn't matter if it was beautiful in its own right or not. It wouldn't have existed at all otherwise. It was created as a means of transferring a beautiful real-life scene into an original work of art, forever immortalised in paint. Because composition plays such a pivotal role in a work of art, I prefer to paint from the photos I have taken myself.

Second week of painting challenge

On Monday I spent over six hours on the Venetian painting. I began it in the morning and finished working on it at 7pm. There had been many interruptions in-between with school runs and such-like. The beginning was like pulling teeth, but towards the end I felt a shift of energy. Suddenly my whole style loosened up and I was in the creative flow. This state of flow showed in the painting. Several people later pointed out the bit they loved the most which was where I had felt the flow in action. It was very interesting and exciting to experience it. I was thrilled with the results as finally I had a painting that fulfilled my internal brief on what I had wanted to get out of the challenge.

There was no way I'd be able to cope with doing a six hour painting every day though, particularly if I wanted the household to still be functioning; or myself for that matter! Now that I had discovered the painting blogs, I was addicted. I surfed around endless different sites sucking inspiration from every lovely picture I saw. Many of the artists painted still life and that was something I'd been itching to explore for many years. I love paintings of not only pretty things but also everyday things that might not immediately scream "art". It's wonderful how a painting can draw attention to the ordinary, like a plain piece of cutlery or a root vegetable, and render the mundane into magic; not just with a still life but with landscapes and urban scenes too – anything at all.

I decided that a little still life would be the way to go tomorrow.

Sleep eluded me again until the wee hours. I was hideously sleep deprived but my body was running on inspiration and enthusiasm. In amongst a hectic morning of domestic chores I got as far as setting up the still life – a wild geranium flower in a tiny green bottle – and I had just enough time to draw in the basic outline before dashing out to run more errands. It was after 1pm by the time I finally got a chance to begin painting. All the while, I could hear the clock ticking loudly in my psyche – I didn't want to fall down and miss a day.

I painted for one and a half hours and was quite pleased with the glass effect, but I spoilt it by adding an absurd background. But as always, it was a productive session and if I'd learnt anything it was to resist over-working things. I had messed up my signature, and when trying to fix it I damaged the background. It all went awry from there, but I had no time to reflect upon it as I had to dash off to get Lola to a dental appointment.

On Wednesday, once the dust had settled on the morning rush, I visited the *Daily Paintworks* website for inspiration. Each day I found myself attracted to a different subject. Initially, I thought I'd do another still life but in the end I felt enthused to do a landscape. Suddenly the perfect photo popped into my head. I had taken it while holidaying on Rottnest Island over five years ago with the intention of painting from it some day.

So many of the photos I took over the years were taken in the hope that I would create a painting from them some time in the near future. It was amazing how I had continued to amass so much photo reference in the face of never using it. So deep down, even as the shutter had whirred and snapped, I'd felt despondently sure this Rottnest scene would inevitably join the one-day-I'm-gonna-paint-this list in my head, which had become so long it snaked through the part of my brain labelled *Yeah right!* A niggle of guilt had assailed me every time I happened upon this photo over the years since taking it. So the realisation that I was about to finally put it into employment felt very gratifying.

It was a photo of a windswept ti-tree on a hill. Every time I saw the tree it reminded me of Vincent van Gogh's *A Wheatfield, with Cypresses* painting. Van Gogh's painting had always been meaningful to me because it channelled a certain place on the farm where I lived as a child, evoking lovely memories. My sister also felt a strong connection with van Gogh's painting for the same reason, although this Rottnest tree didn't call his painting to her mind as it did to mine.

There was some running around to do on Olivia's behalf later in the day so I thought it would force me to be *really* quick with the painting. I was going to create an impressionist masterpiece in one hour flat! Of course that didn't happen, and one hour in it looked more like a paint-spill than a tribute to a cypress bedecked wheat field. After a while it began to show promise, but I had to tear myself away, zombie like, to run my errands. Even while putting my car tyre in for repair and picking up and dropping off children I remained in the thrall of the creative flow and was all but popping out of my skin to return to the painting.

I was delighted with the finished product. I had slipped into a looser style and was in awe that I could complete a fairly detailed painting like this in just one day: it had taken around four hours in three sittings. Driving the girls around really took the guts out of the day, so I was pleased to be able to squeeze the painting in. I would always have this painting now and no one would ever remember that I neglected the washing and ironing. It was a disturbing insight into how much time I had wasted over the years on days such as this one where running around on several separate errands effectively fractured the day into small pieces.

Usually, on these messy chopped up kind of days I felt unsettled due to knowing that I was about to have to go out again soon. Because it seemed there wasn't enough time to make a start on anything substantial, I'd fritter the day away on odd jobs or waste it entirely by procrastinating. While in my creative thrall today I was 100% present: every second leading up to and after each outing was used up and squeezed dry – how rare and joyous that felt. It was true engagement with life.

Throughout my life; since adulthood at least, I had only occasionally felt the lovely fluidity of a day where one activity seamlessly flows into another. I imagined life was often like this for many people and wondered why I made things so difficult for myself. To now discover it was possible to create a whole painting on a day such as this was a gob-smacking revelation. I felt the genius, power and magic in it.

On Thursday I painted a tea strainer from life. Then on Friday, the last day of my challenge, I set up a still life of a mug and a cut lemon. I was reasonably happy with both of these little paintings. After finishing the tenth and final painting, I was too exhausted to savour my achievement and could only manage a lacklustre mental high five to myself. It wasn't until the next day after a night's sleep that I was properly able to appreciate what I had done.

It had been a real challenge having to stare down a glaringly blank canvas each morning. It took a substantial act of will to make the first mark. Ten paintings in ten days didn't sound much in the face of those amazing creatures who painted daily, but I'd had to start somewhere. It was a vast improvement on my one painting every half decade. The challenge format had proved to be a roaring success in finally getting me to paint again. In the past I had relied on making sweeping statements like, "This year I'm going to get back into painting," or "Once the girls are back at school again I'm going to begin painting." I guess these kinds of proclamations never worked because they were too vague and left the way wide open for weaselling out of. The challenge format was akin to writing an oath in blood. The underlying intention to write a book about my journey also contributed to the commitment feeling inviolable. In addition, I had told friends and family about my plan in order to put extra pressure on myself which also proved very effective.

Over the weekend I basked in my success and spent some time evaluating the outcomes of the painting challenge. The second week had been a dazzling triumph compared to the first, whereby I'd lost sight of my original intentions. The Venetian painting at the beginning of the second week had entirely turned things around, reassuring me of the value of the challenge, and putting me on my way to discovering if acrylics, or even painting in general, was still something I wanted to pursue.

Happening upon the network of painters' blogs was also a major turning point and a great source of inspiration. It was hugely motivating to discover so many artists out there painting in styles that I aspired to. Many were very generous on their blogs, offering information and insights into the ways in which they approached their work. It was hard not to feel a little daunted though in the face of the staggering talent some of these bloggers possessed. My abilities appeared rather bony in comparison. But just knowing all those artists were out there in an online community, somehow made me feel there was a clear way to progress. I found myself thinking about the value of setting up my own blog at some point, once I knew what I was doing.

I had felt Goethe's "magic" in the first week – and by the second week I was living in Henry David Thoreau's "uncommon hours":–

"If one advances confidently in the direction of one's dreams, and endeavours to live the life which one has imagined, one will meet with a success unexpected in common hours."

Thankfully, basking in my achievements didn't use up much energy as I was already too depleted and listless to do anything beyond the necessities over the weekend. I'd intended to continue tidying up my art room from where I'd left off the other week, but that didn't happen. Neither did I feel up to making a solid plan for my next challenge. I hoped to still have enough of a pulse to make the most of my "down" week. I'd been horrendously tired every day throughout the two weeks of painting, but the challenge had made me push on. Normally, I would have caved in to such levels of fatigue. The fact that I hadn't this time clearly showed that an act of commitment was a powerful tool not only for motivation but also for bestowing more energy.

However, it must have been borrowed energy as it was nowhere to be found now. In the face of my overwhelming tiredness I resolved that I would use the challenge tool to get my act together with my atrocious sleeping habits. I dared to hope it would work. All my life I'd been trying to orchestrate better routines of retire. Bribery and torture had never worked, so I would put "the challenge" to the test.

An enormous amount had been learnt this past fortnight. While originally seeing it only as a 10 day challenge to be repeated several times throughout the year, I now felt inspired to find a way to keep painting more regularly. It wasn't practical to continue painting every day, because other areas of my life had begun to slide while I dedicated myself to the challenge. However, the thought of not painting again for who-knew-how-long left me feeling bereft. Even though I'd earmarked the following week as downtime – to be spent focusing on other jobs and catching up with people – I resolved to fit another painting in sometime during the week. Having begun to build up my painting muscles, I was reluctant to let them simply wither away. It dawned on me that it would be quite possible to challenge myself to do one painting a week for the *whole* year. This big-picture challenge could run concurrently with my shorter more intensive challenges.

Over the years, I had practically resigned myself to the belief that I would never be a significantly accomplished painter. My painting habits were so terribly intermittent and it seemed to me that most highly skilled painters were single-minded in their craft. They probably didn't dilute their output by trying to specialise in more than one creative endeavour at a time; hence their success and ability to make a living from it.

Throughout my life I'd been very passionate about so many different things: writing, painting and illustration to name a few. Within each discipline my interests diversified even further. When it came to illustration I'd be torn between focusing on greeting card designs and children's picture book illustrations. Within painting I loved *everything*: still life, botanicals, landscape, and portraiture – and had yet to even settle on a medium! Spreading myself so thin had always been my downfall.

Even while deeply embroiled in one creative pursuit, I would at the same moment be pining to spend time on one of the other passions in my life; particularly when I was in the all-consuming, fevered throes of writing a book. But I tried to subjugate the other creative ideas that jostled around in my mind, believing they must be put on hold until I had completely finished the manuscript – otherwise the creative flow would be diluted.

There were other interests in my life that also clamoured for attention. These included my passion for gardening, which admittedly was lying rather dormant at the moment; reading, which I usually managed to fit in around everything else, and also a love of needlework – the most sidelined of all my interests over the past two decades.

Illustration was one field in which I'd seen noticeable improvements over the years, having devoted a lot more time to it – albeit still too little overall. In recent years I had poured most of my creative energy into writing. Even when not writing books, I was writing emails to friends or keeping a journal, so at least one creative muscle was rather buff at the moment. I wish I could've said the same for my real muscles, but alas, they were the most severely neglected of all. Maybe the challenges could see to them as well.

I dreamt of a life where I could regularly include all these interests and still have time to eat. Hopefully, this year of challenges would allow me to incorporate regular sessions of everything I loved to do and thereby achieve creative balance in my life. Engaging in the various disciplines concurrently would enable me to build on my skills in every arena. It was a very tantalising thought that it might be possible after all to become an accomplished painter even while pursuing other interests simultaneously.

But what if all these pursuits were meant to be taken up one at a time, one for each lifetime, and I was greedily trying to fit them all into one? I didn't want to wait until I'd scuttled off the mortal coil before finding out whether or not the Universe subscribed to reincarnation, it would be too late by then if it didn't!

Ultimately, I wanted the challenges to lead towards practical ways to make an income from my creativity, and also to help me sustain a balanced life by implementing all my passions and improvements into it on a regular basis.

Down week
Time to be used catching up on jobs and social commitments – and some rest

Having postponed catching up with people for the past two weeks, I already had three social appointments written in my diary for the week ahead. It had been a rare and glorious interlude having two whole weeks inviolate from extra distractions. Naturally, I'd still had the usual non-negotiable house stuff and taxi duties to deal with. Olivia was in the throes of notching up twenty-five hours of supervised driving time in her log book before she could get her driver's license. This entailed many trips accompanying her to the train station, shopping centres and various other destinations in order to ratchet up her hours. I was excited at the thought of her soon-to-come independence, both for her sake and ours.

In my pre-challenge life, I rarely managed to pace my weeks very well. They'd become overcrowded with trying to keep up with people socially in-amongst all my other commitments. This made it quite the feat trying to fit in any art or writing. Before I knew it, whole months would skitter off into the sunset while my back was turned, never to be seen again. Being inefficient with my time wasn't from a lack of trying: there were periods when I tried earmarking certain days of the week as "work" days to keep sacrosanct for my creative time. But many of my friends worked part-time and all had different days off. Because I wasn't officially employed, I was always "free" to catch up.

It often seemed to work out that someone's birthday or special occasion happened to fall on my work days, or a certain friend could only meet on those particular days because they worked on the others. It felt churlish to hold out when I had no hard and fast structure to my weeks – not to mention the fact that I didn't like to miss out on things. But now I would have to engage a different mindset for the less auspicious social occasions.

I am a very social animal by nature and love spending time with family and friends, but equally I need a lot of time in my own company. Finding the balance has been an ongoing lifelong endeavour. I suspect it might always remain so to some degree. It always seems so simple in theory but is difficult to achieve in the harsh glare of reality. However, I was going to give it a try. Doing the strict challenges would give me more structure and the motivation to stick to rigid work times.

Chapter Three

MARCH

YEAR-LONG CHALLENGES
- Weekly painting challenge – do one painting every single week on day of my choice, or over several days if necessary
- Sleeping challenge – must have computer off by 9.30 and lights out by 10.30pm

The sleeping challenge had begun and, to my own amazement, I was dutifully sticking to it. The computer went off by 9.30pm and I had lights out by 10.30pm. I dared to dream I'd be able to continue with it throughout the entire year. If I could keep it up till December it should by then have established itself into a life-long habit and I would no longer have to exert myself to stick to it.

Despite the success of getting to bed earlier, I still lay awake for hours because my body had yet to understand that I really meant business. It didn't lift a finger to stop the mind running feral into the wee hours. I figured it would work it out soon enough if I remained constant with my earlier bedtimes. Rats were also sent to try me, as they chose that week to seek shelter from the vagaries of the outdoors and cavort around in our roof space all night.

To my surprise I was positively itching to do another painting and was pleased I'd decided to implement the weekly painting challenge. On Sunday I set up a simple still life to work from by popping a few iceberg roses into a plain blue jug. Halfway through, the painting showed brief promise but in the end it looked as soulless as artificial grass. I had overworked it and the outcome was dreadfully amateurish. I felt so flat at the result that it made me question if I wanted to establish a weekly painting habit after all. I chastised myself for being so easily disheartened and reminded myself of how much I had been learning with each work regardless of the outcome. It would be silly not to capitalise on the gains. If I reverted to my old habits and didn't paint again for months or, as was more likely the case, years, every gain would be forgotten and wasted: today's efforts would simply be a bad painting rather than an ongoing building of knowledge. How pathetic would I be to give up in the face of one defeat?

My down week was nowhere near as productive as planned owing to the extreme fatigue, but thankfully there were some positive improvements happening on the hormone front that I hoped would enable me to rebuild my iron stores rather than deplete them further. Even in the best of circumstances it takes several months for iron levels to return to normal, so I just had to live with it in the meantime.

In my mid-twenties I had suffered from glandular fever that went on to become chronic fatigue syndrome (CFS). It had never totally gone away, so something like anaemia possibly knocked me around more than it did for the average person. But of course anaemia was very small stuff in the overall scheme of things. It was certainly small stuff compared to what I'd recently been through with my mental health. I was currently having a great run in this department after years of serious struggle. Being well enough mentally to undertake all these challenges felt like a fresh chance at life – a life that had appeared to be over in many ways only months before. I was the proverbial phoenix and I wasn't about to let my feeble ferrous status send me spiralling back down into the ashes.

During the down week, I made good on my arrangements and caught up with the family and a swarm of friends. But due to my rickety state of health, the long list of jobs that had been planned didn't eventuate. The ironing pile got fatter, phone calls to tradesmen didn't transpire and my car remained un-serviced. But I decided on what the next challenge would be starting on Monday.

It would involve trying a new recipe every day. The recipe could be anything from a meal for dinner to baking a cake. Having not been on top of the domestic situation lately it felt like the perfect challenge at this point in time. As usual, I had been relying on tried but true recipes. It required too much energy to attempt anything overly complicated or to think of anything different. So a cooking challenge would in theory extend my repertoire and also keep my focus on home and hearth. Hopefully, it would give me the chance to catch up on household chores which in turn would make life feel less hectic. It was the year to be more organised and less chaotic – to get more "space" as well as creativity into my life.

In theory, I love the idea of being a domestic goddess, but, having not been blessed with the cooking gene, it has never translated into real life. I cook because I have to. I do enjoy it at times: like when making a hearty soup on a cold winter's evening, but mostly it feels like a chore and a dreaded one at that when I've been busy all day. I envy those who love to cook and who find it a relaxing way to unwind at the end of the day. It is a strange thing then that I love visiting kitchen shops and have a weakness for buying stylish kitchenalia.

Pandering to my lacklustre relationship with cooking, I declared the duration of this challenge to be one week rather than two. Focusing exclusively on cooking for five whole days would be quite enough for me. The second challenge week would instead be devoted to addressing the long list of jobs I hadn't attended to at the beginning of the year as hoped. These were jobs that had been hanging over me for ages – some of them for years! Getting to the bottom of the list would help cleanse my psyche and allow the muse to skip freely around the daisy filled meadow of my mind.

CHALLENGE #3 – New recipe challenge
Cook something new for 5 nights within the course of one week

Monday dawned and I began the cooking challenge. For many years I had collected piles of recipes pulled out of magazines that looked interesting and/or easy. I would tuck them away in a file with the intention of whipping them up one day soon, but at some level expecting I'd die of old age first.

This morning I gave the file quite a shock when I plucked it from the shelf and leafed through its contents. It wasn't long before I found a recipe for a Thai Beef Curry which looked rather delicious. I wrote out a shopping list and got on with the day.

It was a busy week. I'd choose a recipe in the morning and then get on with ferrying people around and attending to household jobs. I was making serious inroads on the domestic front, and because I had geared myself up to it, I really enjoyed trying different recipes; most of which turned out very well and were appreciated by all.

Thursday was the day that Olivia began her regular cooking duties. It had been decided that she would cook one night a week when she began university. Somehow, she had managed to postpone it, but Thursday was her day of reckoning. She wrote out the list, I shopped for the ingredients and then she cooked *and* cleaned up the kitchen. Woo hoo! Luxury!

On two of the challenge days I baked cakes. Recently, I'd been pleased to note a revival of interest at the thought of baking. But it had yet to progress beyond a thought, so the challenge was a great way to turn thought into action. I chose simple cake recipes and did all the mixing by hand. The act of creaming the butter and sugar and mixing in the other ingredients proved to be very meditational. It was extremely satisfying watching the batter develop into the perfect consistency. Good exercise for keeping bingo-wings at bay too! Who knew what cheap exercise equipment was to be found in the form of a wooden spoon and a mixing bowl.

Despite being a fan-forced species, our oven cooked very unevenly, so the outcome wasn't as great as it might have been. We'd been trying to hold out with it for another year or so until we committed to an entire kitchen renovation.

My desire to bake was sated after two sessions in one week. The thought of baking more regularly at some point in the future appealed to me, but who knew when that point would be. And even then, having never been keen on fussing with fiddly cooking procedures, it was unlikely that I'd venture further than simple cake recipes. Not for me the tempering of chocolate or mollycoddling of soufflés.

The fifth and final recipe of the challenge was undertaken on Sunday night. Olivia had cooked one night and we'd had plenty of leftovers another night when Kevin was out, so I'd had to stretch it over the weekend to get my five days in. I did my weekly painting on Wednesday where I made a second attempt at the blue jug with roses and added a cut lemon into the mix. It was a pleasing improvement on the first incarnation.

During the cooking challenge, there had been moments of real satisfaction and a sense of achievement, but because I already devoted time to food preparation on a daily basis, it didn't feel like I was forging new adventures in my life in the way I had with the painting challenge and writing the article. I wondered briefly about making a long term challenge of cooking a new recipe once a week, but I knew I'd only let myself down. Maybe I would revisit the idea when I had satiated myself with these other goals.

Most mornings I had been making fresh vegetable juices. The girls and I had been on a health-kick since late last year and were really seeing the benefits of it. There were improvements in our skin from the better fuel and we were much healthier than usual. Junk food had been cut right back – chocolate in particular – and I suspected the removal of sugar from my diet had a lot to do with the improvements in my mental health. I was also having fish oil and nuts, plain Greek yoghurt and herbal teas, and felt all these things were helping to balance my hormones considerably. The girls and I walked on the beach a couple of times a week in the evenings and Lola and I had started attending a weekly Pilates class. In addition to all this, I was taking in more sunshine as safely as possible since discovering a vitamin D deficiency, and having heard that a lack of the vitamin could impact negatively on mental health. Apparently it is coming to light that there is an epidemic of Vitamin D deficiency amongst Australians due to having been *too* rigorous in protecting ourselves from sun damage.

On Sunday after I had cooked my scallops and signed off on my culinary challenge, I wrote up a list of all the jobs that lived under the impression that they were immune from ever getting done. This would be the replacement for the second challenge week instead of doing two weeks of cooking.

I have an exasperating tendency to let jobs mount up simply because the effort to look up a phone number or make a start on cleaning out a cupboard seems like the sort of effort best left for tomorrow when I'd surely feel a little fresher. Of course, tomorrow never comes. Jobs that get postponed week after week weigh heavily on my psyche and yet when I finally rear up and just get on with them – it's so easy as to be ridiculous. So much wasted time and energy. Why? WHY?

A friend had recently been going through a difficult time, so I planned ahead to give myself an exemption from the challenge on Tuesday in order to visit her. It was the only day of the week she wouldn't be working. Keeping my challenge weeks and down weeks rigidly separate was supposed to be strictly observed, but it seemed eminently reasonable to allow a *bit* of lee-way at times such as these.

I was impatient to do another creative challenge but felt I must delay gratification and first purge myself of these odd-jobs. Indirectly, this challenge would keep things moving in the right direction. The creative juices would flow much better from an uncluttered mind that didn't feel preoccupied about such things as the phone calls it should be making to various tradesmen. The odd-job list included such diverse things as getting my car serviced, carpets steam cleaned, and buying a new toaster. We'd been using the griller for weeks because I hadn't been able to decide on what sort of toaster I should buy as a replacement. Sadly, procrastination was one of my strong points. There was no allocation of particular jobs for particular days – the brief was simply that they must be done by the end of the week – preferably by Friday but Sunday at a pinch.

CHALLENGE #4 – The odd-job challenge
Knock off a prewritten list of odd-jobs over the course of one week

The odd-job challenge began straight after the cooking week and unfolded in a moderately successful manner. Not all of the jobs could be accommodated straight away but at least the appointments had been made for those that needed more notice. They would be coming to fruition throughout the following weeks.

I chose Friday for my painting day and began working on a picture for my father-in-law's 80th birthday. Confident in my new found ability to do a whole painting in one day, I began with the expectation of doing just that, but

I'd underestimated it by many leagues. After three hours, I succumbed to my usual afternoon death rattle of exhaustion and conceded defeat. I had till Sunday to finish within the week and meet the criteria, but I had too much else going on and knew it just wouldn't be possible. I felt quite disappointed, but then I remembered that I was the dictator of this whole enterprise and so I immediately – and despotically – inserted a caveat.

From this day forward, in the event of not completing an entire painting in one day for the weekly painting challenge, the challenge would be considered fulfilled as long as *some* painting had been undertaken. I would still achieve the same objective of keeping my hand in. So having passed that decree, I breathed a sigh of relief knowing I could finish it off next week. While luxuriating in the glow of going easy on myself, I made a mental show of bravado and upped the stakes by defining *some* painting to be at least three hours in order to fulfil the weekly painting challenge. It was easy to make it three hours from the comfort of resting on my laurels, knowing that I'd already fulfilled the criteria this week.

I was excited with the idea I'd come up with for my father-in-law's painting. In the 1970s, Kevin's family bought a holiday shack in a fishing town a few hours north of Perth which has become a family holiday home ever since. A small fibreglass boat: 5.4 metres long (18 and a half feet) is kept there which is launched with an old 1950s tractor. I have always loved tractors of this vintage. They were a relatively common sight in the countryside during my childhood. Such relics could still be found dotting the landscape here and there, if not in use, then rusting picturesquely in paddocks. We'd even had our own pet one corroding quietly in the bush alongside the gravel drive that ran from the main road to our farmhouse.

When I first began joining Kevin's family at their holiday house in the late 80s, the beach was lined with old tractors in various states of oxidisation, patiently waiting for their charges to return from the sea with the unlucky fish of the day. Nowadays, there are more four-wheel drive vehicles than tractors, but there are still quite a few old specimens that dare to be seen in the company of their slick usurpers.

After trawling through some of the photos I'd taken of the boat over the years I found one of Kevin launching it with a couple of his friends. The boat and tractor made for a great composition so I chose it as a reference for his dad's painting. His dad wasn't aware that I'd taken up painting again so I looked forward to seeing the surprise on his face when I gave it to him. It was because his birthday was a special one this year that I'd thought to do a picture for him and it struck me then that it would be nice to offer all the family members a painting for their birthdays this year. My nephew's birthday had already been and gone but I could ask him if he'd like one belatedly.

It's a tricky business offering to do a painting for someone. It puts them on the spot if they're not keen on the idea. Committing to anything sight unseen is daunting. Gifts that don't hit the mark can often be surreptitiously consigned to a cupboard, but a painting that has been created especially for you is not such an easy thing to hide away.

Down week

The plan for the following week was to catch up on the house and to morph into a social butterfly, which I duly did on Monday and Tuesday. During the week I had a bout of hormonal depression which was very short lived but decidedly unpleasant. It reminded me of what terrors lurked within the recesses of my mind. I could feel glimmers of the obsessive compulsive disorder (OCD) returning just a fraction. It was very unsettling after having had such a run of stable moods. OCD had blighted my life for many years, and when at its worst, I'd felt sheer terror that my life as a normal functioning person was over forever and that I would never again know a moment of peace or happiness. But thankfully I'd improved enormously since then; I learnt strategies that helped me to manage the illness and I slowly began to get my life back.

OCD is often seen as a lightweight anxiety disorder – a condition many would imagine to be a little embarrassing and annoying to have, but wouldn't generally understand it to be a serious and traumatic mental disorder. I suspect that many people don't realise that the compulsion to check things and wash hands excessively goes far beyond just being the symptoms of a slightly fussier than average person; or that there is deep mental pain driving these compulsions.

Symptoms of OCD can vary considerably between sufferers and for me they manifested as an overriding terror of harming others due to an exaggerated sense of moral responsibility. One angle of this included a fear of contamination through germs and chemicals – or anything at all that I perceived could be potentially toxic or harmful. These things weren't feared so much in relation to my own wellbeing, but mostly for others. If I thought I'd come into contact with any contaminants I would wash my hands excessively in a bid to be free of accidentally passing them on to anyone else.

I wasn't affected at all by certain aspects of OCD that involved lining things up, counting things or engaging in complicated mental or physical rituals to ensure loved ones remained safe. Thankfully I was spared from those particular forms of the disorder but I had enough of the other aspects to make my life a living hell.

The fear of harming others infiltrated every aspect of my life; not just through contamination but in any amount of obscure ways – from the medical decisions I made for my children to the content of my conversations. I lived in a constant state of heightened anxiety and guilt; anxiety for what I might inadvertently inflict on someone at any moment – and torturous guilt for what I perceived I'd already inflicted through oversight. The most innocuous things escalated into potentially life or death situations as interpreted by my addled mind.

I endured some very dark and unbearable years but thankfully I was able to keep functioning. I was able to raise the girls to be happy, healthy and well rounded people even though they had a *lot* to put up with at times. My level of anxiety regarding their wellbeing was extreme and often irrational. However, so well was I able to keep putting one foot in front of the other that unless I told people of my condition, they didn't have a clue that just a scratch below the surface bubbled a fearsomely anxious, dysfunctional and tortured mind.

Even now I can't say I'm totally cured, because occasionally I am still prone to some aspects of the disorder, but overall I'm in fantastic mental shape – the best for many years and remarkably free of symptoms.

My car went in for a service on Thursday and I worked on my father-in-law's painting for a couple of hours on Friday. I had to ditch the Pilates classes because last time I'd twisted something that wasn't designed to be twisted and my back had yet to recover.

The weekend arrived and I was keen to plan things for the challenge week ahead but then I noticed it was already filling up with various follow-through appointments from the odd-job challenge. So I realised it would be prudent to make next week a second down week.

The sleeping challenge had been under way for about four weeks and I had been fairly diligent in sticking to it. There were still times when I had to collect Olivia late from parties which made it difficult to get to sleep before the wee hours, but that was out of my control for the moment. Despite my diligence, I'd only had one reasonably good night's sleep since beginning the challenge. Every summer I flap around the bed like a fish in a hot frying pan and it wasn't helping that the rats continued to do cartwheels in the roof. One good sleep in all that time wasn't quite the outcome I'd been hoping for and in the past it would have been enough to make me give up – but not this time! I just had to re-educate my body-clock. It would no doubt take time.

On Saturday, having chiselled out time between various outings and happenings, I painted for a total of three and a half hours in three separate sessions. I wasn't able to loosen up with this tractor painting, nor was I feeling the flow very often, but I was pleased with how it was progressing. It was fun painting in a tighter style despite my overriding goal to loosen up. At least now that I was in challenge mode, I knew that I'd finish it off in the next sitting or two rather than never finishing it at all – which until now had been the most likely eventuality.

Because the painting was shaping up rather well I began to make bigger plans for it. I could reproduce the image and create limited edition prints, or greeting cards – or both. It never took much for the idea of translating my art into greeting cards to surface – for me it was primal. Since around the age of sixteen or seventeen I'd dabbled in designing the odd greeting card for friends and family and had begun to dream of designing them for a living – along with writing and illustrating children's books. When I was nineteen I got proactive and designed a comical range of cards featuring frogs, the idea being to sell the designs to a greeting card company. But local options were very thin on the ground in the 80s so I began to look to the bigger companies – such as John Sands. The Australian head-offices of such publishing behemoths were to be found in Sydney and Melbourne, so I hatched a plan to travel to Sydney with my designs. Of course I could have simply made enquiries by phone and sent samples by snail mail, but that option either didn't occur to me, or I was looking for an excuse to go on a rollicking adventure.

I stowed the cards in my backpack and travelled by train on the fabled *Indian Pacific* to Sydney which was a three night journey in coach class (sit up!). Crossing the breadth of the country by land and watching the scenery unfold mile by mile allowed me to really understand the vastness of Australia in a way that flying simply couldn't do.

I visited two greeting card companies while in Sydney. Neither company was interested in these particular illustrations but they were both very encouraging. John Sands kindly gave me a rundown on the types of designs they were looking for and suggested I submit them by mail. I felt disappointed that my frog cards hadn't wowed them but I resolved to churn out design after design upon my return until I hit upon something that they would buy. I'm sure I could have shown more persistence by trying other companies while in Sydney but I was having too much fun being a teenager. I had a very lively time staying in youth hostels while travelling around the east coast. The freedom was intoxicating.

When the dust settled on my return a month later, I didn't set to work churning out designs as I had vowed to do, instead I decided to persist with my frog cards and print them myself. Full colour printing was far too expensive on my limited means, so as a compromise I had only the black outline of the designs printed which left me to colour them by hand. I had 1,000 printed up by a chain-store instant printing company. I registered a business name and began the huge task of painting them individually in watercolour. I made an appointment with the buyer from one of the big retail stores in the city and was giddy with excitement when she put in an order for 400 cards. I felt I'd hit the big time!

It was a very laborious job hand-painting the cards. I set up a production line whereby I'd start with a big pile and paint all the greens then I'd start from the top again and do all the blues and so on. Finally they were finished and delivered, and I remember feeling very pleased about it all, but my memory is a little hazy as to how well they sold. I know there were no subsequent orders from that retailer and seem to recall seeing my cards some time later poorly displayed and forlorn on a discount stand. Thankfully, in the meantime I had found an outlet at the trendy Subiaco Pavilion Markets in an inner city suburb where they sold very well. Bit by bit, I sold most of the remaining 600 cards. So it had been a success in the main but not very lucrative, particularly considering it was so very time consuming and labour intensive.

I didn't feel it was feasible to embark on a second print-run. Towards the end I had found it too soul sucking to keep hand-painting the cards. Thankfully, I hadn't given up my day job.

Second down week

As anticipated, the second down week passed in a blur of activity with the last of the previously arranged odd-jobs coming to completion as well as orthodontic appointments and social outings. It had been a wonderfully productive couple of weeks and it was great to bring to fruition some of the jobs that had been nibbling at my conscience for years. Unfortunately, a couple of the jobs were still languishing on the list: getting a new oven (it had finally died) and organising the sewerage conversion, but I did at least make phone calls to get the ball rolling and hoped to go further with them in-between the coming creative challenges.

On Sunday I was pleased to find I didn't need to open the willpower throttle to get moving on my weekly painting. Nowadays, any little stretch of time at my disposal saw me back at the easel as if in a trance. The weekly habit helped to stop the motivation scabbing over into a state of procrastination. Hopefully, it would remain this easy to keep up with the one-a-week paintings once the longer creative challenges were underway again; I feared that there wouldn't be any creative energy left over. In the past, I always felt it was all or nothing when working on a project, imagining it would be unfeasible to have two things on the go at once. But I was keen to prove that feeling wrong.

During the past week I'd discerned a slight improvement on the energy front and hoped I might be turning a corner with the anaemia. My health-kick was still going well but I hadn't been able to employ much discipline when it came to exercise and had yet to get a regular walking routine going. It was proving very hard to get every duck in a row all at once.

Throughout the week I'd become addicted to looking at the art blogs and was finding them very motivational. If it wasn't for these blogs I suspect I may not have continued with the regular painting. I would never have been aware that people did small paintings on such a frequent basis. These artists made for excellent role models and I was building up a stable of blogs that I visited regularly.

Chapter Four

APRIL

As well as the year-long challenges I also wanted to do some "big picture challenges" which could be achieved by breaking them up into many shorter challenges.

BIG PICTURE CHALLENGE – To get an existing manuscript finished and sent to publishers/agents

CHALLENGE #5 – Devote 15 hours over a one week period to revising and editing book manuscript

Good focus was called for with the next challenge so I would need to keep the week scrupulously free of other distractions. I decided I would only do one week of the challenge for now as the school holidays began the following week. This week's brief was to spend at least fifteen hours working on a manuscript that I had begun writing a few years ago about my experiences of living with OCD. I couldn't base the challenge on word count as the manuscript was mostly finished. It just required rereading and editing. I had all but completed it about six months ago, but had reached a point where I could no longer stomach the sight *or* the thought of it and the manuscript had been enjoying a nice little rest ever since. But now I just wanted to finish it once and for all so I could feel free to move onto other projects. I hoped it had made the most of its down time because the time for lounging around was over!

It was in 2006 that I was diagnosed with OCD. I had thought I was through the worst of it when I began writing about it a couple of years later – but I wasn't. The purpose of recording my experiences of managing the disorder was in the hope of helping others. Such a cliché I know but true nonetheless, and it proved to be a powerful motivator to keep working on it even during the bleak times. There were occasions when I decided to abandon the project, usually during periods when I was deeply unwell, as the very nature of the disorder made me fear the repercussions the book may have on other vulnerable people. I'd suddenly worry that it would harm others rather than help them, and I'd agonise over whether to go ahead or not. But these fears weren't a particular problem when I was feeling sounder of mind. Now that I was feeling so well, I just wanted to finally get the thing finished and launched into the world after having put my heart and soul into it for so long. Despite my recent insights, I still felt that once I resumed working on the manuscript, I would have to complete it before I could feel at liberty to move on to other projects.

It had been all-consuming when I was in the maelstrom of writing the book last year. Whenever I'd had free time that coincided with creative energy I felt compelled to work solely on the book. It would have felt plain naughty and frivolous to even think of focusing on anything else while the book remained unfinished and hanging over me. During that consuming time I had studiously avoided making eye contact with the greeting card design ideas that were simmering patiently and forgivingly on the backburner in my mind. In reality there were plenty of opportunities where I could have devoted myself to other creative activities without detracting from the time I spent on my book. As the painting challenge had recently shown me, there was so much time to be harvested if one was more proactive and succumbed less to procrastination.

At the end of last year when I had first read about the 30 day painting challenge, I told my sister Jenny about it and the concept inspired her too. In fact, the timing was impeccable as she had already been brewing a book in her head and was hoping to make a start on it soon. She thought the challenge concept might help in the motivation stakes. In January she embraced it with zeal and set herself a daily quota of words to aim for. She made it through her 30 day challenge with flying colours and this is what she had to say about it, "By the end of the 30 days, although I was only part-way through the first draft, I had built up a little more confidence. The challenge had helped me to navigate my way through what can sometimes be the most difficult terrain – the beginning."

On the first Monday of April I started my writing challenge at 9.30am. It was slightly overwhelming having not set eyes on the manuscript since October last year. Not long in, I found myself wondering yet again if I really wanted to continue with it at all, but I knew I had to push on to give it a fair chance. Over three separate sessions I managed to do three hours. I had aimed for three hours a day. So far so good!

Midway through the week I strained my neck and shoulders as I got out of bed. The muscles were still skittish from the initial strain at Pilates and were taking every opportunity to buck and spasm should I move too suddenly – I felt very sore. I'd also been grinding my teeth at night, even though I didn't feel consciously stressed. I suspected that revisiting the OCD book was agitating me more than I realised. All the old fears of whether or not I may harm my readers with bad advice had risen to the surface yet again. Not to mention the fact that I was inevitably reliving some very dark times. I knew I had to get serious about exercising more to help neutralise the anxiety, so I called a friend on the spur of the moment to join me for a walk. We set a cracking pace for fifty minutes along the beach paths and I was surprised at how comparatively fit I felt considering I hadn't been very active of late.

The exercise proved to be the perfect antidote and I managed to spend over four hours on the book afterwards. In addition to that, I also sent ten emails to various friends, some of them quite long. I was finding that on the days I wrote a lot, it became compulsive. I couldn't stop even though it did me in mentally.

As the week wore on I became decidedly more positive and could once again see the value of persisting with the book. Most of the week was spent reading through the entire manuscript and editing as I went. It was great having had such a long break since the last reading as it allowed me to see it with fresh eyes. I was bravely removing large chunks without a backward glance and by the end of the week I'd cut out over 2,000 words. That left me with a total word count of around 60,000.

On Thursday, Olivia had an eye appointment that had been on the agenda for a few weeks. This had set off my vulnerability to OCD again. I got into a lather worrying about such innocuous things as the possibility of her needing to have drops in her eyes. However, I'd worried for nothing as she didn't require any in the end. Of course, even if she *had* needed them I had worried for nothing, I'm sure they wouldn't have maimed and blinded her like I'd been dreading. This irrational level of fear was my trademark emotion when dealing with anything health related with the girls. I collected her from Kevin's office afterwards. He had taken her in this time, as I had form for getting wild-eyed and scary when taking the kids to specialist appointments. I always ask too many neurotic questions of the poor unsuspecting specialist – or even a reasonable amount of questions – which for those who confuse themselves with God doesn't go down well. So in more recent years we decided that depending on how weighty the appointment and how unwell I was, Kevin would take them.

Amongst all the angst and other comings and goings I managed to spend over two and a half hours on my book. I got to the end of reading the manuscript from beginning to end, tweaking all the while. Then I continued rewriting certain bits that caught my eye at random as I cruised through the word document. I was enjoying the honing of it more now. Early in the process it was like pulling teeth, now it was more akin to a scale and clean.

Easter Friday was the last day of the challenge and I wrote for just over three hours. I was pleased and surprised at how much writing I was able to do on top of fitting so much else into the week. I exceeded my 15 hour challenge by half an hour.

The Easter weekend followed and it was at some time over those two days that I fell off the chocolate wagon, sustaining rather bad injuries. I had succumbed to eating a whole 100g Easter rabbit in one sitting. I'd reached the stage of feeling sick, but with only such a little morsel left, restraint seemed pointless by then.

Aside from painting and gorging on chocolate, the Easter weekend unfolded with various social outings and attempting to get some down time. I badly needed some rest but because of being in such a sustained frenzy of productivity and activity I no longer knew how to change down a gear or two. This high state of productivity was so very alien to my normal ways; I was constantly amazed at what I was now capable of achieving. Previously I'd have the odd flash of productivity and then go months where nothing creative happened at all, usually because the barrier of inertia would inevitably emerge to squish my motivation and momentum; I could practically hear it grinding and rumbling ominously into place like the closing of a great stone vault. The barrier phenomenon was a common thing for me when any length of time had passed between sessions.

I'd been telling Olivia about this inertia phenomenon recently and she likened it to static and kinetic friction. Having learnt about it in physics she explained to me that static friction is higher than kinetic friction for any object, meaning that it takes more energy to get something moving than it does to keep it in motion. I could certainly vouch for that – it took me a lot of energy (static friction) to push through the state of procrastination but everything seemed to flow (kinetic friction) so easily once I got myself started. It was freaky how neatly this emotional barrier could be interpreted with a scientific explanation.

Down week

Being the start of school holidays, I didn't plan a challenge for the following week as it would be brimming with activities and outings. Instead, I was pleased to get the chance to bury myself in a good book in-between all the comings and goings. I chose Thursday morning for my regular weekly painting session and after two hours of slapping paint around I finally finished my father-in-law's painting. The final touches were completed by adding the steering wheel, gear stick and chimney-thingy on the tractor. I christened it *Launching the Boat.*

It was hard to know what I thought about the finished piece objectively as it had been sitting on the easel looking at me every day for so long now; it was impossible to see it with fresh eyes. I had felt a lot of satisfaction while doing the painting, but by the end I was quite keen to have it finished. The first stroke of paint had swished across the canvas on the 16th of March and the last on the 12th April: I'd worked on it on nine different days over that period taking a total of eighteen hours painting time. So much for thinking I could do it in one day! Maybe the end of the year would see me crowned queen of the quick, loose style, and paintings like this one would be materialising by the hour.

While painting *Launching the Boat,* I rarely entered the true joyful "zone" like I had with my Rottnest tree painting; it had felt more like work – but very satisfying work nonetheless. This made me think that it must be the act of loosening up that got me into the zone – where each stroke felt magical and fulfilling.

Hopefully my father-in-law would like it. I was really looking forward to giving it to him.

I'm not quite sure when it happened, but the sleep challenge had suffered a nasty fall and was now pushing up daisies. After showing so much promise at the beginning it had ended in failure. I'd reverted to my old habits of getting to bed late on a regular basis. The time for "lights out" was creeping up to midnight. It all got too difficult in the end with everyone else rattling around till all hours and then scurrying around early in the mornings. It had failed so gradually that I hadn't even noticed at first.

Despite being a dud at retiring early, at least the sleep I did get was now more solid due to the cooler nights. I'd sleep in till the last possible moment and get up with just enough time to have a quick shower and make a juice before heading out to drop Lola at school. Inevitably I was getting late breakfasts – not eating until after the drop-off which was often further delayed because of stopping at my local shops to grab groceries on the way home. It didn't exactly constitute functioning at the top of my game, but it worked.

Being that I was capable of such diligence with the creative challenges, I wondered why I was less so with the ones based on my health – like exercise and sleeping habits. Hmm, I would need to analyse this further. I continued to juice every second day and walked a little more often but still wasn't as disciplined as I would have liked. Thankfully, despite the poor sleeping habits and exercise, I was slowly building up my strength and growing redder of cheek as my iron stores climbed by the day.

Because I no longer knew where the "off" button was I continued to repeatedly strain my neck and shoulders. My muscles were probably too tense from the hours spent hunched over the computer and easel. Practising better posture would have to be next on my list. Incorporating meditation into my weekly if not daily routine was also on my list but I never seemed able to hold onto the thought long enough to remember to fit it in anywhere. A good idea would be to draw up a detailed plan so I could work out how to accommodate everything. The trouble was that I felt mentally scattered much of the time and seemed to just bounce from one thing to another without much forward thinking – like a pinball pinging around the machine. Over the past few years I'd found that I could never relax as deeply and thoroughly as I was once able to do. I was sure it was due to hormones but the inability to relax had escalated even further this year because of being in this unaccustomed creative frenzy.

CHALLENGE #6 – Spend no less than 10 hours revising and editing in a week

Knowing I had a busy week ahead with Lola still being on school holidays, I decided to reduce this week's challenge to ten hours. Initially, I had considered skipping it entirely because of having too much on but I simply couldn't keep away from it.

Despite my other commitments, I managed to spend over eleven hours on my manuscript and so completed the challenge for the week. Sunday arrived along with my last chance to fulfil the weekly painting challenge. This week's subject matter would be a painting of a bottle of Chanel No 5 perfume for Lola. I'd long thought of doing a painting of a perfume bottle – originally as an illustration for a greeting card – but had yet to get around to it. Now that Lola had expressed a desire for one it would compel me to cough one up.

Glass as a painting subject can be very daunting and difficult what with all the reflections and shiny bits, so I felt a thrill of fear and excitement as I sat in front of the vacantly blank canvas. I tried to think of what the feeling of facing such a ruthlessly expectant expanse of white was like but failed to pinpoint it very accurately. Obviously it would be a *slight* exaggeration to say it felt akin to girding your loins for a bungee jump, but it was somewhere along the "shit scared" continuum nevertheless.

Despite my initial squeamishness to begin, it turned out to be a great success – compared to the misshapen mess that was in my mind's eye at least. I leapt straight in with bold brush strokes and resisted my usual urge to carefully draft the outline first. I simply began with the body of the bottle, doing the colour of the perfume itself.

The directive to "Paint what you see, not what you *think* you see," is a very potent piece of advice that I had heard from various teachers. I took this counsel to heart once I'd seen how it helped improve my own art. It can, however, feel surprisingly counterintuitive at times so a certain amount of trust must be employed in following through with it. Thankfully, I held my nerve on this occasion. By painting the closely observed shapes of the various colours, and not questioning if they made sense or not, a very shiny, reflective perfume bottle began to materialise on my canvas.

It was a thrill to find that I'd lately developed an ability to paint a picture without drawing in the outline first. I suspect that "painting what you see", is what makes this approach possible. *Launching the Boat* had lent itself to the same technique. In addition to this development, I was pleasantly surprised – nay, amazed – that I'd been instinctively producing the colours I wanted with far less fuss and effort than I remembered being the case in the past.

The Chanel bottle was pronounced a success by the rest of the family too which added to my painting high. Since beginning this year of challenges, my mental state had improved from being predominantly anxious and depressed to a pleasant and steady state overall. Today, it was great to note that I had felt joyful – even before beginning the painting. Joy hadn't been a regular visitor in recent years so it was a lovely surprise to perceive the return of this higher emotional state. Having taken time lately to read a good book probably also contributed to my exultant mood by ensuring I rested properly when I needed to.

I planned to do another 10 hour challenge for the following week and almost felt guilty for doing so. I was *really* getting behind on the house, particularly with the ironing and paperwork – and there was a moth plague in the pantry that needed addressing.

CHALLENGE #7 – Spend no less than 10 hours revising and editing in a week

On Monday, groggy from lack of sleep, I hauled my carcass out of bed to face the morning chores and a late breakfast before finally sinking into my computer chair and resuming work on my manuscript.

I'd recently re-established email contact with an old friend called Barbara who was living the expat life in Asia. She too was interested in art and writing and had made the fatal mistake of expressing interest in my book. Before she knew what hit her, I'd emailed her the introduction and first chapter for some feedback. Half a dozen friends and family members had already read the manuscript for me over the last year or so, but it was good to get fresh meat with a talent for words who hadn't already been put upon. My previous readers had all given me great feedback and I had endeavoured to make the improvements they had suggested. But it didn't mean there weren't still other angles that needed improving upon – particularly as I'd been revising since then.

Barbara had some great feedback to offer which drove me to do a total overhaul of chapter one. It was a significant improvement on what I'd originally had, but it did make me wonder if my judgement had been similarly out for the whole length and breadth of the thing. It was hard to imagine ever being able to get the manuscript to a point where I'd be totally happy with it. On further reflection, I remembered that the introduction and first chapter were the bits I had felt least confident about, so it was unlikely the rest would need much more than a few more tweaks – I hoped!

In amongst everything else, I managed to get over three hours of writing done.

Since starting back on the manuscript, I'd noticed a return of some spinal arthritic symptoms that I was prone to at times – along with the teeth grinding. I guess it should have been obvious that revising this book would bring all the mental muck I'd gone through back to the surface. It was only natural it would manifest in my physical state too. I just wanted to get it over and done with. The reason I'd stuck with it this long was because of my aforementioned hackneyed hope that I could help others. I would never have been able to get this far if not for that.

With the book so close to completion, I began to do some online research about likely publishing houses and agents that might be interested in my work. Many publishers persisted with the snail-mail submission process, with each house outlining entirely different submission formats to the next. It was overwhelming just thinking about all the publishing hoops that must be jumped through in order to try getting my book "out there".

Then I discovered that a couple of publishers were offering to read email submissions with the promise of a quick response if sent on a certain day of the week. I decided to send the requisite sample chapters and synopsis to one publisher in particular, and if it went no further than that then I might just wash my hands of it and put it all down to experience. Ha! That thought lasted for two seconds! The thought of having *another* complete book languishing in a drawer was decidedly horrid. I already had an entire 58,000 word – fairly polished – manuscript languishing in a bottom cyber drawer. In 2006 I'd embarked upon writing a non-fiction book that I had felt very passionate about at the time. I'd lived and breathed it on and off for a couple of years only to drop it like a rock when my OCD became too intense; fearing I would harm others with what I was writing about. Once a bit of time had passed I knew that I'd never want to revive it, I had moved on and never looked back. But it was good writing experience so the time and effort hadn't gone to waste.

On Tuesday and Wednesday I managed over five hours around all my other commitments. In those hours I spent a lot of time working on the synopsis and getting chapter one right ready to send off. Initially, I hadn't a clue as to how to write a synopsis. When in doubt – Google! I expected to find the exact formula for writing a synopsis carved in cyber stone, but every site varied considerably to the next in their explanations. After hours of research I remained mostly unenlightened and realised I'd just have to wing it.

By Thursday Lola had returned to school and my day was full with helping Olivia sort out her car transfer and various other matters. I managed to slip in two hours of writing before a late dinner. I was pleased to have already surpassed my 10 hour challenge and *still* have time up my sleeve.

A further two hours of writing were notched up on Friday and in the evening we went out to celebrate my father-in-law's 80th birthday. *Launching the Boat* had been collected from the framers last week and had since been sitting quietly in a corner just waiting for its grand moment. It practically glowed with the sense of occasion – knowing it was to be a special gift.

Kevin's dad was really surprised and thrilled with it – and I was very pleased that he loved it so much. It was hard to go wrong with the subject matter as both the boat and tractor were so deeply ingrained in all of our hearts and minds – they'd become the stuff of family legend.

It had been a lot of fun doing the painting as a surprise gift rather than it having been commissioned or expected of me. I have always found that painting or illustrating to order can block me badly, so I tend to avoid getting myself into that position; probably not the wisest way to go for someone wanting to paint professionally.

Just as I was emerging from bed on Saturday morning, I had a text from a friend to say that she'd enjoyed reading my Melbourne article in the paper. In a flurry of excitement

I grabbed the paper and found the travel section. It felt very strange and exposing to see my name, words and photos in print for all of Western Australia to see. Some changes had been made and bits and pieces cut out because I had been a hundred or so words over target, but that was to be expected. It was a thrill to have it finally appear in print.

Chapter Five

MAY

CHALLENGE #8 – Get submission ready and sent off for the Friday Pitch

The house had gone to rack and ruin through spending vast amounts of time on my manuscript. So, much of this week was spent catching up on badly neglected household chores. The moth plague had moved along apace despite having been on the top of my to-do list *every* day for ages. Each time I opened the pantry cupboard I was assailed by a squadron of moths. Goodness knows what winged civilisations were rising and falling in there due to my neglect. They had probably evolved thumbs by now. I could ignore it no longer.

The challenge for the week was to get my submission ready to send for the publisher's Friday pitch. Thursday was spent honing the synopsis and getting it, along with chapter one, poised right ready to send off tomorrow at the crack of dawn – or when I got up.

Friday the 4th May was rather a momentous day: the least reason being that the submission was emailed to the publisher. Olivia was now a FULLY FLEDGED DRIVER! Yay! Cue *Ode to Joy*. In the afternoon we had gone to the licensing centre where she passed her hazard perception test.

Even though Olivia had driven me around a lot these past few months, there was a tangible difference in the fabric of the universe when she drove me home sporting a "P" plate on her car rather than an "L" plate. We both felt the excitement that attends such auspicious occasions.

A friend rang at some point during the day and told me that the Joondalup shire council was soon to be having their annual art exhibition and that registration was to close next Tuesday. The exhibition had been in the back of my mind for a while now as I'd been thinking about entering something, but I hadn't been keeping abreast of the dates. Upon hearing how imminent the closing date was, I thought I'd missed my chance. Then it dawned on me that I could use my weekly painting time on the weekend to do a piece that would be suitable to enter. This would up the ante in the challenge stakes!

CHALLENGE #9 - Do a painting to enter into the Joondalup Art Exhibition

More than twenty years had passed since I'd put a painting in an exhibition so I was completely out of touch with the current art scene. I had no idea what sort of prices people were asking for their work – or even what sort of work was out there. As luck would have it there was a local painting exhibition not far away this very weekend. The timing was perfect.

Saturday came and I went to the art show. I spent ages soaking everything up trying to store prices and subject matter into my enfeebled memory banks. There were lovely accomplished pieces as well as some slightly amateurish stuff. The quality was very good overall and I thought my work would probably fall somewhere in the middle. It gave a good insight into the cross-section of what would no doubt be replicated in the bigger shire exhibition.

Sunday was the day of reckoning to do my weekly painting which would also double as my entry into the art exhibition – thereby fulfilling two challenges with one piece of work. Yesterday had slipped through my fingers as far as painting went which just left today. The pressure was on! I felt as lively as a bunch of wilted spinach and there were any amount of jobs to be done and preparations to be made for the evening as a friend was coming over for a BBQ dinner at 6pm.

The photo I'd chosen to paint from was of a Rottnest Island beach scene. Just prior to making my first mark on the canvas, I went for a quick spin on the internet to visit the blogs of the painters who had mastered lovely loose styles. With their examples freshly pressed into my brain I felt it would be easier to keep things simple. I began painting at around 11.00am and had every intention of knocking it off in an hour or two. I felt a time constraint because I still had to buy groceries for dinner and hoped to finish the painting before heading out.

But at some point through the haze of creativity and flying paint, I'd become aware of the sounds of Kevin heading out and then returning with all the fixings for the BBQ. This took the pressure off and gave me some extra time. The hours passed like minutes and with only stopping briefly for a bite to eat, I ended up painting till 3.30pm. I was on a painter's high and excited to have been able to complete it in four hours. It looked respectable – not fantastic – but I felt it would pass muster for the exhibition.

It varied between Kevin and me as to who did the food shopping when we entertained. Basically, if Kevin felt in the mood he would do it, and if not then the buck stopped with me. Thankfully, today Kevin was a benevolent paragon of domesticity and organisation and made short work of the shopping and preparation of salads in the time it would usually take me to simply garner the motivation to get out of the house.

Usually when we had people coming to visit, I would spend the day tidying and cleaning with whatever time was available and exhaust myself in the process. But today I was determined not to fall into that trap and gave myself a stiff talking to – the house was already perfectly respectable and only a quick clean of the toilet and bathroom and a short general tidy was necessary. Amazingly – and unprecedentedly – I was able to stick to this self-imposed brief.

I was riddled with exhaustion by the time I'd finished the painting but the adrenalin was still pumping and keeping me upright. I whipped back to the exhibition just before 4pm, not long before it was due to close. Now that I had a piece to exhibit I wanted to have another look to compare things. There were bigger paintings with lower prices than I had decided to put on mine, but I felt that my price wouldn't be *too* way out. And so what anyway, I wouldn't be holding a gun to anyone's head to make them buy it.

I called in to the shops on the way home for a few extra bits and pieces and was home in time to quickly make a salad and tizzy myself up before our guest arrived. Again it made me realise how much time was hiding in the cracks of a busy day. We don't entertain at home a huge amount, and when we do I certainly don't find myself thinking "Oh, we're having people over tonight – what a perfect day to do a painting!" No, usually I fling myself around the house in an obsessive cleaning frenzy. It breaks my heart to think how much time I have squandered over the years by frittering and dithering it away. Not that I believe every minute of our lives *should* be jam packed – far from it. When time allows, I happily devote myself to reading and general indolence in order to recharge my batteries.

Being able to pack a painting into a day that wouldn't normally show itself as having room for such a thing only came about because of the challenge I'd set myself. Again the power of the challenge got me through. It was proving a particularly potent tool for wriggling painting sessions into pockets of time that I'd never before suspected as having room for such things. This didn't mean it was easy, I still had to push myself to a certain degree to get started but it was the challenge that helped me gather the wherewithal to do so. I had learnt never to wait to be "in the mood" to paint or write as that method was too erratic and unreliable. Nothing would happen if I lounged around waiting for the muse to show up, she was far too unpredictable, instead I had to grab her by the throat.

Many people still live under the illusion that we must wait for the muse to grace us with her presence before we can become creatively productive. It's certainly a very romantic notion – sometimes the muse does indeed arrive unbidden, and something beautiful may come of it, but more often it's a case of just getting on with it. Once I've rolled my sleeves up and made a start *then* the muse will arrive bearing gifts of inspiration to keep me going. It seems that if we show ourselves willing to make the initial effort, inspiration and energy will be our reward. I believe that this is one of the universal laws that sits quietly alongside other laws of physics – every bit as immutable as the law of gravity, the only difference being that we can't scientifically prove it or measure it. Of course, the law of the muse isn't quite as well known as the law of gravity, but I believe it is also known as the "God helps those that help themselves" law.

However, as in many other areas of life there do seem to be exceptions to this rule. Occasionally, I find that despite pushing through inertia it seems the muse will not be enticed to appear – no matter what! These are probably the times when other factors come into play; like my state of health. Even though I'm a veteran of pushing through fatigue, there are times when the level is simply too great for the muse to transmute. Another law seems to triumph at these times – the law of "JUST STEP AWAY FROM THE PAINTING/ MANUSCRIPT!"

Not a challenge week as such – more a whatever-happens week but do as much as possible

Knowing the submission deadline for the exhibition was for 9.00am Tuesday, I had anticipated having to deliver the Rottnest painting on Monday – the day after completing it. By Monday though, I was practically immobile with exhaustion and simply didn't have it in me to get it there as it would mean about an hour's round trip. I felt so disappointed at letting myself down on the challenge after having got this far. Then it suddenly occurred to me that maybe it was just the entry form that was due in at that time. After some online investigation I was relieved to see it was in fact the case.

I filled everything out, submitted it online and was excited to know I'd be able to follow through on my challenge after all. It seemed I'd hurried myself for nothing as there were still a few weeks before I had to deliver the actual painting. But the entry form had required the dimensions, subject matter and title, so it would have been too onerous to come up with all that on speculation. The subsequent pressure to follow through to the letter would probably have rendered me creatively impotent; so the pressure I'd put myself under on Sunday hadn't gone to waste.

Because I wasn't used to parting with these creations I gave birth to I felt quite attached to the painting. Having loosened up quite a bit with this one it would be nice to keep it as an example of my early experimentation. So I put a price on it that I thought would almost certainly make it unsaleable but without looking too ridiculous.

After dealing with the attendant hoo-ha for the exhibition and the thrill of being able to say, "I'm going to exhibit a painting in an exhibition dahling!" I spent the rest of the week working on my book with whatever time I could throw it into. It wasn't a challenge week as such and I didn't record the hours I spent on it, but I still racked up a hefty number.

I'd been nervously checking my emails every morning in the highly unlikely chance that one had been sent from the publisher requesting to see the rest of my manuscript. Just the thought of being caught out when it was nowhere near ready made me feel rather uneasy; *if* they called my bluff, then what would I do? I wasn't really expecting anything to come of it and had only sent it off to force myself to just get the bleedin' thing finished!

I continued to work through it slowly and meticulously, chapter by chapter, rather than jumping back and forth and all over the place as I was wont to do. Chapter two was nearly finished now. On the eve of revisiting the manuscript I had known it would be a slow and painful process, but I hadn't expected it to take *this* long to finish. I was keen to get on to some illustration challenges and various other things. From there I wanted to make a start on my main focus for the year – writing the book about these challenges – *Grabbing the Muse by the Throat.*

Checking out the daily painters' websites had become a regular habit and I came across more interesting sites all the time. It was a great motivational tool. There were hundreds of painters' blogs and websites wafting around out there in cyber space. The wealth of talent out there constantly amazed me.

I had begun to think more about the possibility of setting up my own blog once I established a more definite style. To be prepared for such an eventuality, I planned to start painting on the small 15cm x 15cm (6" x 6") boards similar to what the others were using. This would make it both feasible to complete a painting in a day, and lightweight enough for shipping around the world – should I ever get a system in place for selling online. At times though, the thought of offering my art for sale felt far too overwhelming – particularly as I had yet to overcome the problem of finding it difficult to part with my paintings after labouring over them. I lived in hope that this would grow easier as time moved on and I became more adept and prolific.

During these times of little faith, I didn't give up on the idea of creating a blog, but instead thought it could simply be used as a platform to post my latest work for family and friends to see. It would be easier than what I was currently doing by emailing the occasional photo of my paintings to various family and friends. I imagined the latter would be the most likely outcome should I ever take the plunge.

Once again I found myself leaving my weekly painting till the very last minute. It was Saturday, 11th May, and I still hadn't made a start. Today was chock-a-block with other activities so it had to be tomorrow – but that was Mother's Day which would be equally groaning at the seams.

Thankfully, on Sunday I was able to weasel a painting in by beginning it the moment we returned from an early breakfast with Kevin and the girls and Kevin's parents. Last week I'd placed a pink rose from our climbing specimen in a mustard jar and photographed it at night. I'd discovered that the down-lights in the kitchen threw off some great shadows. That light source was more exaggerated than what I was getting through my art room window. Having seen the wonderful results some of the online painters were achieving with the artificial lighting set-ups they had in their studios, I hoped to organise something similar. I had been relying on the light from my window which wasn't capable of casting impressive shadows.

The painting began with my usual wildly unfounded optimism of expecting to knock it off in an hour or so – along with visions of dashing the paint across the canvas with the deft strokes of a master. I had no idea why I clung to these delusions when they flew in the face of all previous known evidence. Despite my misplaced optimism I really enjoyed the painting of it. Not so much the rose – as that was laborious and long-winded – but the glass jar, surprisingly, was nothing but pleasure to paint and surprisingly easy to do.

Again I was thrilled to find that I was able to get the colours quite close and without too much fuss – and without drawing anything in first. I was painting by impulse and enjoyed seeing where it would take me. I had always considered good drawing skills to be a prerequisite for being able to paint well – and still do. I believe you must have a good understanding of perspective and scale whether drawing anything in first or not. I just thought I'd loosen up better with the painting if I didn't start off with a detailed drawing.

My passion for art began with an early love of drawing and I always credit my mum for having fostered the drawing talent and am very grateful for it. As children, my sister and brother and I would ask her to draw things for us, and even though drawing wasn't her particular strength, she would always have a go. She would never say, "Oh, I couldn't draw that!" so it never crossed our minds that we couldn't do the same. We were always impressed with her pictures.

Whether art came naturally to me, or whether it was fostered by the "can do" attitude that Mum modelled for us, it came to be one of my main passions in life. We had a wonderfully creative backdrop to our lives as Mum would always have something imaginative on the go that we would get involved in, from Hobbytex fabric painting to making plastic beaded handbags that were quite the thing at the time. Dad played his part too by always being suitably impressed with our creations.

I painted for three hours straight and it was nearly 1pm by the time I finished. I cleaned up the brushes and photographed the painting. I nipped outside to cut some chrysanthemums that were flowering in the garden from Mother's Days past and harvested a surprisingly plump bouquet. I popped them in a vase and got organised for my family's visit for afternoon tea at 2pm. After the excitement and activity of the day had abated, I spent another hour or two on my writing in the evening. It had been a truly lovely day catching up with all four parents and my sister and nephew – and being so in the thick of my creative life as well.

A just-get-as-much-done-as-possible week

Over the next week I gingerly continued to check my emails each morning. And each morning the relief at having heard nothing mingled with the disappointment of having heard nothing.

In-between the bare essentials of keeping the house functioning, I spent as much time as I could on my writing. Again, I hadn't made a challenge week of it because I no longer needed a whip to keep me going – if anything I had become *too* obsessed and would soon need the whip to keep me away from it. The structured format would feel more like a hindrance than a help at the moment in the face of this obsession. The "challenge mode" would be wheeled out again once the book was finished and I was ready to implement the next creative goal.

By Friday there was still no response from the publisher. The deal with their Friday pitch was that if they hadn't been in touch within two weeks, then I wouldn't be hearing from them at all. I felt a wisp of disappointment, but barely. After all, I had really just sent it in as a motivational tool, rather than with any real expectation of a response. Just knowing, however, that a reply *was* within the realms of possibility had been enough to motivate me to write fast and furiously.

In the absence of a reply, I wrote harder still and was pleased at how much I had achieved over the past two weeks. Submitting the first chapter is a motivation tool I'd highly recommend to anyone wanting to up the ante in just getting something done. Knowing I could *only* submit the first chapter forced me to get it into the very finest of fettle. I'd already known the beginning would need reworking and culling, but hadn't quite known where to start until I had to look at it as a self-contained piece that could make or break the whole thing. Having Barbara's feedback had been a great help as she had drawn attention to a few things from a slightly different angle.

Giving myself a deadline also forced me to be more methodical with the editing instead of the time-wasting, ad-hoc approach I usually employed – as if I had the rest of my life to get it right. I'd been in the habit of working on bits anywhere and everywhere, and if I came upon a spot that looked too tricky I'd skip over it to return to later. This time I was going from beginning to end thoroughly and wouldn't move on until it was as tight as a facelift.

There were only a few chapters left to work on and they were already quite well honed; so the light at the end of the tunnel began to look more like daylight than the headlights of an oncoming train. Another solid week might just be enough to conquer it. But, now that the pressure of a potential response from the publisher was off, I felt the need to come up for air for a bit.

Next week, I would make the house a priority in order to catch up on the growing backlog of jobs and I would just wedge in a bit of writing if I got any spare time. A different publisher took email submissions on Mondays, so if I began to procrastinate and fiddle with it too much again, I would use their pitch to continue with the hot-poker approach.

Sunday was upon me and yet again it was my last day to paint. I painted an ocean-scape from a photo I'd taken the day before while walking along the coast. I'd had my camera with me in the hope of getting a good shot of some waves for painting reference. As luck would have it the waves were so perfect and tubular I could practically hear the pounding intro of a Beach Boys song. Having begun walking a little more regularly I found it doubled well as a means of scouting out good painting subjects.

The painting only took around an hour and a half to complete. I was thrilled – and somewhat shocked – that *finally*, a painting had actually lived up to my wild optimism. The elusive loose style I was after finally came through. I'd used a small 15cm x 23cm (6 x 9 inch) canvas covered board, and laid the paint on rather thick so the brush strokes could be seen. I was frolicking with excitement and christened it *Perfect Conditions*. It was a far cry from painting on location, but there was still something organically lovely about creating a picture of a scene I had just enjoyed in the flesh the day before.

The other week when I had finished working on the Rottnest painting, I realised with disappointment that my ocean looked flat and lifeless. So, while painting *Perfect Conditions* I was mindful of bringing in more green, and it was very satisfying to see the vast improvement from one painting to the next.

Despite my intentions to spend this week catching up on the house and only squeeze in a spot of writing here and there, in the end I spent many hours on the writing and only squeezed in a spot of housework here and there. I just couldn't keep away from the manuscript. A few social occasions further interfered with the housework, and the week was topped off with a rollicking family outing to see the stage production of Mary Poppins on Saturday.

On Friday alone, I had done four hours of writing which left me with just the last chapter or two to go through. There were still a number of hours of work ahead of me, but I hoped to have it entirely finished by next week. As time wore on, I was becoming increasingly skittish and desperate to get back to the more varied and structured challenges. I was beginning to feel that the book had hijacked the challenge idea and I had to keep reminding myself that getting it finished this year *was* one of the challenges. It was simply taking far longer than I had anticipated.

On Sunday I did my equal worst painting yet. It was the last day of my self-imposed painting week yet again which put me under pressure. On top of that, I left it till late in the day to begin – having spent time in the morning trying to work out what to paint, and after lunch being accosted by Lola. She strong-armed me into going shopping against my will for a couple of hours. She was determined to acquire some doo-dad or another that turned into a wild-goose chase. It ended with me feeling like a goose – and a wild one at that – for letting her talk me into it. It was 3.30pm by the time I began the painting and I worked on it for about two hours. With the shorter days I was practically painting in the dark by the end. I never took my eyes away from the canvas for the whole of the frenzied duration. Big mistake!

Once I'd cleaned up and put the light on, I discovered what a shocker it was. Even as I was painting I'd known its vital signs were fading, but it was worse than feared. There was a point where it was actually a decent little painting and it was then that I should have walked away. But I hadn't noticed the light fading at first and kept feeling the need to intensify the colours. In the end the lemons were a cacky green instead of the nuanced yellows that I had achieved earlier. Oh well, I reminded myself that the main thrust was to stick to the challenge and that each painting, good or bad, would teach me something. I resolved yet again to try to paint earlier in the week in order to take away the pressure that came with leaving it until the last day.

The volume of creative energy was hard to handle at times. I was constantly in motion, driven by an overwhelming onslaught of creative derring-do. Not that I was complaining of course, but it probably wasn't terribly healthy to be *so* hyped up all the time. I needed to practise moderation and get a bit of down time. It was like a creative light had been switched on at full blast, and while I certainly wasn't interested in finding the off button, a dimmer switch would have come in handy.

Another get-as-much-done-as-possible week

Much hefting and honing of words took place the following Monday and on Tuesday a friend and I visited some local bushland to do some drawing. It was a classic late autumn day, crisp but sunny, with a breathtaking clarity to everything. The exact conditions that inevitably have me waxing lyrical about everything I set eyes and nose upon. I hadn't known this woman very long so I reined in my loquacious observations. I didn't want her running screaming for the car. Not before we'd done our drawings anyway.

We moseyed along the paths admiring everything, but keeping our eyes out for perfect specimens of banksia flowers and nuts. We knew where to find good stands of *Banksia menziesii* which were currently flowering prolifically. I'd had it in my head for some time now to do a sketch of a *Banksia* nut on a tree. However, it proved too difficult to position ourselves where we could get the right view; because I wasn't familiar with sketching in the wild, it hadn't occurred to me that I could try to draw while standing up. So in the end we sketched the interesting texture of a tree trunk. While we were there I took photos of the banksia flowers and nuts to use as reference material for my next painting.

On Wednesday, I raced around all morning running errands before trying to wrestle things into shape on my book. To my dismay, I discovered that the chapter I had thought worked well on Monday needed a *lot* of rewriting. But then I was finally up to reworking the conclusion and I could smell freedom in the air. I was on a mission to just get the bleeping thing finished and every spare moment was taken towards that end. Most of Thursday and Friday were taken out with it as well; I was truly back into hyped up mode and found it impossible to relax.

Despite giving the keyboard a pounding, I wasn't able to get the conclusion of my book finished on Friday, but I retained a particle of hope that I'd have time to tap out the final words over the weekend. In the end there was just too much on – including delivering my Rottnest painting for the pending exhibition. I felt ripped off as I'd counted on being able to take the coming week off in order to get some rest and bask in the manuscript's completion. Well, that wouldn't be happening now, but come nuclear holocaust or plague of locusts, I was going to finish the sucker off this coming week!

Chapter Six

JUNE

CHALLENGE #10 – Get conclusion finished and ready to send out to publishers and agents

On Tuesday 5th June, Kevin flew to London. He was meeting up with friends in Europe where they would ride their vintage Ducati motorbikes through the mountains of Italy and France. Since his last European ride in 2010 his bike had been kindly stored by cousins in Suffolk, so that's where his journey would begin and end. He would be away for six weeks in total. Late last year when the plans for the trip were originally taking shape, we were planning that the girls and I would meet up with him in Paris or somewhere equally exotic after he'd finished with riding around the mountains – as we had done in 2010.

But for many different reasons, including trying to fit in around school and university holidays, it just didn't lend itself to the same format this time, so we wouldn't be joining him. Initially, I was disappointed that we'd miss out on swanning around Europe, but in the end I realised that I was actually happier at the thought of not taking out months of the year with the planning, organising and executing of a big overseas jaunt. Owing to the keyed up state of creative frenzy I was in, I might have found it impossible to tear myself away – even for Paris! At this stage I was happy to settle with enjoying Kevin's exploits vicariously. The poor girls didn't quite join me in this equanimity though.

After the flurry of activity in the lead up to him winging off on his adventure, my creative escapades continued, and having so much work to do stopped me from missing him too much. So this was the week of reckoning. I had to sign off on my OCD book once and for all – no matter what! I knew I could end up rewriting and making changes forever if I wasn't careful.

Finally, the conclusion was finished to my satisfaction and then I spent time trawling through lists of agents and publishers to check out their submission criteria. As anticipated, it was all quite depressing. I'd been there before in the past with other submissions. It always felt like attempting to scale a brick wall – one with razor wire on top and hungry crocodiles frolicking in the moat below. I still wasn't 100% sure whether or not I even wanted to get an agent and/or a publisher, or if I would try to do it myself. If I self-published (such a dirty word!) then I would retain the power over every aspect of the process and could take or leave any promotional hoo-ha that might be expected of me. But of course I might never sell a single copy either.

I decided to approach literary agents first rather than publishers. In the off-chance that I *could* engage a publisher, the thought of having to negotiate my own contract was terrifying. There weren't exactly swathes of agents to choose from in Australia and to further deplete my options I would only consider those who were members of the Australian Literary Agents Association. Many stated on their websites that self-help books would not be considered. The purpose of my book was certainly to help others, or to offer comfort at least, but I was unsure if mine fell into that genre or not due to the style of delivery.

Over the course of the week I rang a few agencies and, as expected, the brick wall proved as daunting as always with very little interest being expressed in response to my enquiries. At one agency the receptionist was mildly encouraging and said to send it through, but the submission process was so deeply onerous I thought it wise to explore my options further before investing in such vast tracts of time. By Thursday I felt demoralised and mired down in not knowing how to move from there.

The thought of sending it to the ever dwindling list of publishers who continued to accept unsolicited manuscripts, and having to jump through all their peculiar and precious hoops of manuscript presentation, unique to them alone, simply felt too overwhelming. On Thursday afternoon I decided to ring just one more agency, thinking I should at least check if their no-self-help criteria did or did not include my book. I wondered too, if the subject of mental illness would be off-putting. I had been taken aback when speaking with one agent who said they'd once considered taking on a book about OCD but didn't see how it could be marketable. Quite an unimaginative response I thought when there was such a push these days to promote mental health awareness.

So with this final call, I was surprised when the woman who answered the phone turned out to be the eminent agent herself and not a receptionist. I had seen mention of her name previously when researching Australian literary agents. She sounded very interested when I told her what the book was about and she said to email some sample chapters through – no more than sixty pages in total.

When I got off the phone I was all aquiver. Something was tangibly different about this phone call. Knowing the manuscript would be looked at by the person who actually made the decisions made it seem very possible that something might come of it. Usually, after listening to the impersonal spiel of a receptionist it was hard to imagine the eventual fate of my manuscript being anything other than one of wallowing miserable and unseen on a slush pile. What also made this submission seem so easy was the lack of preciousness about the manner in which the agent expected to receive it.

After feeling so demoralised the morning before and wondering what my next move would be, it seemed rather miraculous that I could be so energised and hopeful the very next afternoon. The strong gut feeling that something would come of it felt very similar to the one I'd had after speaking to the editor at the newspaper in regard to my Melbourne article. The agent had been very approachable, relaxed and interested which made it seem that anything was possible. Deep down I wondered though if my book would have enough mainstream appeal for a publisher to invest in – but I guessed I would find out soon enough.

After speaking to her on Thursday afternoon I worked at a blistering pace and had my submission ready to email by Friday afternoon. It was such a relief to make delivery of it.

I made a point of trying not to think about it over the weekend as I knew it could take weeks before I received a reply, and in the meantime there was all the usual house and family stuff to keep me occupied.

On Sunday I began a painting for Kevin's birthday which was still a couple of months away, but with him being overseas I could work on it without having to keep it hidden. The reference material I used was from a photo I'd taken of the petrol tank on his favourite motorbike. I couldn't stomach the thought of trying to paint the meticulous detail of a whole bike, it would take me years. A little section felt more interesting and achievable. Three hours in I realised it would be one of my more long-winded paintings. It would require quite a few sessions, even though in theory it should have been possible to complete more quickly. Not with me at the helm of the brush it would seem.

Planned as a down week

This week was to be a break from the hectic pace of the previous weeks. I *badly* needed some down time. Monday was a social day, and then on Tuesday morning, as I was emerging from the shower, I heard someone speaking on the answering machine. I managed to grab it before they hung up and to my surprise it was the agent calling from Sydney. She said she'd enjoyed reading my submission and wanted me to send the rest of it through to her. Somehow I managed to sound quite relaxed and chatty while we spoke, but underneath I was thinking, OH. MY. GOD! She asked if the manuscript was completed. I told her it was, but that I had intended to do one last read through before I could really sign off on it. She said to go ahead with the final read but in the meantime she would email a contract through for me to sign. We talked a little longer and all the while I hoped I was coming across as an articulate and urbane kind of creature; as if discussing contracts was an everyday occurrence for me, while surreptitiously I was *FREAKING OUT!!*

Once I got off the phone and finished hyperventilating, I rang everyone to tell the exciting news. Frustratingly, many people I rang were out at the time and I had to cool my heels before I could squeal about what had just unfolded. I was particularly in awe that the agent wanted to sign me up before even reading the whole of the manuscript. I was on such a high. This was real validation that my writing was fit for human consumption beyond family and friends. Another thrill of excitement shot through me when I received an email not long later with a contract to sign – the very same day!

In the meantime, Perth was expecting a huge storm to pass through in the evening so I pulled myself together and scoured the yard, front and back, to make sure outdoor furniture and other objects were secure for when the high winds arrived. Later in the afternoon, I picked up where I left off to make a few more excited, squeally, phone calls to friends about the conversation with the agent.

The storm was in by 9pm and it wasn't long before I heard a dripping noise. There had been a weak spot in the living room ceiling for a couple of years where the TV aerial was attached to the roof. Now its old war wound had come back to haunt us and I worried that particles of old rat bait in the roof space would find their way into our living room along with the dripping water.

I lay awake till the wee hours worrying about the ceiling caving in, but then the worst of the storm was over and I had time to reflect on the phone call I'd had from the agent. Now, instead of unadulterated excitement, terror had begun to creep in to the mix. I recalled how she had touched on the subject of publicity and what the agency's expectations entailed. Because I hated the idea of having to put myself out there, I guess I had conveniently glossed over that aspect of things. The thought of having to go over and over the details of dealing with OCD when all I really wanted was to put it behind me was not an appealing one. But if my aim was to make a success of the book and to help others, then I'd just have to suck it up.

Lately, in a more objective manner than usual, I'd had a profound understanding of just how short life is. I could viscerally understand how silly it was to fear everything, when we'd all be dead soon enough and our brief little flicker on the world stage as the unique creatures we are, would be over and done with forever. So I swallowed down my anxiety and resolved to seize the day by living fearlessly and embrace everything that came my way.

Fulfilling the challenges so far this year had made me much more confident about what I could achieve in life. It helped facilitate this tangible shift towards embracing life more fully and fearlessly. Obviously I still had a way to go, or I wouldn't have been fretting over the leaking roof. But right now, I felt more than ready to take on this wonderfully exciting opportunity for mainstream publishing without dreading public exposure.

The following morning I had lunch with my sister Jenny and a friend at the shopping centre where the shire art exhibition was being held. Before eating we sauntered through the roped off area where the art was being displayed. My Rottnest painting looked like a midget between two enormous canvasses. There were certainly a lot of finer works than mine in the show but it didn't overtly disgrace itself.

Jenny came home with me afterwards to stay for a couple of nights. We'd planned to create a health-spa like atmosphere here for a few days, making fresh juices and going for invigorating walks along the beach. But that was before the pressure was on to get the manuscript finished and the roof began leaking. Instead the visit was chaotic and overwrought. The whole house felt contaminated with rat bait (all in my imagination I realised later), my hormones were raging and there was a power failure the first night due to storm damage. If that wasn't enough to scupper our plans for a relaxing idyll, Jenny was press-ganged into listening to the tweaks and changes I was agonising over on my manuscript which I wanted to get off to the agent ASAP. Thank God for sisters!

Jenny left on Friday morning (trying not to look too relieved) and I had one last fear to face as this tumultuous week came shrieking to its end. Brunette, a friend of mine, had organised for me to pay a visit to the school where she worked part-time. She had been filling in for another teacher some months before and had been charged with the task of reading a book the teacher had chosen for the children as a launching pad for their activity. The book in question just happened to be one of the children's books that I'd had published over half a decade ago. I had written and illustrated a series of five stories based on an education program called *You Can Do It! Education* by Professor Michael Bernard. Brunette mentioned to the children that she knew the author (me). They were all agog so she thought it would be fun for them to meet me.

It had been years since much interest had been shown in the books, so it seemed poetic that this visit timed in during the very same week where a career as an author might be on the cards after all. When the books were first published I had spoken at my daughters' primary school on various occasions but a few offers to speak at other schools never eventuated.

It wasn't long after they were published that my mental health went into serious decline, and speaking in public was the last thing I was interested in pursuing. In fact, during the worst of it, I had assumed my creative life was dead and buried forever. The OCD had turned me into a creature who feared that her every word and action may harm others, and everyday outings felt steeped in the danger that I could cause harm and disaster at any moment.

When Brunette had first put the idea to me a month or so earlier, I feared I wouldn't be capable of doing it. Having not long emerged from the thick of my mental maladies, I still felt a bit delicate mentally and emotionally. But when looked at it in the cool light of day, I couldn't see any reason why not and knew it would do me good to face my fears. Up until then, I hadn't had cause to revisit the idea of speaking in front of people, but in light of recent developments the timing was perfect to get back in the saddle of the speaking-in-public horse.

I gussied myself up and met Brunette at the school at the appointed time. I read a couple of my books to the class of six and seven year olds and they were encouraged to ask questions afterwards. Their enthusiasm and curiosity made for a very enjoyable interlude. All of a sudden I felt like a real author and it revived my interest in my series of children's books.

It felt wonderful to have the stresses of the week behind me. As I drove home in a haze of contentment born of having faced a fear, an overwhelming sense of everything being right with the world washed over me. Things were going great with the family, and life felt so full with the agent's contract and all the new milestones I was making with my painting skills. How quickly my life was becoming like that of my dreams. I realised that I just hadn't been resilient enough in the past. I had always given up too soon.

In the afternoon, I sent the signed agreement off to the agent and spent an hour working on the manuscript after dinner. On Saturday a social occasion had to be cancelled in order to free up the time needed for writing. After four hours of tickling the plastics, the manuscript was *finally* finished! I sent it to the agent in the afternoon and what a buzz it was hitting the send button!

On Sunday, as requested by the agent, I wrote a mini-biography and found a photo of myself to accompany it. I pottered with a few jobs and then reluctantly decided to miss doing my weekly painting. I knew I'd cause myself grievous bodily harm if I kept pushing through the exhaustion. It was the first time I had missed my weekly challenge but I didn't even have enough energy to feel disappointed, although I knew I was in theory.

Down week

The following Monday I was surprised and thrilled to hear from the publisher of my children's books to say that he'd just had an order for 1200 copies from an education group. It had been seven years since the series was published, but he still had several thousand copies warehoused, even after originally selling around 45,000 copies in the first year or so. There hadn't been many sales since then, so the timing of this recent sale seemed really freaky.

I had a nice long email from Kevin who was now spinning around Italy on his motorbike. He'd met up with friends from Australia as previously arranged and they now numbered six or so. He waxed lyrical about the beautiful scenery they were soaking up as they roared around the mountains. They were enjoying glorious sunny weather in the low 30s, after beginning the holiday with a sodden week in England.

He ended the missive by saying he was sitting on a terrazzo as he typed, overlooking rustic villages while sipping a glass of vino bianco in Mediterranean comfort. He was doing it tough! But I was pleased to hear that he was having such a great time and I was content to enjoy it all vicariously. Thankfully, the excitement I was having in my own life restrained me from making a voodoo doll of him out of an old sock and sticking pins into its nether regions.

Amongst other things, the week was spent getting the house respectable after too long of just nodding in its general direction. Tackling the ironing and paperwork proved to be a particularly strenuous workout. The only creative element to the week was working on Kevin's painting for an hour or two, and there was an exhilarating moment on Friday when I received the signed agreement from the agent.

The last week of June was upon us – half way through another year! Usually this was my cue to bewail, "Where does the time go?" and I'd feel a familiar ripple of alarm at the thought of my life rocketing by at the speed of light and without much to show for it. But not this year! For the first time in a very long time – if not forever – I felt that I was really living my life thoroughly and fully; sucking every minute dry. It was hard to resent the days passing so quickly when they were passing in such a pleasant and fulfilling manner. Finally, I was seizing the day(s).

Second down week

Mid-week I got an email from the agent. Both she and her colleague had read the entire manuscript through and she suggested I make a few small changes. Much of the day was taken up with working on them. Thankfully, she didn't pressure me to change the few small things I didn't agree with.

While speaking on the phone with her later in the day, she told me about the plans she had for my book and the name of the publisher she would be sending it to directly. She sounded very confident that they'd take it with open arms; so much so, that I excitedly and optimistically began mentally rearranging my appointment diary with the expectation that I might well be tied up the following week doing rewrites for the publisher.

After catching up with only the basics last week, I used the remainder of this week to tackle the house with a vengeance. I got to the bottom of various jobs and clutter that had been long ignored. It was nice to change gears and focus solely on the house and garden for a while. However, I tipped into obsessive mode and lost sight of moderation because we were expecting visitors. I opened the throttle and powered on even though I was declining by the minute with fighting off a virus and dealing with hormone horrors.

Chapter Seven

JULY

***Third* down week**

My brother and his wife came to stay for part of the week. We had a lovely time together chatting and eating and generally catching up. I was mindful that my shorter challenges had fizzled out while occupied with getting the book over the last hurdles. Getting on top of the house and having visitors had also taken its toll. While I had thoroughly enjoyed the interlude, I was keen not to let the dreaded barrier develop. I intended to set a new challenge for the coming week – on top of the weekly painting. Of course if a publishing offer came through and more changes to the manuscript were required, then I would need to put the other challenges on hold for a while longer.

The busy, but uncreative week rolled into the weekend and I was finally able to do my weekly painting session on Saturday afternoon. The morning had been spent lazing in bed and finishing off the book I was reading which was most relaxing! But something I read in it reignited my bear phobia.

You might wonder how an Australian could develop such a phobia when in a country devoid of these creatures, but I guess it was due to being exposed to too many gruesome stories in my childhood of people being mauled by bears.

I was hoping to visit the US for the first time in a few years hence, and had recently been horrified to hear that bears were more widespread than I'd previously realised. I'd thought that they only lived in the deepest, darkest, woodiest type places like the Rocky Mountains. Such places were not on my hypothetical itinerary, but now I began to wonder if *any* forested areas could potentially be frequented by the creatures. I emailed my new American painting blog friend in the hope she could reassure me that there would be no chance of bear encounters in states like New York and Massachusetts – which *were* on my hypothetical itinerary.

Other countries' beasties always seem scarier than our own because of being unfamiliar with them beyond what we've seen and heard about them from afar – and often it is the scariest and juiciest of tales that find their way into the news. I guessed my fears were similar to those who freak out at the thought of visiting Australia because of what they've heard in relation to our poisonous spiders and snakes. We perversely pride ourselves on stocking the most venomous on the planet *and* in the most numerous of varieties. But I would rather be bitten to death than eaten alive. There are of course a respectable amount of Australian predators that *do* like to eat people, such as sharks and crocodiles, but at least they don't climb trees!

A few nights later I dreamt that I just got the garage door down in time before a rampaging bear could get to me. I began looking sideways at teddy bears.

I was disturbed to find it becoming increasingly difficult to motivate myself to sit down and paint. I had to break through the barrier of inertia afresh, even though there was only a week between each session. It was mid-afternoon by the time I began working on Kevin's motorbike painting and I continued until around 5pm. I hoped that one or two more sessions would see it finished. I was thankful that I'd enjoyed this stint of painting as I hadn't felt properly engaged with it on the previous two occasions.

CHALLENGE #11 – Paint every day for 5 days

On the first day of this new challenge week I felt energised to be returning to the more structured format after the wishy-washy, albeit highly productive approach I'd taken while finishing off my book. I challenged myself to paint every day – five days at least.

I made a sluggish start by sleeping in until 10am. Being that it was school holidays, it was hard to resist. I did some housework in what remained of the morning but by then it was lunchtime. I began reading a book while eating my meal which was a bad move as I got swept up in the story and read for an hour or two, all the while knowing I should be getting on with my painting. I wriggled deeper into the couch, and as I turned the pages I could practically hear the "fear of starting" barrier rumbling along in its tracks and clanging into place. It was around 4pm by the time I made a start. I spent a happy hour continuing on with Kevin's motor bike painting, but it was getting too dark to keep going. I'd initially decreed that I had to paint for at least two hours a day to meet this five day challenge, but after today's effort I decided I would be pleased with a minimum of one hour. Not quite the fresh-faced early start I had been anticipating for the return of the strict challenge format.

After getting through the domestic chores on Tuesday, I once again fell into my book. It had been foolish to begin reading a novel this week as I knew only too well that I had little self-control in such situations and could easily squander large slabs of day by reading. I began painting mid-afternoon and worked on it for an hour and a half. It was an enjoyable session but not in a really creative-flow kind of way. There was more a feeling of satisfaction rather than one of exhilaration.

I thought I'd be safe to read my book briefly before cooking dinner, but I couldn't put it down. I wasn't able to peel myself off the sofa until I had finished it. It was after six by the time I started cooking. Later in the evening I rang Kevin for a short chat. He'd be home again soon.

On Wednesday, after two hours of painting and with a sigh of relief, I declared the motorbike picture finished and signed my name. I hoped Kevin would like it.

The next day I began a new painting. It was fun to start something different – a still life of some old china tea-ware. This time I painted from a photo that I'd taken earlier in the year one afternoon when Mum and Dad had been over for a visit. We'd had tea on the balcony and I'd served it in the lovely vintage china cups that I'd collected over the years to create a "crazy tea set". This was a term used for the latest trend in tea-ware back when Mum was a mere slip of a girl and squirreling things away in her "glory box". Rather than buying a complete tea-set with every piece in the same matching pattern, it was fashionable at the time to collect at least six different trios – a trio being a cup, plate and saucer from the same china pattern. With no two trios alike, it made for a very colourful table setting.

Since I was a child I had loved Mum's assortment of pretty teacups, and after getting married I too began to collect mismatching trios. But I never really used them; it was too easy to throw a teabag in a mug. Five or six years ago one of my friends was admiring my china and suggested we get them out of the cupboard next time she came for afternoon tea, which we did. The teapot was most startled to be plucked from hibernation, and was even affronted when it discovered that I was only using *teabags*. I would have been cross too if I was it, but I hadn't thought far enough ahead to buy tea leaves. We loved the sound of the china cups clinking genteelly against saucers and teaspoons.

After that I made a habit of using my fine-china more regularly. I also began using loose leaf tea *and* sugar cubes no less. That wiped the haughtiness off the teapot's face! Doing tea the old-fashioned way had become quite the trendy thing to do of late in society at large. At first it seemed strange to see the young ones lapping up all the old-fashioned, grandmotherly stuff while still glued to their iPhones. It was heartening to see that the slower traditions could exist amidst the "instant everything" era. I was so pleased to be using the beautiful things that had been stored away for so long in cupboards – or even worse – boxes. Besides, the Queen wasn't due to visit any time soon, so there was no need to keep them pristine in the meantime.

Anyway, back to the painting. I painted for three hours and finished it off in one sitting. Even though the outcome was questionable I really enjoyed the process. I had loosened up this time to the point of absurdity, but it was such fun and I learnt a lot in the process. I found myself swimming in "the flow" with this one. As was becoming my habit, I hadn't drawn anything in beforehand. Usually the perspective somehow seemed to work, but not this time. When only ten minutes in, it looked likely to be an unmitigated disaster, but in the end it was just a disaster, but one I'd enjoyed creating.

On Friday, the thought of doing a whole painting felt too overwhelming. Instead I added a background to yesterday's picture which I hadn't originally intended to do but had since thought I should. It only took twenty or so minutes but it completed my five days of painting. Even I could see that it was a total cop-out to count today's effort (or lack of) as part of the challenge, but I felt terribly washed-out. Besides, I was Queen and creator of these challenges. I had no compunction changing decrees at will – as long as it was within reason.

Kevin returned home over the weekend and it was great to have him back again. While he recovered from jet lag poor Olivia went down with what appeared to be the flu.

Down week – with the goal of making a start on Olivia's birthday card

By Tuesday Kevin was back at work and Lola was gadding about. I had hoped to get a lot done but it seemed that I too was succumbing to Olivia's virus. I spent a while wallowing on the couch watching DVDs with Olivia. Later on, Lola kept Olivia company and they watched a few episodes of *Buffy the Vampire Slayer* on DVD. I asked them how they were enjoying it. They said, "Oh yeah, it's good in a 90s kind of way." I was taken aback by this comment as it had yet to occur to me that the 90s were far enough removed to even have a "look". Wasn't it only last week? I'd only recently been able to visually define the 80s as a decade – and that was simply because 80s retro had become so trendy it was impossible not to see the overall theme of it. When you live each day, one after the other (as you do!), it's impossible to feel the era until another decade or two has passed by to remove it and define it separately from "now". Two years into the 2010s – how could we even begin to imagine the face of this decade?

With Lola being on school holidays, Olivia sick and me fighting off what she had, not much was happening on the creative front. I had earmarked the week to get onto Olivia's birthday card. I always feel a great deal of self-inflicted pressure when it comes to the girls' birthday cards. When they were very small I started a tradition of illustrating a card for them that reflected their interests at the time.

Guilt often trickled through my veins when birthdays came around as I rarely made birthday cakes for the girls. They are not my forte. I rarely bake at all – let alone make show-stopping birthday cakes. I feel far more competent to draw a picture of a cake than bake one. Throughout their childhood I'd made one or two that passed muster, but most years one of their capable grandmothers would make one for them or I'd get one professionally made – so they never went without an eye-popping birthday cake. Instead, my way of doing something special for their birthdays was to do a personalised birthday card for them which had become something of a cherished tradition, and as an added bonus survived longer than a birthday cake. But I had come to feel a weight of responsibility to live up to their expectations.

The bright spot of the week was receiving an email from the agent to say there was an update from the publisher. My manuscript was to be discussed at an acquisition meeting next week. I was abuzz with excitement. It was great to know that there was some progress, and it sounded positive to my ears.

I finally made a start on Olivia's birthday card. An idea had come to me to do an illuminated Celtic style letter "O" featuring various symbols from her life. I did some rough sketches and thought it showed promise. Afterwards I went for a short walk through local bushland with Mum and Dad and my sister. It was a vivacious day with the foliage sparkling and glittering in the crisp sunshine. There was enough heat to release the smell of eucalyptus from the marri trees, and the purple pea-flowers of the hardenbergia vines were beginning to emerge. A little dose of the natural world was always good for feeding the muse.

Olivia had recovered her health and was out kicking up her heels with friends. She returned at 11.45pm and I felt grateful for the midnight curfew that new drivers had to abide by for the first six months after getting their license. Even still, midnight was late enough for those parents (ie: me) who couldn't sleep until their progeny were safely tucked up in bed.

I did my weekly painting on Sunday from a photo I'd taken of a vineyard. It started off okay but trying to translate the main part of the picture into any sort of coherence on to the canvas became as frustrating as dealing with a computerised phone receptionist. It was at this point that I wondered why I kept painting at all. There were times, and today was one of them, that I loved and hated it in equal measures. I was hoping that sooner or later every painting attempt would transport me into the zone. Most paintings had their moments at least, and there had been a few which had felt very right regardless of the finished product, but I would have to analyse those moments more closely sometime soon to see if I could find a pattern and know which direction to move in. I wondered if I should be making more effort to get some painting lessons so I didn't keep relying on luck for getting things right.

I had begun to feel a bit flattish lately. The amazing productivity and enthusiasm that had consumed me in the first half of the year had begun to dissipate. Admittedly I'd had a lot of other things demanding my attention these past few weeks, and at least I had been continuing with my weekly painting challenge; but after the dizzying heights of living in the uncharted territory of extreme creative output, I was now feeling pretty much back to my old "blocked" state. I could get to things eventually, but only after much vacillating and employing of delay tactics. I'd do a million other things before I felt I could devote myself to the job at hand – or worse – I'd fritter the time away doing very little at all. I hoped this sluggishness wasn't the first sign of the beginning-of-the end for my new way of living.

Finding it so difficult to get on with Olivia's birthday card was a perfect illustration (ooh a pun!) of my increasing reversion to the old ways. In fact maybe that was partly what had started it in the first place. Creating the girls' birthday cards often came with this sort of listless angst. I would put too much pressure on myself because of wanting to get it right for them which inevitably led to a fear of failure and finding it difficult to start at all.

So with one thing and another, my year of challenges that began so brilliantly seemed to have wound down to "creative business as usual". Yet again, like the bad old days, I was feeling that all the ducks had to be in a row before I could get on with anything arty. My phenomenal weeks of feeling compelled to paint or write every day – no matter what, and squeezing the creative sessions into every nook and cranny, had again been replaced with having to get on top of things first before I could feel free to devote my time to the challenges. I was frittering so much time away and being far less productive, despite the fact that I had no more to contend with now as I'd had while in the thick of the challenges. Neither was my physical state any worse than what it had been then. So I had no good excuses at all!

The recent decline in my mental state was most likely due to no longer having the preventative medicine of creative juices pumping constantly through my body. It had been replaced with the gutless juices of procrastination. It was time to get things revved up again. Even as I thought this I could feel the old "yes, buts" come into play. Instead of the euphoria of believing I could take on the world, I found myself worrying about how I'd be able to fit in anything at all next week.

Down week and continuing with Olivia's card

The second week of the school holidays continued in much the same fashion, with outings, visits and taxi runs to the station. I also continued to fight the feeling of aimlessness with my challenges.

Olivia's birthday came and went along with all the attendant gatherings of family and friends. The winter weather took a break and put on a glorious show of sunny mildness for the duration. It seemed I'd hit the spot with Olivia's card as she raved about how much she loved it. This of course was music to my ears and I basked in her delight.

In the end, I had really enjoyed designing and painting it, despite having to break through the barrier afresh each day before working on it.

Olivia's card had been the impetus to finally make use of some books on traditional Celtic art that I'd borrowed from my father-in-law a couple of years ago. I'd been keen to try my hand at some Celtic themed artwork but it had yet to happen prior to designing her card. I'd suffered that dreaded "unfinished business" feeling every time I'd happened across the books so it was great to exorcise that feeling and finally return them to whence they came.

When it comes to my illustrative work I have always used fine ink waterproof pens and watercolours, and when working on Olivia's card it was unadulterated pleasure to return to the more familiar painting accoutrements. Unfortunately, half of my very expensive tubes of paint had hardened and fossilised, due to old age I think, rather than lack of use. Just the tinkle and clink of the paintbrush swishing in water and watching the cloud of delicate pigment infuse the jar was a sensual delight after the more robust sludginess of acrylics. But they are very different animals of course and shouldn't really be compared. They both have their own unique qualities and are both delightful to use. Did I just say that about acrylics? Hmmm, maybe I will be sticking with them for the long haul after all.

Monday 30th July heralded a new challenge week. We'd watched the opening ceremony of the London Olympics on the weekend and loved it. Particularly where the Queen "jumped" out of the helicopter with James Bond! Olivia was back at university, and last week Lola finally succumbed to the virus just as Olivia had recovered from it. She had conquered it by the weekend and then Kevin got a touch of it and was couch-bound for a day or so watching the Olympics. Such fortuitous timing for him to be laid up!

CHALLENGE #12 - Write an article about the disappearance of greenery in suburbia with the intention of getting it published in the opinion pages of *The West Australian*

For five years, or maybe more, I had been threatening to write an article about the declining trees and native bird populations in the suburbs in the hope of getting it published in the state's newspaper. The hope being that it might make people sit up and smell the wood chips. I wanted to make them think about growing more trees and shrubs in their gardens. With the latest minimalist trends, many new houses and their renovated counterparts were replacing conventional gardens with a scanty smattering of designer tufts and severely coiffed shrubs. They could hardly be called gardens – more like garnishes, placed artfully to highlight the main dish of the house – and not at all bird and insect friendly.

The whole feel of our neighbourhood had changed enormously over the years. There was an increasing decline in the general lushness of many of the older suburbs that previously enjoyed leafy reputations. It seemed to me that our high-tech population was inexorably becoming more and more removed from nature and could only see trees and shrubs as optional extras in the world – and messy ones at that. If we were to save our planet and our wildlife, we needed to reacquaint ourselves with nature and understand that it wasn't something separate from us.

There is nothing more beautiful than a tree that is free to stretch its limbs freely in all directions without exciting guilt on its own or its owner's behalf. On a hot summer's day one only needs to walk under the canopy of a tree to feel the temperature drop by degrees. For a city with such a hot, dry environment in summer it would be so refreshing to be able to walk the streets in the shade of street trees and be awash with the sights and sounds of birds and butterflies frolicking through the greenery.

Every time I noticed that a tree had been chopped down I felt sick, particularly if it had been innocently growing in a perfectly benign situation with no previous form for menacing gutters or power lines. Nausea would also come upon me when I noticed trees that had been hacked back to stumps as if the owner thought a nice bracing prune would be good for its constitution – only to find it dying shortly afterwards from the kindness. I'd find myself grieving for all the lost trees and plants on the latest block to have a house demolished – of which there were many in this area. It was happening constantly. I began to realise I'd developed a strange obsession about the declining leafiness quotient and was finding it almost impossible to go out in the car without railing against the negative changes in people's gardens.

Not only was I upset about the increasing disappearance of trees from gardens and roadsides in older suburbs, but new suburbs were proliferating from north to south and taking all the native plant life with them. Our beautiful native bushland, previously untouched for millennia, was being wiped out forever in a brutal, short-sighted rampage. Nothing would be left standing once the bulldozers had been let loose. All this to allow featureless, carbon copy suburbs to pave over where beautiful grass trees, banksias, orchids and tuart trees once thrived. The populace in general appeared either oblivious or unconcerned at the unchecked urban sprawl that now rivalled some large American cities. Of course, I knew that we all had to live somewhere, and Perth had an exploding population, but there were other places in the world that put a lot more foresight and sensitive planning into urbanisation. With it becoming more clearly understood that trees attract rain, continuing to wipe them out wholesale was short-sighted madness. We'd be working harder than ever to supply fresh water to a burgeoning city.

I'd bleat about these things repeatedly, particularly while driving past recently massacred greenery, but the family got *so* fed up listening to me that I was forced to rein in my tongue. Over the years I'd written the article a million times in my head, and now, my day of reckoning had come.

Thankfully, the recent creative torpor I'd been wrestling with appeared to have vanished, but it still took me till 11.30am before making a start on the article. At least this time the late start was from getting necessary jobs done rather than from wading through pools of procrastination. I worked on the article for about three hours and in the strange way that time loses all meaning while thoroughly engaged, those hours melted away like minutes. I was very much in the creative flow and pleased with how the article was coming along.

Despite the satisfying progress, I was concerned about how the article would be received if it did find its way into the opinion pages and wondered briefly if I should put it out there at all. I wanted it to encourage people to grow more trees rather than have it interpreted as a criticism to what was already going on, if I got the tone wrong I might find myself alienating the readers. With the lingering vestiges of

OCD, I felt rather ambivalent and neurotic about the whole thing, but after all these years of thinking about it, I had to follow through now.

I continued on it after dinner but found I'd lost the tone that had been gelling well earlier. I realised it was too late in the day to be in top form. Instead, I caught up on the diary I had been keeping erratically for the purposes of writing this book.

It was great to have my original challenge format up and running again – *and* to be eliminating something that had been clogging my to-do list for years. I was back in business! On top of all this, I was pleased to be feeling somewhat livelier of late with my iron stores growing fatter by the day.

On Tuesday morning I attempted yet another beginning for the article as I didn't feel happy with the last two. I was tying myself in knots and making things too complicated. Having created too many different tangents on the same points, I felt I'd made it unworkable. Nonetheless, I pressed on; I couldn't give up on it owing to it being a challenge. Then suddenly it all fell into place. There was nothing like the thrill of nailing a few well-crafted sentences.

When I had rung the paper prior to beginning, I was told they'd consider a word count of 800. I now had around 798 words and it was pretty tightly honed, so I sent it by email to a few family members and friends for them to cast their eyes over it. After getting their feedback I decided I would tweak it a little further tomorrow.

During the day an email came through from the agent to say she still hadn't heard back from the publisher but had sent an email to enquire as to the current status. I was surprised at how long the publisher was taking to get back to her.

Before I knew it, it was time to enter the real world again and collect Lola from school. Both ends of my writing day were crammed with back to back activities and that night I fell into bed like a sack of anvils. My mental state had changed dramatically due to hormonal influences and in the evening a bleak OCD style anxiety had taken over. It had begun to creep back lately and was intensifying somewhat, but it was still at a level that I could handle. I knew unequivocally that it was hormonally driven so I was able to endure it in the knowledge it would pass like anything else unpleasant but inevitable.

Chapter Eight

AUGUST

The following morning I spent an hour and a half polishing the article until I could see my reflection in the sentence structure. All the while I was still unsure as to whether or not I would go ahead and send it to the paper. But after getting some updated – and positive – feedback, I went ahead and sent it through in the afternoon. The editor responded shortly afterwards with a quick note to say he'd get back to me soon. It was out of my hands for now.

CHALLENGE # 13 – Rewriting and resubmitting children's book manuscript *The Golden Glitter Girl*

Now the article had been sent off, the afternoon was free to make an earlier than expected start on another challenge. Something else I desperately wanted to eradicate from my to-do list this year was to revise an unpublished children's picture book story I'd written some years back. Entitled *The Golden Glitter Girl*, it's a story about a young girl who is guided wisely towards self-esteem by a friendly mermaid.

Upon unearthing it, I was surprised to note how long ago I had written it – 2007. I'd sent it to a few agents and publishers at the time but hadn't had inspired reactions: one complaint being that the text was too long. Another agent had accused it of being too didactic. Unfortunately, the publisher of my *You Can Do It!* books had ceased to handle children's publishing so the potential to get a foot in that door had closed.

The *You Can Do It!* series had sold very well, with many people telling me how much they loved the rhyming aspect of the stories. So I thought I should stick with what worked and try to rewrite *this* story in rhyme. But the muse had left the building! I wasn't able to compose a single verse. Either my rhyming ability had deserted me or it was too difficult to translate previously written prose into rhyme. I'd written the other stories in verse right from the beginning and I began to wonder about leaving this one in prose after all. The story worked well as it was, it was just too wordy. I would try the rhyming again tomorrow, but if it didn't gel after giving it my all, I'd concentrate on honing the prose and cutting back the word count. All the pictures were at the stage of fairly good roughs. I felt very motivated to get it moving again and then make a start on writing *this* book.

Straight after breakfast on Thursday, I fired up the computer and to my amazement my old rhyming groove was back. It was a stark contrast from just the day before. The muse was back! I was feeling a little more even in the head today so no doubt that had something to do with it. Yesterday, it was odd how I'd been in the zone while working on the article in the morning but felt blocked with the children's story in the afternoon. Maybe it was due to feeling weary by the afternoon and the need to change mental tack had possibly been just one mental manoeuvre too many for my overtaxed synapses.

Even though it was possible to rhyme today it still wasn't easy, but I found it satisfying and fun, like trying to solve a puzzle. By the end of the morning I had converted about four pages of the story, but it still needed more honing.

When I stopped for lunch I checked my emails and saw there was one from the agent. I held my breath as I clicked it open. The publisher had declined! Huh! I was quite surprised considering it had got as far as the publisher's acquisition meeting and that the agent had felt so confident about it. I had always heard it was harder to get an agent than a publisher, so once I'd got my agent, I thought getting a publisher would be a fait accompli. Feeling surprised *and* disappointed, I rang the agent straight away to pump her for more information and hopefully reassurance. She assured me that it would be snapped up by another publisher in no time and she had everything in hand to send it to a different one tomorrow.

That was the wonderful advantage of having an agent – they have open channels to keep things moving. If it was in *my* hands, I may have spent weeks or months licking my wounds before being able to face the laborious preparation for the next submission. Having to heed the onerous, one-off requirements of the next publisher's submission criteria might have been enough to keep me immobile indefinitely.

While on the phone, I also mentioned to the agent that I was reworking my mermaid story. She sounded interested and said to send it through when I had it ready, but she let me know that she didn't handle much in the way of children's literature as a rule. Our conversation motivated me to stick with it until it was ready for submission. It would be great to have one less unfinished project skulking in the shadows. Unfinished projects have haunted me all my life and weigh me down mentally. Particularly when I see them lounging around the place.

I rang a few hapless people to unload my disappointment upon and then continued on with the day.

I had pulled right back on the socialising this year and loved how it had freed up so much time. As the year progressed I no longer had to manage my outings so carefully by declaring it a social-free zone when on a challenge week. I was becoming more able to fit in the high level of creative output amongst my everyday activities without having to compartmentalise everything.

Although I wasn't being so proactive socially, I felt sure my friendships could handle it. Those that you connect with well can withstand less frequency easily enough. Everyone has such busy lives these days that the months seem to pass like weeks, so it doesn't feel like we've been neglected or been neglectful. In the past, I had been too obsessed with always trying to do the right thing – in that I'd think, "Oh, I haven't seen so and so for a while now – I must organise something". I'd often overlook the fact that others didn't necessarily run on the same time frame as I did. I found that with some friends, if I didn't initiate things, more time would pass between catch ups, and vice versa with other friends.

In the past I had often endeavoured to cut down on socialising time, but it always seemed to conspire against me in that as soon as I tried to let things fall a little fallow, a deluge of people would be in touch, with all their inner time-frames synchronising at once. Somehow, it was working out well this year without much overt planning on my behalf. Initially, I'd had to adhere rigidly to my self-imposed socialising rules, but it seemed that once my commitment had been registered as the real deal, the God of social butterflies orchestrated things to feel like no effort at all. I'm not quite sure how it worked but I now had swathes of time to devote to my passions while still seeing enough of my friends to not feel that too much time had passed between visits. Some of my closer friends had recently returned to full-time work or more time-consuming pursuits so that had also made an impact on making things easier.

Overall, the challenges allowed me to see that with diligence and commitment, there was an awful lot of usable time to be carved out from around all the usual things that fill a day. The genius, power and magic of commitment also manifests in synchronicity, which I found had increased enormously over the year. Some weeks more than others, but certainly when I actively stopped and reminded myself to go with the flow of life, it was almost spooky how synchronicity emerged from the woodwork.

When we relax and "let go, let God" it is not only our self that reaps the benefits. I've heard of the concept that the energy we generate via our state of being, whether it be sunny or sullen, happy or hateful, contributes to the tone of energy of the entire planet. We only have to be in the company of someone in a foul mood to tangibly feel the unhealthy vibes emanating from them, so it isn't that far fetched a notion at all. I like to imagine that when I feel happy and jolly, any good vibes surplus to my own requirements will be siphoned off into the planetary good-vibe grid. In the same way that surplus electricity generated from solar-cells on roofs go into the energy company's main grid.

On Friday, I continued with the rhyming, and had an easy and spacious day with it being Olivia's night to cook. It was such a luxury for me to get a whole night off a week from being responsible for dinner, a luxury I never tired of. It allowed me to wring a little more productivity – or rest, out of the day.

While Olivia cleaned up the kitchen, I snuggled up in bed to catch up on my diary. I had been luxuriating in bed before dinner too. It was the height of decadence that my most onerous activity of the evening had been to lug myself out of bed when summoned to eat.

The publishing disappointment had mostly dissipated and the horrible anxiety of the past weeks had released me from its grip. When I stopped to analyse it, I could see that my mental state had become wobbly sometime after Olivia got sick. In my robust state of mind I had weathered her convalescence fairly well, but a succession of ailments was too much for me. Olivia had only just shaken the virus when Lola succumbed to the same thing – and Kevin after her. It took Lola about a week to totally recover and she'd needed a couple of days off school. Then Olivia's birthday was upon us and a skin condition arose on her face which required cortisone cream treatment. They were such little things for most people, but it was all classic OCD material for the irrational part of my brain to feast upon. Having been comparatively free of it for so long, it was extra unpleasant and difficult to deal with. It was a great relief to feel such an improvement this last day or so.

It was very satisfying to have such a productive and successful challenge week but I had to fit some painting in too. I didn't want to fall off that wagon now that I was once again deeply embroiled in the writing.

The weekend was a busy one and I only managed to spend half an hour on my painting. The vineyard picture wasn't inspiring me at all. I knew it had nothing to do with the actual image but more to do with having got off to a bad start. It was all wrong colours and poor perspective and I didn't know how best to proceed from such inauspicious beginnings. Hopefully, I'd feel more enthused as I got further along with it.

Kevin's birthday had come and gone and he'd been thrilled with his motorbike painting. It's a great feeling to know that an idea has hit the spot. Knowing him so well, I could be sure he wasn't just putting on a brave face and pretending to like it.

Continuing with the challenge of rewriting *The Golden Glitter Girl* (mermaid book) in rhyme

The next week began frenetically. The intention for the week was to work single-mindedly on the mermaid book until I'd perfected it in rhyme. On Monday, I powered through a long list of jobs in the hope of working on the book once they were done. But then I had to run Lola around for various outings and escapades that spilled into the evening. In the end, there had been too many non-negotiables to deal with and I had to concede defeat.

When the girls were babies and toddlers, people were always saying, "Enjoy every moment, as they grow up too fast," and of course they were right. But when up to my elbows in dirty nappies, and deranged from lack of sleep, there were times when I did catch myself wishing it away to some degree. Some days, time actually seemed to go *backwards*. The responsibility for two totally dependent little children 24 hours a day while dealing with poor health was at times so overwhelming, I found it impossible to imagine having real time to myself – or a good night's sleep – ever again. But naturally, that level of intensity fell away after a while and much was savoured over the years.

Even not so long ago, I'd occasionally find myself imagining a dreamy future where both the girls had their driver's licenses and I'd be swimming in extra time. But the reverie would only last a moment. I didn't want to wish this stage of my life away; it was too precious and fleeting and, overall, so rich and rewarding. Time was passing *so* fast I feared getting whiplash.

Besides, their full independence was no longer some hazy concept in the distance – it was right up close and in my face. I could practically smell the exhaust fumes as they roared off into the distance of their independent lives. I was very mindful these days of savouring my taxi duties and other calls on my time. It was all part of the privilege of having children to love and the thrill of being in the thick of life. Soon enough, I would be an empty-nester looking back longingly on these full and busy days.

My endeavours to compose verse continued over the next two days until it became obvious it wasn't going to work. Trying to convert long-winded and profound prose neatly into rhyming verse was proving tricky. Rather than condense the text, it was further lengthening due to trying to retain the same meaning. At 1900 words it was already way too long for a picture book. I rang the agent to tell her of the difficulties I was having with the word count *and* the style. She kindly suggested I send it to her to see if it looked viable as it was in prose.

After sending the original version through, I decided to take a break from it until I heard back, which I thought would be sometime later in the day. I downed tools and ensconced myself in a good book.

We were finding it difficult to get out of bed on these cold winter mornings and Thursday was no exception. The mercury had shimmied down to 2.9 degrees Celsius! Nonetheless, it was a lovely crisp, sunny day and after dropping Lola at school, I went for a twenty minute walk along the coast to get my corpuscles cavorting. The day was making a spectacle of itself with perfect tubular waves crashing onto a glittering blue, green ocean. Purple hardenbergia flowers trailed amongst the scrub in the foreground and an impossibly blue sky brought up the rear. Conditions were divine and made for a lovely walk, but I felt like I was missing an appendage – my camera!

I've always felt a compulsion to capture the beautiful things I see around me; either by taking photos or creating a work of art based upon it. It causes me physical pain to be without my camera on a gorgeous day, or when seeing beautiful things of any sort. The angst of not being able to capture what I see often overshadows the enjoyment I should be having by being in the moment with the beauty; even though I *know* that a photo can never possibly do justice to the real thing (not the ones I take anyway). Somewhere within the angst, I'm mindful that I should be savouring the present moment and just accept that life is fleeting – I can't keep trying to bottle it.

That being said, the compulsion to record things has certainly led to many an artwork, so I wouldn't want to deny the deep pull I feel to create something from what I see. I just need to find the balance between capturing the moment and savouring the moment. The idea of painting en plein air (on location, out doors) really appeals to me and would probably satisfy both needs at once.

Living in the moment and appreciating the flow of life had been so much easier as a child. The need to capture everything probably only began to develop sometime in my early twenties, and once the kids were born, my camera went from part-time to full-time employment. I was constantly trotting to the shops to put film in for developing. But at around the age of forty, I went through a stage whereby I all but gave up taking photos. I had already stopped videoing quite some time earlier as I felt there were times when I was just watching life happening through a small screen. The changeover from film to digital had cooled my photographic ardour somewhat, as learning to upload and retrieve in the new format was initially quite intimidating. But the critical moment for dispensing with the still camera had come during Olivia's primary school graduation night when she was up on the stage making her speech. I had wanted to capture the moment for all time – for her sake in particular – but the camera was malfunctioning and wouldn't focus properly. While I furiously manhandled it, trying in vain to get it to work, I missed hearing part of what she was saying. I was left without a decent photo or a decent memory of the special moment. I vowed to experience life first-hand and without the camera for a while.

On Friday I was yet again in the grip of the worst type of OCD. For most of the morning I was unable to turn off the insidious thoughts, but thankfully, the distraction of having visitors over for afternoon tea began to erode them. It seemed they weren't cutting quite so deeply these days and tended to shift more quickly. The intrusive thoughts continued to recede to the point where they had all but evaporated by evening. I was surprised at how such an intense psychological state could abate so quickly, it certainly wasn't what I'd been used to during the worst times, so I was truly grateful for this evolution.

By Saturday, I was entirely free of the OCD torment. Even the usual hangover feeling that would come after an episode was absent. In fact, I had a particularly pleasant day which began by returning to bed immediately with a cup of tea and my book.

Later on, I went for a walk along the beach path – this time *with* my camera. It was warm and sunny and the sea air smelt too divine for words. One of the neighbours at the end of the street caught me on the way to the beach to ask where she could buy a set of my children's books. This was the third enquiry about my books in a very short space of time after going years between any mentions of interest. Very strange!

I had intended to paint at some point in the day but left it too late to start. Knowing there wouldn't be time to paint tomorrow, I realised I'd let myself down on the painting challenge this week. It was disappointing but I had really needed the rest.

Some days, I felt the need to get away from my every day environs and rejuvenate my creative spirit. Sunday was looking like a good day to tack on a few extra excursions to an outing that was already on the agenda with the girls. It was a shame that the weather forecast was looking ominous.

We went to an open day at a university campus that Lola was considering attending once she finished high school. The day served up torrential rain in an over-generous manner and we got wet and bedraggled even with our brollies at full sail. It poured with attitude and the wind got in on the action too. It was a terribly bleak day in which to be out and about, but we persisted with our plan and from there visited a few antique shops in a nearby suburb. From there we hydroplaned to another old suburb to have a bite to eat at a cafe and to look through the adjoining art gallery where a friend was exhibiting her beautiful pottery. It was an enjoyable outing and it had jollied up the muse, but we'd really had to work at it in the face of the inhospitable weather.

Down week – and doing a painting for Mum

It was a relief to have an excuse to stop working on the vineyard painting. I put it on hold in order to start a painting for Mum's birthday which was fast approaching. I decided to do a still life. I popped a few violets from the garden into a tiny chintz patterned jug and set it next to a china figurine Mum had given to me as a child. After setting everything up ready to paint from life, I made the decision to work from a photo instead as I didn't feel confident at being able to capture the shine and colours on these particular pieces. It is easier to work from two dimensions than three, but it is a compromise. When painting from life, it's a bigger buzz knowing that something a little more difficult and more real is being undertaken. I took over fifty similar photos of the set-up. By the time I'd finished agonising over which was the best one to work from, I'd run out of time to start painting.

Tuesday was Olivia's allergy specialist appointment which had been weighing heavily in my psyche for weeks and contributing to the return of my OCDish anxieties. I'd been living in fear that the specialist would discover something that would trigger off a full-blown OCD episode.

Along with having her skin condition examined, Olivia would be having an updated test to see how her shellfish allergy was faring – amongst other things. I'd been freaking out that even the most microscopic amounts of crustacean juice molecules used in the prick-test would send her into anaphylaxis. But all went swimmingly, and to our excitement her shellfish allergy appeared to have abated somewhat. She still needs to carry an EpiPen with her, but should she be exposed to anything it was now less likely to be an anaphylactic reaction. Whatever the case, we couldn't lessen our vigilance with the EpiPen.

Against all expectations, it actually turned out to be a nice little outing. Having arrived early for the appointment we'd had time beforehand to enjoy a coffee together at a nearby café. All that wasted time and effort worrying for nothing – would I ever learn?

After a busy social day on Wednesday, I racked up nine hours of painting over Thursday and Friday. It was quite a tight picture but I was very happy with it.

Eventually, I heard back from the agent with feedback on my mermaid story. She agreed that it would need to be cut back in length and that it wouldn't work in rhyme. Once I had it ready she would try it with one publisher in particular that I had requested, but that would be the only submission she would make for me.

Some time back, I had retrieved my painting from the Joondalup art exhibition. There had been a lot of better art on offer and at better prices so I wasn't surprised or disappointed that I hadn't made a sale. In fact, there hadn't been a huge number of sales overall, so I was pleased that one of my friends had been among the lucky minority. It had been a good experience for putting my toe in the water.

I'd had a rejection regarding the tree article, but here too I hadn't felt terribly disappointed owing to my ambivalence about it. Shortly after writing the article, I had noticed that new street trees were being planted by the shire on various roads. I began to worry that what I'd written may have been a little jaundiced because of being an obsessive tree hugger – something I was proud to call myself – but deep down I knew it had nothing to do with that. I'd had legitimate fodder for the piece because even though good green deeds were being done in certain areas, many dirty deeds were being done elsewhere.

At least some good came from writing the article; in that it had a positive outcome for the family. The act of converting my whines and bleats into the written form was somehow cathartic for me. My obsessiveness over disappearing greenery evaporated. It was healthier for everyone and I could enjoy myself more when I set out in the car.

But then it wore off. The therapeutic effects dried up while chatting with an acquaintance some time later. She was telling me about friends of hers who had just moved to an outlying suburb. Upon hearing the name of the locale, I asked if her friends had bought one of the larger acreage blocks that were common in the area, not realising that it had already fallen victim to encroaching suburbia. She said no, as it was now all new housing developments. I said how sad it was that the outskirts of Perth – which were recently old market gardens and bush blocks of ten acres plus – were getting wiped out to make way for cheek by jowl suburbia. She gawped at me as if I was from a far flung galaxy and said rather snarkily, "Bring on the development I say!"

All she could see when looking at native bush was that it needed urbanising. All I could see was a unique and beautiful ecosystem that was found nowhere else on earth and would be destroyed forever after taking millions of years to evolve. What made it worse was the fact that this part of Western Australia is one of the planet's biodiversity hot spots. I wish I could say that hers was an unusual viewpoint, but obviously it wasn't or there wouldn't be such wide-scale destruction as if our bush went on forever – or was just some annoying thing in the way of the bulldozers. I'd heard enough people over the years call it useless scrub to know that it was a fairly endemic viewpoint among those who had no affinity with nature – which seemed to be a good proportion of the population.

I'd been gradually formulating a plan to set up a blog of my paintings with a link to my children's books. I felt the need to be in control of my own creativity, or some part of it at least. It was horribly deflating to always be in waiting mode, compulsively checking emails to see if a long awaited response had come through. Not only from publishers via the agent but also checking for other awaited correspondences. Of course, I was very excited and grateful to have my book and other things in the pipeline, but I'd had an inelegant sufficiency of the waiting process – and of being dependent on others' yays or nays. It was very disempowering and I felt stuck.

I had begun an email correspondence with one of the daily painters in America after buying one of her small paintings. She happened to ask if I had a blog she could look at, and I told her I had yet to create one. Somehow, her enquiry vaporised the last fibre of procrastination standing between me and making a start on it. I'd been thinking about it for ages but had been ambivalent about committing to it while I was still unprepared to offer original paintings for sale. But I decided I could begin by posting my latest paintings for friends and family to view and see what happened from there.

CHALLENGE # 14 – Set up a blog

I continued painting over the weekend and on Monday began work on setting up the blog. It took me ages to figure out how to get the header right and I became almost unhinged in the process. It was an exercise in sheer frustration having to rely on my own computer savvy which was barely a smear. My technical consultants (the girls) were too "busy" and indifferent to respond to my cries for help. I only got as far as establishing the name, address and header, but it was quite a thrill getting it to that point.

I was firmly planted in front of the computer again for most of the following day while I worked further on my shiny new blog. It took my pterodactyl brain whole Neolithic periods to work out how to create every new component while it would have taken mere minutes for anyone under twelve to do the same thing. How humiliating it is for our generation to be seen as dinosaurish know-nothings. Throughout most of human existence, the natural order of things has always been that the elders in society have it all over the young ones with their extra years of experience – not to mention the choicest bits of meat from the campfire. Of course we oldies know that we still rule, but unfortunately we're the only ones who know it! Another generation in history that had the natural order upturned so unceremoniously was the one that saw literacy become a birthright for every child. As the children learnt their three Rs, they soon outstripped their parents' knowledge in something that had great cache in the modern world. Their parents' only mistake was being born a generation too early at a time when literacy was still the preserve of the wealthy classes, and often only the males amongst them at that.

I created my first ever blog post by uploading some photos of the paintings I did in the 10 day challenge. When I was about to add more photos in the afternoon, the computer had a hissy fit and I was forced to abandon it. It was probably for the best: I was depleted from all the unaccustomed mental effort but had been unable to pull myself away from the computer.

In amongst all the blog wrangling, I finished off Mum's picture. Having missed doing a painting the week before, I made up for it this past week by painting every day until it was finished. In the end I spent just over fourteen hours on the jug and green china doll and thoroughly enjoyed myself in the process. The recent slump in enthusiasm for painting disappeared with Mum's picture. It made me realise that it had been the vineyard painting causing the motivation problem. The inspiration to revisit it just wasn't there and I suspected it was because the photo reference hadn't resonated with me for some reason. Hopefully, I would feel enthused to return to it at some point as I didn't want to add anything to my "unfinished" list.

Once again I marvelled at how great things were panning out this year overall. I had come through to the other side of my recent unproductive spell and was achieving more than I could ever have dreamed of when living in the common hours of my start/stop/wallow artistic career. But I was yet to master the art of balance.

Every day lately, my goal was to sort out the paperwork before slinking into my art room. But every day I resisted my responsible intention and headed straight for the computer instead. The pile of bills grew more menacing by the day, pulsating with the imminent danger of overlooked pay-by-dates. I could hear the ominous screech of violins every time I glanced nervously in their direction.

On Wednesday morning, I worked feverishly on my blog before popping out to meet friends for a quick bite to eat. I was home by 2pm for more heated blog construction.

When I first began cluelessly setting up my blog, I was still under the delusion that the girls would help me once they were flush with free time and benevolence towards their mother. I had pottered with it endlessly and often fruitlessly to see how far I could get before they'd be ready and available to kindly do my bidding. I had it practically up and running by the time it dawned on me that they'd had no intention of helping me at all – any more than Kevin had. I'd only half-heartedly asked him in the first place as I'd thought the girls would be my best bet. It seemed I hadn't backed any good horses! "Having a go" in the face of something that initially appeared insurmountable reminded me of the time I'd had a flat tyre when I was around nineteen years old.

I had owned a car that was considered a big vehicle for a girl to drive in those days. Power steering was yet to become a common feature and it was long before the arrival of the four-wheel drive fad that many women took to years later.

Ironically, I turned to a slightly smaller make as I got older while many of my friends ditched their cute little numbers to cruise around in beefy but stylish fuel-guzzling rides.

The nineteen year old me had already been shown in a hands-on manner how to change a tyre, but that had been a year or so previously and it seemed a bit daunting to have to do it in a real life situation on my own. Luckily, I'd noticed the tyre was punctured before heading out, so the car was still in the car park of the apartment where I lived. It crossed my mind that one of the neighbours I knew vaguely would possibly be free to help, but I felt embarrassed to ask him before I'd made it look like I'd at least *tried* to do it myself. I scrabbled around in the boot for the jack and positioned it at the rear of the car and wondered if that small act would look pro-active enough.

As I fiddled with the ratchety, lever thingy, I thought I could probably even jack it up if I made sure it was secure, "Yes, that did the trick! Now where's that socket wrench?" Once I loosened the wheel nuts just so, *then* I would go and knock on Mark's door. "Whoa! This baby's heavy!" I thought as I wrestled the tyre off and manoeuvred the spare one into place. "Mark, Shmark!" I thought as I tightened the last bolt, jumped in the car and drove off in a cloud of smugness.

Over the years, having that experience in my archives was a good reminder to be more proactive in the face of things. Although, I'm sure Kevin would never guess at the lesson I'd learnt in light of all the occasions I go running to him to do my dirty work.

No doubt, I was now a contender for taking out the record for the-longest-time-ever-taken-to-create-a-blog, but I'd had such a wonderful time doing it and felt a great sense of achievement at having launched it by myself. It was a draining process though. What is it about computers that makes them so drop-dead exhausting? I couldn't imagine ever preferring to read books electronically to the real thing as it would defeat the purpose of trying to relax. There is nothing like a good old-fashioned paper book… Oops! And just when I was beginning to feel like a hip blog designer!

What with the painting and creating the blog, the last two weeks had been great for getting back on track with the creative challenge. It had been a long-term plan to get a blog or website (or both) up and running by the end of the year, so it was good having recently found the impetus to set it up earlier. There was another good reason to do it sooner rather than later: the commitment to my weekly painting had begun to wane and I could see the habit might fall away entirely if I wasn't careful. I hoped that a blog would force my hand to paint more frequently. Making the commitment public would be a great way to keep the weekly discipline inviolable: it would be much harder to weasel out of in the full glare of any potential followers. I thought it would also help keep the OCD at bay. With my creative exploits having fallen a bit fallow in more recent weeks the OCD had had a chance to come to the fore again. I needed the full-on creative inoculation. Just doing bits and pieces here and there wasn't cutting it any longer.

After the frustration of feeling at the mercy of waiting to hear back from others, I'd had a fabulous week of taking things into my own hands again. But the empowerment didn't last long because I soon realised I had fallen into a similar trap. Now that my blog was launched, I was *constantly* checking to see if anyone was visiting it.

On Sunday, Kevin and I set off at 9.00am for a drive into the country. It was a glorious day in the low twenties and we stopped for a couple of wildflower appreciation interludes along the way. The girls had better, teenagery things to do, so they stayed home to do them. Our destination was to visit Auria – a property not far from the farming town of Dowerin – which is around 160kms from Perth. The property is owned by David Kennett who has transformed around 243 hectares (600 acres) of degraded farmland into a vista of thriving trees. I had read an article about him a few years before and was interested in his vision of researching better ways to grow trees on salt-degraded land. I'd recently spoken to him on the phone and he'd offered to give us a tour around his property should we like to come and visit.

David Kennett is a lovely man and very enthusiastic. He welcomed us with homemade soup for lunch and then took us for a tour of the property in his four-wheel drive. He's had remarkable success with the survival rate of his plantings with many areas now bristling with well established trees. It was great to see the impressive results he'd achieved through experimenting with his own unique methodologies.

While bouncing over the rough terrain and admiring his results, we were also entertained by great numbers of pink and grey galahs wheeling around the sky as one. I had forgotten how huge the flocks became when in their natural habitat. And their distinctive, almost deafening trills en masse was another joy to behold, made all the sweeter being that it was a remembered sound from childhood.

The first photo I ever remember taking, was as a young child on our wheat farm in a landscape not dissimilar to this one. With Mum supervising I had carefully held our box brownie – which was black – at waist level so I could look into the view finder. I aimed it towards the trees in the chook pen and clicked the button, immortalising in print forever a cohort of pink and grey galahs as they chewed the fat together in a stand of tall trees. I still have the grainy black and white photo in an album.

In recent years I'd been thinking a lot about wanting to buy some cleared acreage in the wheat-belt in order to revegetate with original and endangered species. The old saying, "You can take the girl out of the country, but you can't take the country out of the girl" certainly pertained to me. Not that I often ventured into "my country" as it happened, but my heart and mind still held it especially dear. Wisps and echoes of a beloved landscape permeated my very being. But it was neither practical nor financially viable right now to take on such an enterprise and there was a fair chance it would never happen, so it was great to be able to enjoy someone else's exploits vicariously. In the face of my less than robust specimen-hood, I often wondered that I could take my dream so seriously.

Variations of this dream have been with me since youth, reclining comfortably in my "one day" basket. "One day" had belonged to a future that appeared to stretch out forever in my imagination, because time was on my side then. But now I am at an age where I clearly understand there is nowhere near as much time in a lifespan as I had imagined when newly hatched. I now know that some things in my "one day" basket are definitely never going to happen, and others may just be wriggled in somewhere in the itinerary. It hit me today that it's very similar to when you're on a holiday. You start with a proposed itinerary but inevitably you run out of time to see and do everything – unless you're on a package tour of course where everything is mapped out by the minute. But life never works out *that* way!

Continue with blog

On Monday, I continued working on my blog by uploading a photo of my children's books and creating a link to where they could be bought. Aside from that, the first half of the week was devoted to all things domestic rather than creative. By Wednesday I was free to pursue more pleasant things. I had earmarked the day for doing my first painting on one of the small 15cm x 15cm (6" x 6") boards I'd bought a month or so ago. I'd decided to paint in the smaller format for the purposes of standardising my work for when I was ready to start selling. I'd been holding off using the small boards while I waited for an easel to arrive that I'd ordered especially for these smaller sized boards. I'd either underestimated the shipping time or it had gone astray so I decided to wait no longer and planned to begin painting sometime before lunch. To my surprise the easel was delivered with consummate timing that very morning. Synchronicity had shown its hand so immaculately I could practically hear the cogs and levers whirring in the ether as the parcel arrived at the door.

The little burst of excitement over the timely delivery soon trickled away and the underlying fatigue I'd felt all morning regained the upper hand. I pottered lethargically with paperwork and various things while trying to muster the energy to make a start, but it began to look like I wouldn't have the wherewithal to paint after all. Would my failure to paint be a slap in the face to the Universe after it had perfectly choreographed the timing of things? If it wasn't for Olivia taking the easel out of its packaging in the afternoon in a burst of curiosity, I probably wouldn't have done a painting. But once it was unpacked and I'd set it up with a board right ready to go, the sight of the blank board got my creative juices flowing, and the attendant energy that seems to accompany the muse was enough to get me painting.

The subject matter was the same backyard succulent I had painted on the first day of my 10 day challenge, but this time I did a stylised version. It was much more satisfying painting on board rather than canvas which I'd been doing until now. The paint felt buttery and easy to manoeuvre, whereas the rough texture of the canvas had impeded my brushstrokes. It probably wouldn't have been so frustrating painting on canvas if I'd been able to apply the paint in the generous, luscious manner of my imaginings. But from today, I was a convert to the board!

I was very happy with the finished product and loved every minute of the one and a half hour painting process. There was still ample daylight remaining, so I photographed the painting and posted it on my blog. I enjoyed the immediacy of posting my first "live" one. Up until now I had been uploading photos of work I'd done previously. Having begun the day so wrong-footed it was a surprise to find it had transformed into a very satisfying afternoon. It was even more satisfying knowing I hadn't turned my back on the synchronicity of the easel arriving at the perfect moment.

The next day was back-to-back entertaining. In the morning, it was a mad rush of vacuuming, mopping and tidying; the usual frenzy I go through to make it appear that our home is always effortlessly clean and refined. A friend came for morning tea and then several friends came for afternoon tea. I brought out all the lovely china and threw some tea leaves in the pot. It was a very agreeable, albeit tiring day, but I had enough life left in me to continue the socialising bender the following day as well.

It was at around this time that I began to notice something. After regaling the fourth person for the day with the same colourful description – almost verbatim – of something I'd done earlier in the day, I realised that I'd begun to compose my anecdotes as if I was writing dialogue in a script. I was even tweaking them a tad with each retelling. I wondered how many kinds of weird this was. Also, I'd find myself recounting to friends, anecdotes that I'd recently been writing about in my book and practically using the sentences word-for-word. Did that mean I was a natural writer, or again, just many shades of odd?

Chapter Nine

SEPTEMBER

My Dad was a wonderful writer and often wrote poems and short stories when I was growing up. We loved listening to him read them out to us in his animated style. He had a great talent for making the characters come to life. I'm sure his enthusiasm for writing brushed off on me right from the beginning.

I used to think my desire to write was something that had only come upon me in recent decades. But looking back I realised I've enjoyed writing since my earliest years, from the unfinished novel I wrote in primary school (heavily plagiarised from Enid Blyton's *The Magic Faraway Tree*) to the many journals I kept at various times throughout my life. There are numerous people within my extended family who are also consumed with a passion to write, so it's probably more than just a conditioned interest: it's in my genes.

Over the weekend, I referred back to the first few pages of my challenge diary to remind myself of the original objectives. One was to make more use of the wealth of art-reference material I had squirreled away over the years. This material came in various forms: multitudes of photos, both digital and hardcopy, and decade's worth of pages pulled from magazines that had inspired me in one way or another. I had also bought books and magazines to keep solely for the purpose of art reference – I'd even collected the odd shopping catalogue! I still do from time to time, but I chastise myself heartily even while in the act of adding to my stash.

Occasionally, a piece of art would spring from the loins of my reference material, but not often enough to justify continuing with the collection. The time had come to either validate it for clogging up my art room for decades – or get rid of it (Yeah right!). This would be the basis for my next challenge. Then on the following week I hoped to begin writing the book that would document these challenges. I had intended to begin it weeks ago but the blog-frenzy got in the way.

Even aside from reference material, my art room was getting unruly again and needed attention; it never seemed to stay tidy for long. It wasn't just *my* mess clogging it up: David Tennant of Dr Who fame appeared to have found his way there after his latest terrorising exploits. The girls kept leaving a life-size cardboard cut-out of him around corners or placing him behind me when my back was turned. Lola had bought him as a birthday joke for Olivia who is a Dr Who fan, but he was becoming a menace. Just when I thought I'd become immune to his sudden appearances, the girls would up the ante. I'd find him suddenly standing at the kitchen bench or waiting for me as I came out of the bathroom. I'd jump-back in alarm as a surge of adrenalin shot up my spine. Our stress hormones are supposedly so toxic that if one were to extract and inject them into a guinea pig (as you do!) it would die on the spot! Due to a piece of cardboard my body was pumping out enough adrenalin to kill a whole Andean village full of guinea pigs.

Hmm, the recycling bin was to be collected soon and there was plenty more room for a bit of cardboard!

CHALLENGE #15 – In one week, create 5 illustrations to be used as greeting card designs based on existing art reference

When trawling through the daily painters' blogs last night I felt so inspired by all I saw that it made me think I'd rather paint in the coming week than do illustrations from art-reference. It made more sense to go in the direction of my current passion. So, as a compromise, I decided I would work in acrylics but the painting must still be suitable for a greeting card – or a mug design – and be inspired by something from my reams of art reference material. I had begun to do some research into the online shops that do print-on-demand (POD) to see about getting my designs set up in that format.

It was disturbing how quickly I forgot things lately; I had a mind like a rusty colander. By morning I found myself arranging my favourite china teacup, plate and saucer in a beguiling pose before heading off to look for some fabrics to include in the set-up. I had already forgotten that the challenge was to work from long held reference material. It was only later that I looked back in wonder at my blatant lapse in memory. I hoped it was just because I was so deeply connected to the muse these days and following my heart blindly when it came to what it wanted to create at that moment.

After messing around for a while with the still-life arrangement, which wasn't gelling to my satisfaction, I remembered a series of photos I'd taken some years ago of this same green china pattern. I had arranged the pieces with some flowers picked from my garden. The plan at the time was to use the best image for a greeting card. But I realised belatedly that the camera wasn't capable of taking the quality of photo I needed. Shortly after the photo-shoot, I'd happened upon a greeting card site that gave the minimum size requirements for submitting photos. They had to be at least six megapixels in size in order to get the right quality for reproduction, and mine could only spit out three. Nonetheless, I had been very happy with the composition so I would now convert it into a painting.

After agonising for a while as to which photo to paint from I decided to paint only a portion of the picture as it would work better that way on the 15cm x 15cm square board. So it was only by a circuitous route that I ended up working from long held reference material – even though it was digital rather than the hard copy that I'd wanted to work from. It wasn't really in the spirit of what I'd intended for this challenge, but I felt secure enough in creativity's embrace to bend the challenge rules. I liked to think I was adept at turning a blind eye to my transgressions only if it meant I would remain on track for the ultimate goal, which was to be productive and create something.

Despite occasionally playing fast and loose with the rules, I continued to get the same productive outcomes as when I had observed the strict challenge format. This started me wondering what *was* the magic ingredient that had enabled me to make such grand changes in my life? When I reflected on it more deeply, I concluded that of course it had been due to the strict challenge format that I'd become more disciplined and creative. I had begun to organically move away from the stringent approach only because it had been so successful in initiating a significant increase in creative output. I no longer had to crack the whip on myself. Having continued with the format long enough for a natural momentum to set in, it was now so well established that I could afford to take some liberties with the challenges. They had set the creative juices flowing, and should the momentum begin to slow, I'd simply trot out the strict challenge format again in order to reawaken the muse.

I put brush to board at around 11.00am and worked for two and a half hours before stopping for lunch. I was so in the zone while painting this picture I was practically doing breaststroke in the stream of creativity. As the paint glided dreamily onto the smooth board I realised it no longer mattered that I rarely achieved the elusive loose style I had been trying for. The regular painting sessions were definitely helping me to feel more at one with the process. I was delighted to discover that I could get into the zone on a tight painting too.

The flow was interrupted with the school pickup and running other errands, and all the while I was desperate to get back to my painting. I managed to slip another hour in before cooking dinner. Despite working on it for four hours in three separate sittings, the teacup painting remained unfinished until the next day when I was able to spend a further two and a half hours on it; a disappointing outcome considering I'd aimed to do a painting a day this week.

However, I was very pleased with the painting itself and everyone who had seen it so far loved it. Kevin and the girls are usually brutally honest with their feedback which is fine by me: when they say they love something then I know they mean it. If they say they don't like something – and I do – then I simply put it down to them not knowing what the "bleep" they're talking about. A good system I think.

As per the challenge, this painting was to be used as a greeting card design to (hopefully) sell on whichever print-on-demand (POD) site I decided to sign up with. Because I like square cards I had especially painted on a square board. But last night after doing further research, I was unable to find any sites that offered a square card format. It was demoralising to realise I'd overlooked something so basic.

On Wednesday, Jenny came over for the day, and we went through a manuscript she was working on. It's great having each other to go over our writing with, particularly when our work is still in the embarrassing early draft stages. Also, it's invaluable having each other to cast a fresh and critiquing eye over our more developed works to be sure we're not straying into "you call that writing!?" territory. Because of our shared passion for writing and concurrent book-writing exploits, our conversations are often littered with interruptions. Should a funny anecdote or descriptive phrase find its way into our chatter, we make a point of noting who came up with it first in order to correctly attribute exclusive rights for any potential inclusion into current or subsequent oeuvres. Not that we often remember the phrases for long anyway, being that we both suffer from hormone induced dementia.

Jenny left at around 3pm, and at 3.30pm I began a painting of a hibiscus from a photo I'd taken earlier in the year. Because of Jenny's visit there had been no expectations of having time for anything creative today; I'd thought that in order to fulfil the brief, the challenge would need to spill over into the weekend, as was often the case. So it was thrilling to find it possible to seize the small gap between Jenny leaving and having to get dinner organised. I finished the painting just before 5pm then took a photo and posted it on my blog. I was very happy with the hibiscus and decided it would make a perfect little gift for one of my friends who was currently unwell.

After dinner, I continued with my research into POD sites and became increasingly bewildered and stressed about which company to sign up with. I badly wanted to just choose one, but my pathological fear of making decisions made it feel like a leap into the abyss rather than a leap of faith. I was frozen with indecision. One of the stumbling blocks was believing I must first buy a better camera to get the quality of reproductions I thought would be necessary for the POD site.

Even though I was often productive while on the computer, a lot of time was wasted with checking emails and Facebook. It was time that could have been used to get jobs done around the house – or even spent resting. Having recently added the blog to my online activities I'd increased the amount of time-wasting to ridiculous levels – it was *so* addictive.

Usually, the computer remained on until I was ready to retire for the evening, but that made it too easy to hop on for a "quick" check of things. Of course, it never ended up being quick, and by the time I'd checked each site, so much time had passed between the first and the last that it felt timely to revisit the first again before logging off. It could become an endless loop and was like being sucked into a whirlpool type vortex that took a formidable effort to emerge from. I had been feeling rather bewildered and ashamed of this propensity for compulsive site checking, but I had recently heard of others of my own vintage who were coming out of the woodwork to confess to the same sort of behaviour. With nerves of steel I turned the computer off at 8.30pm and put an end to it.

Making good use of my computer-free evening, I folded some clothes and did a spot of paperwork before heading to bed. The elusive early night was within my grasp! As I settled into bed it suddenly occurred to me that I could catch up on my diary: being that the night was still in its prime. A little unwinding time followed in the form of a short read, and by the time I turned out the lights it was 11.30pm! Sigh!

When it came to implementing more discipline and structure into my evenings and bedtimes I despaired of ever behaving like a grown-up. Having managed to become *very* disciplined on the creative front, I thought it strange that the same level of resolve didn't extend to the nuts and bolts of my life in the form of good sleeping habits and regular exercise. At least it was better than being unorganised in *every* aspect of my life, which was my usual default setting, but it frustrated me no end.

During the week we had a man over to do a sewerage conversion and it was completed on Thursday. The septic tanks had served us well for nearly twenty years since having the house built, but they'd just begun to show alarming signs of revolt. The timing was suddenly right to get onto a job we'd been meaning to do for years – connect to the sewerage system. It had been an option for some years now: ever since sewerage connection points had been made accessible to all properties in the metropolitan area. Ours had been one of the last suburbs to get the upgrade owing to the difficulties posed by the rocky limestone terrain.

The tank was unnervingly full, and when the contractor said he'd had to let a bit of sewerage run into the trench he'd been digging, my brain began to ripple with obsessive contamination-style thoughts. What if his boots had made contact with some microscopic particles of poop? What if they'd subsequently contaminated the lawn right where *I* was walking while delivering him cups of tea?

Over the years, I had built up a wealth of mental techniques in which to draw upon that helped enormously in disabling these anxious repetitive thoughts. One of the techniques was to ask myself if I'd taken all reasonable steps to physically and morally guard against contaminating anyone. Once I could see that I had, I then had to accept that if a contamination incident did occur it wouldn't be due to a lack of vigilance on my behalf, it would simply be one-of-those-things. After all, we can never guard against everything in life no matter how hard we try. Over the years I had discovered the efficacy of employing the short-hand slogan of "shit happens" as a quick reminder to let-go in circumstances such as this. It proved to be a *very* apt one-liner in this situation.

By midday I had pulled myself together and resumed work on the mermaid manuscript. Having wrung my imagination dry in a fruitless attempt to rework it in rhyme, today I simply worked on condensing it as much as possible. I had come within a whisker of giving up on it entirely, but I'd put in too much effort over the years simply to give up on it now. I managed to trim several hundred words of fat, but it needed to lose more.

At some point during the week I had decided to dispense with the art-reference challenge and instead just continue with a general week of creativity. I didn't allow guilt to come into the equation for my change of tack. As long as I was powering along in top creative form, which I was, then I could afford to put that particular challenge on hold. Other things had rudely elbowed their way to the front of the queue and writing had gained the upper-hand. It seemed counterproductive to squelch down the writing fire, when the whole point of the challenges was to ignite my creative fire in the first place. Also, I was still in the thick of blog-fever, and distracted with researching POD sites.

The contamination concerns that I'd battled with and vanquished in the morning suddenly rallied and triumphed in the evening when Olivia announced that she was having friends over the next day for a study session. The whole house and yard once again felt contaminated and I feared it would be potentially dangerous for her friends to visit.

The next day, I hosed down the paving near the front door in the hope of putting my contamination fears to rest. Taking this precaution would rarely have stopped the obsessive thoughts in the past – it would often just perpetuate them – but because the condition had weakened so much in recent times, it seemed to do the trick and I could let it go.

I worked on the mermaid text for a few hours and then steeled myself to tidy up the painting area in my art room. There were squeezed and pummelled tubes of paint strewn amongst spiky-haired paintbrushes. It was a disgrace! Once it was basically tidied, I switched the easel with my light-box. Now I was ready to rework the pencil illustration roughs that I'd originally done for the book years earlier – but where were they? After a frustrating half hour of searching and dark mutterings I was only able to unearth two of them. The search for the others would need to be resumed at a later date.

It was amazing how much time I could waste searching for critical items that I'd placed somewhere without thinking – or even worse – placed somewhere "safe". Despite taking pains to file things away in a logical and organised manner, it never seemed logical and organised later on when I was looking to retrieve them.

But Frustration hadn't finished toying with me yet, I finally sat down to begin work only to realise that the pencil I'd held in my hand mere moments ago was nowhere to be found. Aaaargh! I discovered it shortly afterwards near the kettle. I couldn't count the times I'd been right ready to begin an illustration or painting, hot cup of tea to hand, only to find I'd somehow mislaid the pencils/brushes that I'd just spent twenty minutes searching high and low for in the first place. Dashing off to make a cup of tea was often the culprit for these farcical scenarios, so why I didn't automatically think to look near the kettle for missing items by now I didn't know.

Years ago when I had been working on the illustrations for my children's book series, I'd regularly surface from my work to make myself a cup of tea. I began to notice that I always felt very joyful while I was waiting for the kettle to boil – probably because my mind had stilled for long enough to register the warm creative glow that I had just been ensconced in while doing something I loved. Some time later, it inspired me to write the poem you will find overleaf.

Joy is a Freshly Boiled Kettle

Flagging from my duties and the morning almost gone,
I headed to the kitchen and put the kettle on.
With the sound of bubbles boiling, I took a teabag from the tin,
I popped it in my favourite cup and poured the water in.
I was right there in the moment while I made my cup of tea,
And a lovely wave of joy rose up and washed all over me.

...

Once I finally began reworking the two roughs that I *was* able to find, I had a wonderful time getting back into illustration mode.

After all my freaking out earlier in the day, Olivia's study session didn't end up coming to fruition. On a teenage whim, plans were changed and she ended up going to someone else's house to study; giving strength to the saying "Don't worry! It may never happen!" Not that I hadn't already lived through many vivid and disquieting verifications of this saying over the years, but it seemed I always had room for more.

On Saturday, I attended a propagation class at Kings Park that I had been excitedly anticipating for weeks. Kings Park comprises Perth's botanic garden as well as large tracts of native bushland. It plays host to an annual wildflower festival and is a great supporter of conservation and research. *The Art of Propagation* class was part of the University of Western Australia's extension program in conjunction with the Kings Park wildflower festival. It was being delivered by one of the park's horticulturists. First she discussed various aspects of seed collecting and then we were given seeds and punnets in which to plant them ourselves. It reminded me of cooking shows where everything has already been neatly chopped and measured and the chef just pours the ingredients into a bowl making everything look so easy. Our native seeds had been variously pre-boiled, scarified or treated with smoked water. This had been done to replicate all the necessary brutalities, like bushfire, that some Australian seeds must endure in nature before being able to germinate.

After we'd finished planting the seeds – some which were mere specks – we moved on to learn how to propagate from cuttings. We got to cut our own specimens from swathes of large branches that had been cut previously ready for our use. I particularly loved this bit and felt an amazing at-one-with-everything peace wash over me. I was very much in my element. At 4 o'clock the class finished. Being so totally engrossed in what I was doing, it felt like only five minutes had passed. We were then all invited for a behind-the-scenes tour of the Kings Park nurseries. Being that we were all native-plant-tragics we found it fascinating, and oohed and aahed at every turn. It was 5pm by the time I headed home. I'd had a *really* wonderful time but felt utterly drained once I got home – so much so that I was in bed by 8.30pm which was unheard of for me. I could hear pigs' wings flapping as they flew past my window.

The next day we were up early as Kevin and I had been invited to visit friends, Bob and Kelly, who live on the outskirts of Perth. I'd first met them a few months back at a restaurant when celebrating the birthday of one of Kevin's motorbike mates. I had been fascinated to hear about the lovely bush block they live on and the surrounding reserved land nearby. They'd promised to invite us down when the spring flowers were at their most spectacular and today was the day. In fact Bob had been a bit concerned that the best was over, but we hadn't been able to work in a visit until this weekend.

It is always a tricky job catching spring flowers at their best due to the seasonal variations from one year to the next. It's the same scenario the whole world over of course, from the cherry blossoms in Japan to the bluebell woods of Blighty.

Their property boasts nearly five acres of native bush that backs onto a huge area of reserved land and semi-rural properties. Housing developments breathe down their necks from all directions – one literally across the road from them. We enjoyed a cup of tea together before embarking on a long amble through the bush. There were flocks of orchids everywhere, particularly donkey orchids – and very beefy specimens they were too. Even Bob and Kelly said they'd never seen so many before. It was perfect weather, and such a delight seeing all the wildflowers in their prime. It was great to be with others who were equally interested in spotting orchids and other flower gems hiding in the scrub. Kevin could openly admire them in company for a change – he was no longer the only man to be tiptoeing through the undergrowth. And I found myself in the unprecedented position of being outdone by someone (Kelly) when it came to taking the most wildflower photos in one session.

After walking along the firebreaks on their land which offered a great vantage point for spotting specimens, we continued into the neighbouring derelict semi-cleared farmland where death lilies proliferated. It was very beautiful in a degraded kind of way: as in it was no longer original bushland. Weeds had replaced most of the understorey.

Considering how compromised the native bush was here, we were surprised and pleased to discover a wealth of pink orchids growing in the area, even amongst the weeds. An old car-wreck in the midst of it all looked very picturesque and I took some photos for art reference. Unlike in previous years, this time I took the photo knowing that there would be a fair chance it may actually get used for a painting.

Bob displayed rather too much zeal when it came to pointing out the many fresh snake tracks crossing the sandy paths we were walking along. They appeared at alarmingly frequent intervals, but the serpents were nowhere to be seen. Thankfully, it seemed they had better things to do than hang around livening up the local foot traffic. It was a lovely morning spent in very pleasant company.

After my weekend of immersion into spring and wildflowers, I felt hugely inspired to get my own garden sorted out. For years I'd been planning to get an understorey growing beneath the large eucalyptus and peppermint trees we have in our garden. When we first built the house, I had created a pretty understorey in parts of this area. But it eventually became choked with leaves, bark and neglect when I no longer had the time and energy to look after it properly, and all but the trees had gone on to meet their maker. A decade or so later I had been keen to revisit the idea but knew I'd have to wait until the sewerage had been connected. I hadn't wanted all my plants to be dug out again later to make trenches for the connection. Now it had finally been done there were no more excuses.

No hard and fast challenge this week – just be as productive as possible

The week began with an hour or so of weeding and making a start on the seemingly endless job of clearing leaves and bark from under the trees. It was wonderful to finally have the time and motivation to administer some love to this neglected part of the garden. The layers of bark were so many years deep; anything from snake colonies to ex-pat leprechauns could have been hiding amongst it. The rest of the day was spent pottering with various jobs in an inefficient manner. By contrast Tuesday was very productive on both the domestic and creative fronts. I continued with the mermaid book, tracing the cover illustration and outlining it in ink ready to paint. This was my third attempt to get the cover right. I wanted to change the look of the main character a little.

I did my weekly painting in the afternoon and used one of the donkey orchid photos I'd taken at Bob and Kelly's place for reference. Now that the days were getting longer, it gave me more room for manoeuvre when it came to fitting in my painting sessions. It was fun painting the orchid but I thought the finished piece looked old-fashioned and fusty. I hoped it was just due to the lighting. Nonetheless, I felt pleased at how productive my day had been and was thrilled to be able to go from one project (illustration) to another (painting in acrylics) in one day.

My hope for the following week was to make a start on my new book (*Grabbing the Muse by the Throat*) while continuing to work on the mermaid book, and also do at least one painting. If I could achieve all that, I would have truly arrived at my creative goal of writing, illustrating and painting all in one day. I came close to achieving it today and felt so enriched at having fully seized the day through a variety of endeavours. I realised too that I was feeling very energetic. The fatigue I'd been plagued with for the past twenty-plus years felt almost absent. My theory was that it was due to the high-octane creative juices frisking through my veins.

A few of my friends and relatives were currently battling cancer and it was a sobering reminder that I must seize the day while I was able. Even the longest of lives is a very brief interlude in eternity. This insight galvanised me into making the most of the day. I resolved to take on this philosophy as a permanent thing, but it may have lasted until lunchtime.

Despite all this creative glory, I'd felt a flat emotional undercurrent all day. Olivia was feeling much the same and I wondered if we'd picked up on the worldwide vibes of remembrance for September 11. I didn't let my mind go there. I was still in total lock-down from news and current affairs since my recent resurgence of less than robust mental health. When I was much younger I felt compelled to be plugged-in on a daily basis to what was happening around the world, but now I rather enjoyed living under a rock. I had been actively doing so for a few years now, just coming up for air here and there if something particularly newsworthy or juicy filtered through the fissures and trickled into my awareness.

It's funny how often the term "living under a rock" is bandied around in the media – "You'd have to be living under a rock," the smooth baritone newsreader's voice would intone, "if you haven't heard that so and so is in town." Always said with a twinkle in the eye, because of course no one on the planet could *really* be unaware of the latest rock star visit, royal birth, politician's disgrace, movie star's wedding, devastating earthquake, sport star's downfall, etc, etc. But actually they could – I was!

At times it was very embarrassing when looking blank faced at someone when they began talking about a recent news event with the obvious expectation that I'd be up to speed with what they were talking about. The zenith of embarrassment came when I caught the tail-end of a news item on TV one day while coming in to chat with the girls. I noticed a man in a suit that looked familiar amongst a group of people at some function or other. He looks familiar, I said, is he an Australian politician? The girls gawped slack-jawed at me.

Apparently he was a *very* famous person whose identity I'm too embarrassed to admit to. I had become the sort of person I used to sneer about in derision in my more finger-on-the-pulse days. I felt very ambivalent about this decline in my general knowledge as I used to pride myself on having a good one. But the improvement of my mental health due to the elimination of daily news reports was monumental. Of course, I did still hear about a lot of what was going on around the world – a rock is not totally impermeable – but at least I didn't have to endure all the gory details of *every* natural and man-made disaster. Neither did I have to hear *every* detail about *every* individual rape, murder and financial scam.

I have already lived long enough to have heard in gritty detail about every possible type of adversity and atrocity capable of occurring on this planet, so I am still aware enough to champion people's rights, make donations and petitions to worthy causes, and exercise my right to vote. I doubt I am any less involved in the world now than I was when imbibing frequent news reports and being buffeted with the stresses and horrors of the entire world.

As a natural animal we were only designed with the capacity to take on board the sorrows and adversities of one small tribe where it was within our capabilities to help and contribute effectively should it be blighted by misfortune. It is the natural human reaction to want to help those in need, so it becomes very stressful and overwhelming when we are exposed to a whole planet's woes while knowing it is beyond our powers and reach to be able to help more than a mere fraction of them.

I had sworn off chocolate yet again. There was no longer any in the house and I wasn't buying any more to restock. My sister Jenny had once made a very insightful observation about willpower, which initially seemed too obvious to have teeth; nevertheless, it proved very effective. You only need to exercise willpower when in the shops. You can pine all you like for the contraband when at home but if there is none in the house, you can't eat it. Those with the weakest of willpower muscles are in no danger at all if the chocolate cupboard is bare. If you pine so hard that you find yourself making a zombie-like trip to the supermarket, then you simply fire up the willpower again once you enter the shop and ensure it holds fast until you vacate the premises. I guess a slightly different approach is needed when you are out visiting, but I mainly observe the total crackdown in the discomfort of my own home. I wouldn't feel too guilty to let my hair down in the face of someone's homemade chocolate cake or an offer of after-dinner chocolates.

Unfortunately, no good intention lasts forever – at least not for me. The last time I re-succumbed to buying chocolate, I was quite surprised to see my regular brand of chocolate still on the shelves. Owing to the large quantities I was in the habit of consuming, I'd thought that losing my custom in the interim would have been enough to send them into receivership. Maybe this time I'd go cold turkey long enough to tip them over the fiscal cliff!

On Wednesday I photographed the donkey orchid painting and posted it on my blog. I was enjoying the blogging more than appeared seemly. My stats showed that I was getting a couple of views every day so it was nice to know it wasn't languishing totally unseen out there in the ether. It was hard to comprehend how people ever developed a solid following.

Over the next few days I felt very bad mentally. Knowing that it was entirely hormone driven I engaged the mental tools that allowed me to tread water rather than go under while I waited for it to pass. Over the last couple of months there had been an intermittent escalation of chaos with my hormones. The premenstrual tension was getting worse and certain aspects of the OCD were becoming more strident. I resolved to reassess my diet to see if I could revisit some of the mental improvements I'd enjoyed earlier in the year.

The weather was glorious and I pined to go walking through the bush to spot orchids, but I felt too decrepit. It wasn't a terribly productive day, but I did manage to keep up with domestic and taxi duties. I finished the mermaid picture which only took an hour or so. I was delighted to be painting in watercolour again and felt I'd made a significant improvement on the previous version.

On Saturday evening, Olivia's plans for the night were becoming rather unwieldy and I didn't like some of the arrangements that were beginning to gain traction. She was talking about meeting a friend at the train station but dusk was fast approaching. The only way to ensure she wouldn't find herself waiting alone on the platform in the dark was for me to collect her friend from his far flung suburb (an hour's round trip) and drop them at the station together. They were meeting other friends there and then going to see a band in the city. Retiring as a taxi service was a gradual process it seemed.

My reward for these efforts was to lie awake worrying until 2.45am when she finally arrived home in a taxi. I didn't get a wink of sleep until after 4am which is when I was finally able to settle and drift off. No wonder I was finding it hard to get early nights. The relief that came with her having her license was tempered by the inevitable worry of waiting for her to return home safely. The natural lot for some parents – Kevin slept like the dead whether Olivia was home or not.

I assumed that this overwhelming worry for her safety would lessen as time wore on – at least I hoped it would. After all, I was still brand new to being the mother of an independent teenage girl/woman who was constantly in and out, and this was only the second time she'd ventured into licensed premises in the city with friends. I dreaded to think what lay ahead.

CHALLENGE #16 – Begin first draft of *Grabbing the Muse by the Throat* – also be productive with writing, illustration and painting all in one week

On Monday the 17th September, the big moment arrived. I began writing *this* book – yes, the one you are holding in your hot little hands right now!

At the very beginning of the year I began keeping notes of my challenges to use as reference for this book. I had been in the habit of keeping diaries in the past which became more long-winded and elaborate by the year. They graduated from simple appointment diaries with extra notes jotted near the appointments, to bigger volumes that contained all the drivel that I felt compelled to record. There was, however, a lot of stuff amongst the dross that was worth keeping. The later tomes also doubled as scrapbooks, where I pasted in artwork the girls were doing at the time as well as tickets and clippings from various outings we'd enjoyed.

After fifteen solid years of compulsive record keeping, I stopped. This was largely due to being so unwell mentally. I'd begun to worry about what I'd written over the years, fearing that my seemingly innocuous words would later turn out to be evidence of my ineptitude as a mother in ways I had yet to realise. For example: I dreaded seeing it written in black and white that I hadn't taken them to the doctor straight away when they got colds or had fevers etc.

At least keeping a diary for all those years had allowed me to build up a good facility for getting words down. When I stopped keeping my daily diary, my writing energy spilled over into writing emails to friends – one long-suffering friend in particular.

When deciding to document *this* year, I had worried that I might relapse into my obsessive record keeping habits and rekindle the aforementioned neurotic fears. So I took the precaution of making it only a weekly thing to begin with. Thankfully, being that I was no longer entirely at the mercy of the OCD, no angst was reignited.

Now that I was making a start on this book, I reacquainted myself with the beginning of the diaries and tried to decide on a format and style for my story. I created a word document and after three and a half hours I only had one page to show for it, but I had a clearer idea of how it could begin and how it might unfold.

After dinner, I was glued to the computer and indulging in my bad habit of obsessive blog surfing. One blog belonged to a writer I liked, and I read with amazement that she'd written one of her books in just *six* weeks; it wasn't a particularly slim volume either. I was very impressed because this particular book had been a good quality read. I found myself wondering if I could possibly write my own book in such a short time. Now *that* would be a challenge! I entertained the idea for a microsecond or two and then reality bit me where it hurt. With my poor health and stamina, trying to keep up with the painting challenge *and* having a family to look after, as well as writing a book in record time, wasn't anywhere near being a realistic ambition for me.

Still, it was very inspiring to see that some people were capable of such feats. I'm people too of course, but of a slightly less robust species. With a more sober-sided assessment of things, I decided I would aim to have my book finished by the end of the year. Still wildly ambitious of course – even ridiculously so, but what the heck! My OCD book took a few years to write from beginning to end, but that was because I fretted and fussed over it so much and had long rests from it in-between. I had also approached it in the most ad hoc manner imaginable. It was a traumatic subject and it had felt very onerous trying to explain everything, particularly while still in its grip.

This book would be dealt with in a chronological manner for which I had been keeping notes. I was determined to approach it more sensibly, which through experience I felt I was now able to do. Also, the subject matter for this book would be mostly uplifting and creative rather than bleak and difficult.

It was a shame that my young teenage self – the one that had *loathed* typing classes and was told off constantly for talking to her friend Karen – couldn't see what a great asset it would prove to be. At that age I never imagined myself becoming a typist, and indeed I never did, but computers weren't exactly on the radar in those days. I couldn't have foreseen that typing would become almost as useful as a set of lungs with the advent of the computer keyboard.

On the old clunky typewriters of my youth I wasn't the fastest typist in the West, but now when it came to zapping out words on a computer keyboard, I reckoned I could give anyone a run for their money. Or so I had thought until recently. One day I was amazed to notice the velocity at which Lola was typing on her laptop. Her speed appeared similar to mine – the speed I prided myself on because of my hard-earned touch typing skills. How was this possible? She'd only ever had a few touch typing lessons at school, and that had been in year two! So surely she had to look at the keys? But no, it turned out that she could type without looking – and without having to endure hours of repetitiously hammering out "the quick brown fox jumps over the lazy brown dog" – *and* without traversing Dante's nine circles of hell doing speed drills and learning how to tabulate. I had considered my typing skills to be a feather in my cap; a skill from the pre-computer era that for once gave me an edge in the face of all the whippersnappery, computer-savvy arrogance of today's youth. My feather suddenly looked very limp and moth-eaten.

As I made a start on the book and reread back through my notes, I saw that the beginning of the year had started off quite differently to how it was progressing now. The beginning was full of very strict challenges to keep me on the straight and narrow – to become more consistent with creative output. The challenges were like trainer wheels while learning to ride a bike. I now felt I no longer needed them and could ride the bike with only an occasional wobble.

I'd settled into a very productive groove and felt the strict and varied challenges would be almost counterproductive at this point as I was mostly achieving what I set out to do. However, should I start to slacken, I had the challenge approach to fall back on should I need to entice the muse back out of the woods. I had actually set myself a structured challenge again this very week, but there was a lot of room for movement within it. The challenge was to be productive with my writing, illustration and painting all in one week. The painting component would simply involve my regular one day of painting.

The morning was spent working on my sparkling new book, and after lunch I began reworking one of the mermaid roughs. The momentum on the mermaid book had practically come to a standstill. It had been wallowing in the backwash of my other creative goals.

I'd had to search high and low for the "safe" place where I'd inexplicably stored these particular roughs. For some reason I had filed them away separately from the others I'd found recently. I didn't have a lot of time to spend reworking the illustration before collecting Lola from school and getting on with dinner, but long enough to be productive.

I basked in the ongoing amazement of how much extra time there seemed to be in a day when squeezing as much from it as possible. I was sure I had more energy because of doing what I loved; it was an elixir. It hadn't totally trumped the endless fatigue but I definitely felt able to do a lot more than I used to.

On Tuesday I felt very fine of fettle. I spent half an hour on my illustration and afterwards did a painting of a spider orchid. It was duly photographed and posted on my blog. I did some writing later in the afternoon and wrote a further 1,000 words after dinner. It was very much pig swill at this stage and definitely for my eyes only, but I was really enjoying thrashing out words again. It felt strange to be writing about something other than OCD for a change after having spent so many years on the other book. It and writing had come to seem synonymous.

The act of writing and checking my word count felt so familiar, but so alien at the same time because I was starting from scratch. Having been through the process before, I knew it would be a while before I could pummel all my ideas into some sort of order, so I'd have to stay brave in the face of some very bad writing initially. I felt reasonably confident that the idea had legs – and possibly shapely ones at that – but it was a case of having faith that I'd be able to find them.

With today's output, I achieved my goal of the week by doing all three things in one day – illustration, writing and painting. Even though I wasn't aiming to do all three *every* day, I was excited to see how easy it was to become equally engaged in each discipline. It was proof beyond a doubt that it would be possible to successfully have all balls in the air at the same time. I wouldn't have to feel one was being neglected for months or years while another was in hand.

The next day was like walking through mud in fluffy slippers. I only managed to fit in a couple of hours of writing around the domestic slog. Thursday wasn't much better for output, but I was making steady process in establishing a direction I wanted to take with my book. I'd spent a productive two hours crafting a solid beginning by rearranging and honing what I'd put down yesterday. I was able to resolve problems more quickly than when working on my previous book due to the experience I had gained from writing that very book.

Lately I was spending far more time in the garden – some days almost as much time as I spent behind the computer screen. On one such interlude, I was excited to find that a potted trigger plant (stylidium) I'd bought from the plant sale at Kings Park last year was in full bloom. It hadn't been in flower at the time of purchase so this was the first time I had seen it bedecked in all its finery. I poked the flowers with a stick to see if they would "trigger" but nothing seemed to happen. I thought they were supposed to snap shut on contact.

A couple of weeks later another trigger plant I'd bought more recently began to flower. I was showing it to my friend Corinne – a fellow native flower enthusiast – and thought I'd try my luck with this one. I poked at the centre of the flower with my little finger and, with an exclamation, jerked my hand away suddenly, thinking a spider had jumped on me. But then I realised that it was just the little hammer springing across my fingernail. I'd finally hit the right spot to trigger it off. I hadn't known that the hammer would pounce from the side. We cackled like witches at the revelation – but mostly we laughed at me for being such a scaredy cat.

On Friday there was an update from the agent about a few minor developments with my OCD book – although nothing of note. However, it was exciting to dip back into that rarefied world knowing that things were at least in the pipeline, and gurgling a little as they went.

It was evening before I got a chance to work on my manuscript. I made myself a stiff cup of tea before starting to write, and while doing so was startled to hear one of Olivia's friends' voices in the dining room. I looked over to the table where Olivia was sitting with her laptop and realised that she was Skyping. We didn't tend to Skype much in our household for some reason, in fact, I had never Skyped at all, although I'd been meaning to sign up for years. It was so taken for granted that we could do these things now that I didn't even bother to do them! When I wanted to speak with my overseas friends and relatives I still used the phone. Thirty years ago I would have marvelled at my nonchalance in the face of something so amazing and accessible.

Sometime in my teens, in the late 70s or early 80s, I heard the boffins announce that we would have visual telephones in the not-too-distant future. This was before computers were prevalent in society and still entirely non-existent in my day-to-day life. What came to my mind's eye as my brain struggled to visualise such a staggering innovation was a picture of me sitting on our existing telephone stool, holding the clunky olive-green receiver to my ear while dialling the numbers on the whirring, plastic rotary dialler. Somewhere nearby (my imagination was a bit confused about exactly where to put it) was a small TV screen 1970s style where I'd be able to see the person I was talking to. My main reaction to the whole concept was one of amazement, but at the same time, I found it rather disconcerting that I would actually have to look respectable before I could make or receive calls. No falling out of bed to take a call with my hair sticking out in all directions looking like a Gonk!

Saturday was busy catching up on mundane jobs interspersed with a little reading and an hour and a half in the garden weeding and pruning. Gardening never felt like a chore – I *loved* it. It was a thrill to be gardening regularly again. My dormant passion had been reignited since immersing myself in the spring wildflowers. I certainly hadn't foreseen it developing to this level of fanaticism – or that I'd be able to fit so much of it in while doing all the other things.

After dinner I wrote for an hour and a half and ended up with sixty words less than when I started. In a moment of weakness, I'd slipped back into default mode and honed what I'd already done. Having now written two full length manuscripts, I had developed a very definite working pattern, but one I wasn't keen on persisting with if possible. The plan was to wean myself off the previous approach of premature editing and foster more effective writing habits.

I admired the way Jenny went about things with her writing. She'd write each draft in one fell swoop, with very little honing until going through it again as the next draft. It was all so neat. I, on the other hand, would write a bit and then go back over it – and over it – until it shone like the sun. That wasn't bad in itself as I believe all writing must be laboured over intensely to get the sentences singing like a bluebird, but only once you're sure it is right to keep it. Often I would spend hours on a single paragraph only to delete it mercilessly later on when realising belatedly that it didn't serve the whole. But despite reverting to this habit, I felt that overall my manuscript was progressing well.

Simply do as much as possible on all fronts – no official down weeks anymore now that it's possible to integrate everything without needing to delineate between "on" and "off" weeks

I'd managed a spot of writing on Sunday, and on Monday I wrote for a couple of hours before squandering the afternoon by finishing off the novel I was reading. Once I'd emerged from my reading stupor, it was too late to embark on the painting I had intended to do after lunch: it was time for the afternoon and evening rush. After dinner, I was too tired to resume writing, so instead I read through what I'd written earlier in the day. I had been pleased with the content as I was writing it, but when I read it back in the evening it didn't seem so good after all – quite dire in fact! I wallowed in despondency. I'd thought it had been coming along so well. I hoped my assessment of it was simply due to lack of sleep and fighting off a virus. It's very disconcerting how our impressions of the quality of our writing can vary so greatly depending on the mood we are in when reading it. The same phenomenon had played out when writing the previous book.

Not only did I feel despondent because of adding nothing but swill to the manuscript, but also because of squandering the few free hours of the afternoon that hadn't been committed to non-negotiables. In defeat, I wasted even more time and vegged in front of the TV. Olivia wasn't due home until late so knowing I wouldn't be able to get an early night didn't help overcome my bleak mood either. Both Olivia and Kevin were in the habit of staying up late but often not on the same night. Retiring early was difficult when one of them at least rattled around the house until all hours.

Kevin regularly stays up till all hours and then gets up early. He can burn the candle at both ends without ill effects, and in-between sleeps like a log. Or at least like he is cutting a log – he snores like a chainsaw! I, on the other hand, am still waiting for someone to establish my royal lineage – Princess-and-the-Pea style. I notice every little thing – the slightest noise, or pea-sized discomfort – and it keeps me awake. On the one or two nights a week when no one else is up late, then it seems to be *my* cue to get a ridiculously late night. The saying "I'll sleep when I'm dead" will undoubtedly be my lot. I'm afraid not quite in the way the saying implies though. The saying brings to mind a kicking-up-your-heels-and-raising-hell kind of philosophy rather than the eyes-hanging-out-of-your-head debacle I was running with.

Despite Olivia's late night, I managed to get enough sleep and felt back to sorts on Tuesday. I spent some time combing through various painters' blogs and checking out the *Daily Paintworks* challenges. *Daily Paintworks* is the American website I had stumbled upon while doing the 10 day challenge. It appears to be the mother ship for many of the art bloggers I have come across. Started by Carol Marine and her husband David, it's a place where artists can set up online galleries and sell their work by auction. The site also hosts challenges that anyone can enter whether they are a member or not.

I thought I could take things to the next level by entering one of the challenges and putting the resulting painting up for sale. There was a "Birdbrain" challenge which invited artists to either paint from the photograph provided or from any bird reference of their choice. The subject for the challenge changes each week with a different artist providing the idea and reference photo.

I settled on a photo I'd taken of a seagull. While painting, I felt a shift in the way I approached the subject matter. Also, I'd felt very much in the zone which showed in the finished piece and I was really happy with the outcome. There is no way I could have painted so adeptly even a few months earlier. Finally, I was beginning to see tangible evidence of improvement and felt a growing confidence in knowing how to manipulate the medium.

I began to think that if I persisted with the weekly painting it would be within the realms of possibility to become a moderately accomplished painter some day. This was something I'd only ever imagined being possible if I dedicated myself to it solely – living and breathing it daily like the true masters do – rather than spreading myself as thin as Vegemite. The artists I most admired seemed to approach it on a full time basis. I was unlikely to reach their giddy heights, but I was thrilled to see real progress nonetheless.

I ached to paint more frequently, but I knew I had to fit other things into my life as well.

I photographed the seagull painting ready to upload it for the challenge, but Olivia entreated me not to sell it. She said she loved it too much. High praise indeed and I confess that having just done it I also felt it would be hard to part with. I was hoping that the more prolific I became the more I would think nothing of parting with my paintings. Because of our emotional attachment, I decided not to put the seagull in the challenge. I felt disappointed though, as that had been the goal for the day – and a much anticipated one at that. If we felt differently about it in a few days I could still put it in. There was nothing to stop me posting it on my blog though. It was a shame that the photo didn't capture the lovely buttery texture of the original – or the nuance of colour. It wasn't until a week or so later that I realised it could have been entered in the challenge without needing to offer it for sale.

After a late lunch, I wrote for two hours and did another hour after dinner. In the end I had to remove myself by force – it was all-consuming. Instead of rereading and honing today, I'd held firm and continued from where I'd left off last time. It was very freeing. I was able to type much of it straight from the diary today as I was currently writing about my initial painting challenge and felt it lent itself to close-up detail. I now had around 5,700 words.

Since beginning work on the book I felt very grateful for having kept a diary of the challenge as it would have been hard to remember so many details otherwise. It galvanised me into writing in my diary *every* day from here-on-in, rather than just recapping after several days or even after a week which I had been doing up until now. Being so intermittent with my entries had meant I also needed to consult my appointment diary and revisit my archives of sent emails to fill in the chasms of my memory.

Emboldened by my increasing productivity and the successful wringing of more and more time out of each day, I again found myself thinking that it might be possible to do a session of both art and writing *every* day. How wonderful it would be! Painting in the morning and writing for hours in the afternoon and evening had seemed such an easy and natural thing to do today. But on further reflection, I realised it had only been so achievable because of the day being freer than usual. For one thing, I hadn't needed to cook this evening due to having substantial leftovers from last night.

The rest of the week continued in a moderately productive manner. A clean break was made from my bad habit of having to reread things through from the beginning before I got cracking. No longer did I hone endlessly and fruitlessly things that might later find themselves on the wrong end of the delete button. The first draft was now unfolding in a smooth, organic – albeit drivel-ridden – manner. It was all about getting the skeleton down at this stage. Not that I was getting down *just* the bare bones – my skeleton was looking a little overfed. I was notoriously prone to including reams of mundane minutia in my diary about what I got up to in the day, for example, how many loads of washing I got on the line and other riveting details along those lines. So I was trying to sift through and sort out the worthy bits as I went, but I knew a lot was slipping through the net in my frenzy to simply get the words down. For some reason I was finding it hard to let go of the minutia. Much of it would need to be removed wholesale, but that was okay. Okay until I had to face the second draft!

Determined to get my paintings uploaded onto a POD site, I continued with my online research, but after wading through the legal-speak of various companies' terms and conditions, I felt even more daunted. It was frustratingly difficult to make the leap of faith and just sign up with one already. Some of the shilly-shallying was due to believing I must first get a good digital SLR camera in order to get top quality reproductions of my paintings.

Just before I was about to log off and go to bed, I happened upon a blog whereby the artist was selling images via one of the sites I had just been researching. Suddenly, I was able to make the decision on which one to go with. So too, the camera problem was suddenly no longer an issue. I decided I could start my site by uploading a few photos I'd taken over the years with my automatic camera. I knew I had some lovely flower shots floating around in amongst all my snaps. They would do until I got myself a decent camera, and making a start of any sort would motivate me to buy the camera sooner rather than later.

Buying the camera was another thing I had agonised long and hard over as to what choice to make. I could procrastinate for Australia and win gold! I always look on in wonder and envy when I see people making quick decisions when it comes to choosing things. I make a meal of deciding between colours with differences barely detectable to the naked eye, and then feel sick at the thought that I may have made the wrong choice.

In order to work out a plan for overall life stuff, I felt the need to step away from my writing briefly. Exercise had gone by the wayside and I was getting endless late nights as usual. Why I hadn't made any progress on that side of things when I was breaking new ground on other fronts was still hard to fathom. But I suspected it could be due to being utterly addicted to my writing: not only would I try to squeeze it into every stray minute but also into every last minute. On reflection, I could see that getting moderation into my life remained my Achilles heel. Yes, I had achieved unprecedented improvements in some facets of my life, but I guess it didn't automatically follow that the improvements would infiltrate in to every fibre of my willpower muscles.

Looking at it with a clear eye, it seemed I was still living my life in a rather obsessive manner, only now the obsessiveness was taking the form of something good and productive rather than bad and wallowing, so it hadn't been as easily recognised as being obsessive. If I had no option but to be obsessive then this was the best way to go about it! I was finding it very healthy in the main.

While consulting my diary, it reminded me of how thrilling the sense of achievement had been with the early challenges. Even though I no longer needed the hot poker approach to get painting and writing, my early diary entries made me want to revisit some more specific challenges. Rereading about my first sleep challenge motivated me to give it another try.

I noticed again, that some of my original ideas were quite different to what they had since evolved into. At that time, I had been considering doing real print-runs of greeting cards and buying spinner-racks to put in any shop that would have them. This wasn't to say it might not still come to that if it ended up proving more viable than POD card publishing. But until now, I'd almost totally forgotten about having had the idea in the first place.

I'd begun to succumb to the first-draft horrors: where the writer feels embarrassed that they ever thought they could write in the first place. Equally undermining was the fear of not having enough fodder for a whole book. I'd been in this position before where an idea for a book would clatter around in my brain for ages, seemingly viable – even best seller viable – but when I finally began to transfer the ideas onto paper it seemed more like a penny dreadful. However, I forged ahead knowing I just had to trust it had potential and allow it to emerge from the marble, Michelangelo style. He famously said he didn't carve his statues, but instead simply used the chisel to release what was already there. Not that I thought I was in his league *obviously*, but I liked the metaphor – albeit paraphrased!

By the end of the week, Kevin had left to go on a fishing weekend with his dad, Olivia was at a party, and Lola was on Facebook. Having decided last night that I must commit once and for all to setting up with a POD company, tonight was the night I actually signed up. Once I'd registered all my details, I trawled through my photos to find the ones I'd been thinking would be suitable for uploading. Upon finding them, I began to wonder if the quality and/or composition would be good enough after all. It didn't help my confidence when, in a rare moment of device-disentanglement, Lola came up for air from her laptop, peered over my shoulder and said, "No way – are you joking!?"

But having just gone through the throes of setting up an account, I wanted to put *something* on. Eventually I chose just one photograph of a still life I'd taken last year.

It felt great to be moving forward on something that I'd wanted to set up for so long. It would force my hand to buy the good quality camera that I'd had on my to-do list for at least twelve months. Being able to offer prints and greeting cards of my paintings had always been my goal. It would be a good way to get my art out there while I continued to wrestle with the concept of parting with the originals.

On Saturday morning, I collected Mum and Dad and we went to Kings Park to enjoy the wildflower festival. One of the main objectives was to buy some native plant seedlings. I was on a mission to get the understorey planted amongst our Eucalyptus trees before the hot weather set in. The line waiting to get in to the plant sale enclosure rivalled the queue to see the Eiffel Tower. So we continued on, resolving to see if it had improved on our return to the car. We looked at the various floral displays and admired the cultivated gardens where the regulation acres of everlastings rippled in the breeze; everything was at its stunning springtime best. It was impossible for me to visit Kings Park without giving a heartfelt nod of thanks to the ghosts of the early colonists who were instrumental in reserving the 400 hectares (1000 acres) of land for botanical gardens and public use. Apparently, it is now one of the largest inner city parks in the world.

We went further afield to walk along the natural bush paths and enjoyed seeing the kangaroo paws growing rampant in the understorey. Unfortunately, we were only able to spot a few late blooming orchids. The flowering season must have been earlier this year. Last year during the wildflower festival they were still in their prime. The bush was infested with orchids and each and every one of them had called out to my camera as we walked along, "Look at me! No, look at me!"

Thankfully the line for the plant sale had evaporated by the time we were ready to head back to the car. There were still things to be bought so we jostled with everyone else for our druthers. I bought half a dozen specimens including some red-and-green kangaroo paws, a dwarf banksia and a trigger plant.

That night I went to bed feeling I was coming down with a cold, and the following morning it was upon me proper. A heavy malaise had settled upon me and I dreaded the day ahead due to the fact we had visitors coming in the afternoon. It meant I had to clean the house! It was an eyesore of the first water due to having only kept up with the bare minimum of late.

Strangely, after beginning the day feeling I was on the endangered list, a short time into the vacuuming I realised that the malaise had gone. I was amazed as the cold had really had its claws in me and gone well past the usual point of no return. I mopped and scrubbed and did a couple of loads of washing – and was able to enjoy the visit all chirpy and chipper.

Having had so many physical and mental problems over the years I'd never previously had the stamina to just keep going all day. I had always needed a lot of rest time to be able to tackle the next thing – and to hold on to what little sanity I had. Usually if I pushed myself when I was run-down or sick, I'd go under badly in true chronic fatigue fashion. It would take longer than ever to recover or I'd succumb to an OCD episode that could take days or weeks to get over. But I had found in the last few months that my body and mind were far more resilient than ever before. It was such a joy being able to wring more out of each day in the way I used to before succumbing to glandular fever at twenty five years of age. I still often felt very tired, but not to the point of being entirely overwhelmed by it. Whether that was due to less sugar, more good quality food and fresh juices, or simply from pumping myself high with creative juice every day – or all of the above – I didn't know, but whatever it was, it felt like magic! It certainly didn't belong to the reality I'd been accustomed to up until now. While this might be the way that most people's bodies responded to pushing through exhaustion and malaise, it was a new and exciting development for me.

It continued to be a very full day on the domestic front and it wasn't until after dinner that I was free to do some writing. I was tempted to leave it until the next day, but feared that if I let too many days pass without doing any, "the barrier" would develop and my current obsessive need to write at every possible moment would swing alarmingly to the extreme of not being able to write at all!

Chapter Ten

OCTOBER

Another unstructured week, but with the expectation of a high output – or else!

I paid the price for staying up late to write. *Good Sleep Hygiene 101* – don't engage in mentally stimulating activities right before bed! I slept badly, woke too early and felt like some of my vital organs had been stolen in the night – but I still managed to get things done. I staggered into the garden to do some weeding and raking, and again, in a strange twist of my own personal laws of physics, I found it banished the worst of the fatigue.

I had to drive Lola and a friend to a barbeque birthday party that was being held at a beach park not too far away. It was a perfect day for the beach which meant the traffic was horrendous and parking impossible, so the plan was to drop them on a side street on the other side of the main road from the beach. As we were driving along, Lola asked me to drop them in a street further along than I'd originally intended, and

I realised too late that the visibility for them to cross wasn't so good from there. In the rear-mirror as I drove off, I saw them in the middle of the median strip waiting for the now bumper-to-bumper traffic to thin before they could cross. In reality it was nothing untoward for two nearly-sixteen-year-olds to deal with, but I felt sick about it. An unpleasantly familiar wave of heat shot through me – suddenly I felt like a negligent parent who through incompetence had put her daughter and her friend in mortal danger through having to cross an impossibly busy road. This type of OCD reaction had become very rare these days and it caught me off guard.

After not receiving the text I had asked Lola to send once they'd met up with their friends, and not getting a response to my own text, I couldn't let it go.

I rang Jenny, hoping she could reassure me that I was worrying for nothing, but my mind had become too unbalanced too quickly for her sensible words to have any traction. The only way I could put my mind at rest, was to drive back down to check that where I'd last seen them wasn't now the scene of an accident. Twenty-five minutes had passed by this time, and it struck me that even if I saw a comfortingly normal road, I *still* couldn't be sure that they had crossed safely: what if there had been time for an ambulance to arrive and depart the scene already? So as I drove, I began calculating the possibility of the ambulance scenario having unfolded in that time and decided that it probably couldn't have – and even if it had, there would surely still be a pool of blood on the road. So having driven past and found no evidence of ambulances, pools of blood or lingering by-standers, my insane mind was finally convinced that the only possible outcome was that they had crossed the road without incident. I drove back in relief thinking I could now get on with things.

Unfortunately, OCD doesn't let the mind off *that* easily. It suddenly occurred to me that I hadn't offered Lola's friend sunscreen to put on and worried that she'd get burnt to a crisp – and it would be ALL.MY.FAULT. Obviously, at her age it was her own responsibility to have put some on already – and she probably had done so. But even if she hadn't, she could have spoken up when I was reminding Lola about it. Again, common sense was unable to gain a foothold in my mind and now I couldn't let *this* go. I didn't like to bother Jenny again so soon, so I rang my friend Barbara to reassure me that it wasn't my responsibility. Like my sister, Barbara was a veteran of coming to my aid at such times and it didn't take her long to give me the swift verbal kick I needed to enable me to let it go. It seemed only right to dilute the impact of my madness by sharing it around.

I felt very shaken and disappointed by this fully fledged OCD incident. It was a horrible reminder of what every waking moment was like only a year or less ago, when no sooner was one mad fear allayed than the next one rose up to fill the void. It was another good reason to get the sleeping under control. Once again, I reminded myself that I must also meditate regularly. I could get myself started again by attending a meditation workshop and get the girls to join me. It would give me a boost, and hopefully Olivia and Lola would learn good skills to navigate through life's difficulties without the same level of dysfunction and fear as I did.

Thankfully, by the afternoon I had recovered mentally, and I pottered with my POD site – adding some photos of flowers that I thought looked card-worthy. It amazed me how time-consuming doing these sorts of things on the computer could be. There was time for a short read afterwards, and then it was back to more domestic toil. Kevin cooked fresh fish for dinner – the triumphant spoils of his weekend away. It was nearly 8pm when I finally put pen to paper, or finger to key at least, and worked for an hour.

After feeling like a fallen soufflé all day I resolved to resuscitate the sleeping challenge as of tonight. Observing my newly self-imposed curfew, I turned the computer off smack on 9.30pm only to remember that I hadn't sent a backup email for the book. I was in the habit of religiously sending a copy to Jenny as a safeguard should the computer get struck by lightning or contract a virulent memory-sucking virus overnight.

I rebooted, sent the email and then read till 10.30pm.

The week unfolded in a fairly productive manner. I ordered ten copies of my photos from my POD site to be printed up in card form so I'd be able to see what the finished products looked like. On my painting day I did a picture of a Macaw which was respectable enough to put up for sale, and so I entered it into the *Daily Paintworks* challenge. It was an exciting step closer to actually selling my paintings. Not that I held high hopes of getting a buyer for this one as there were an awful lot of beautiful paintings on the site to compete with, but I was happy just to get one "out there".

Later in the week, I was more social than creative, and I *finally* bought a new camera! Having recently done a soupcon of research on digital cameras I had narrowed the field to a couple in particular. I ended up with one of the new-fangled mirror-less types which was much slimmer than its older DSLR brethren. While it was exciting to get a new camera, it was also daunting having to learn how to work it. Having never operated anything but an automatic camera in my life, I wondered how easy it would be to use. Thankfully, it also came with an automatic option should I be slow to learn how to use it properly.

Sunday began with grand plans for getting a lot done, but in the end I frittered it away on nothing in particular. Because I was usually *so* productive these days it really irked me when I wasn't, and it left me feeling rather flat by the end of the day. I did a last quick whiz through the sites I liked to check. Having now added my POD site and *Daily Paintworks* on top of two email addresses, Facebook, and my blog, it was a wonder I got anything done at all! Less than a week into it, my revived sleep challenge had *already* bitten the dust – I so badly needed to take a stick to myself!

This week dedicate to writing as much as possible, but no throwing down of gauntlet for any prescribed challenge

After being in the creative doldrums yesterday, the new week began on a more positive note. I was able to write for hours without feeling drained. I floated through the day, arm in arm with the muse. This was becoming a more frequent occurrence as the year wore on.

The next morning, hours were wasted while searching for a particular photo to use as painting reference. To make things worse, when I finally located it, it didn't live up to my memory's high praise at all; it was unusable. Rather than allow despondency to get a toehold, I skipped off to spend a few hours in the garden; making paths, moving rocks and clearing leaves and weeds. Gardening was fast becoming an all-consuming passion, which was only kept in check by my other all-consuming passions.

On Wednesday, with the frustration of yesterday's "failure to launch" still lingering in the air, I had a real job trying to inspire myself to paint. Sometimes it was terribly difficult to settle on a subject or image because inspiration simply wouldn't come – the muse could be a very fickle creature at times! Usually, when the right idea or image presented itself I would get an instant "knowing", but for some reason nothing was doing it for me today.

I spent forever cyber-sifting through my photos and in the end had to force myself to decide on something – anything! It was a picture of a bucket of cut banksia flowers at the wildflower florist that I'd taken at Kings Park the other week. I decided to work on a slightly larger canvas for a change – 40.6cm x 50.8cm (16 inch by 20 inch). I was determined to stylise this picture as it would be quicker to do. I didn't want to spend forever on it as I felt so tired. Today was the perfect example of the potency of the challenge. Once it had been demonstrated that I was willing to put my back into it, the energy and inspiration arrived courtesy of the law of the muse. But pushing through didn't always work, sometimes my health was just *too* beyond the pale, and on those occasions, even if *I* didn't know better than to try to force matters, the muse did!

Once ensconced in the painting process, I sort of enjoyed myself, but I also found it frustrating. The flowers were shaping up nicely – loose and stylised, but then I sabotaged it with too much detail and by striving for exact colours. I worked on it for over three hours but wasn't able to finish it. I'd had enough, and I ached all over from yesterday's gardening; I'd forgotten what a great workout it could be.

After dinner I repaired to my art room where I procrastinated about whether or not to post the unfinished and embarrassing painting on my blog. Could I be so brave? But I felt I must in order to prove that I had achieved my weekly challenge. The blog had certainly fulfilled the brief of keeping me to my painting challenge. I felt certain that my weekly painting commitment would have died a terrible death by now if I hadn't set it up. I was getting a few visitors every day – the tally had rarely peaked beyond single digits but it was enough to feel I wasn't blathering into the wilderness.

Thursday morning disappeared in a puff of mundanity. On Friday I felt out of sorts, with things deteriorating into one of those messy kind of days where you feel clumsy and out of alignment with the flow of life. Anything that can go wrong will most certainly do so – and with spite. The sort of day that had I been out shopping or in a crowded space I would have inexplicably found myself weaving and wending my way through the crowd, getting in everyone's way even when they were originally coming towards me in their own lane. I'd find myself dancing in front of them trying to get out of their way, wondering how it was humanly possible that I'd managed to get into their flight path in the first place. Today I seemed to be having a particularly ungainly day. As I went to put the milk back in the fridge, my jacket caught weirdly on the door, flinging me back into it unexpectedly. I banged my knee on a sharp corner that didn't even exist. I felt like I'd been beaten up – by the fridge!

On Saturday I slept in until 10am, made myself a cup of tea and retreated back to bed with Jenny's manuscript hot off her printer which she had dropped over to me yesterday. I had a good feeling about it and a little thrill of anticipation rippled through me as I held the crisp white pile of papers in my hands. In fact I felt quite joyful in the morning. It was a nice contrast after the bleak day yesterday; my hormones must have swung back to some sort of equilibrium. Sometimes I felt like an ill-fated puppet dancing on the end of strings manipulated by a maniac.

Jenny's writing really impressed me; it was the first time I'd read it in typed form. After reading her first draft which had been handwritten, reading this was as smooth as silk. I rang to tell her that I loved it so far and we discussed it from various angles. I had only reached page nine mind you, but I knew she'd be keen to hear any feedback.

I started on my own writing in the early afternoon and with a few short breaks wrote for two hours. I now had over 21,000 words and was averaging around 1,000 words an hour. Some days I did considerably more in the hour but that was no doubt due to having the diary as a starting point. But I still had to sift through the entries for the pertinent bits and elaborate upon them. Having now adopted the new approach of writing in a steady flow without revisiting and honing, I was loving every minute of it. It was exciting at how quickly the words were adding up in my manuscript even though it still mainly consisted of droning banalities. It would need to go on a crash diet in the second draft.

My preoccupation of late with my blog, POD site, book writing and gardening had been the perfect distraction from waiting to hear back from the agent on the latest publisher's decision. The way things were going I began to think my work in progress might get published before the OCD book. Because of being so deeply ensconced in writing this book at the moment it would practically feel like an imposition to attend to the OCD book if a publisher *did* want to take it on. In reality I knew I would of course be ecstatic if they did. Life felt so full right now. I was at one of those much sought after times in life where the journey is so rewarding that the goal is practically an afterthought. Which is how life should be lived after all – as the hackneyed phrase "life is a journey not a destination" constantly reminds us.

It suddenly occurred to me that the time I had been investing into researching a POD site had interrupted my plans for the *Daily Paintworks* idea. But I came to see that it was less an interruption and more an organic shift in priorities. I continued to feel out of my depth with taking things further with selling my original work. In the off-chance that I was actually able to sell anything online the thought of dealing with the logistics of sending original paintings off in the mail seemed a bit daunting. In reality I preferred the idea of selling prints so I could either keep or give away the original. I just wasn't ready for the next step it seemed.

It was such a delight to give my Macaw painting away to a friend who I knew would love it and was pleased that I hadn't sold it after all. It was nice to be able to put a face to the recipient. Maybe that's what it boiled down to for me – if I was able to eyeball my buyer I would find it rewarding to part with the paintings. I felt confident this ambivalence would go once I became more prolific and accomplished in all matters art.

I'd resolved to concentrate on getting on top of the house today, but instead I was very unproductive and listless. Subsequently I felt depressed by the evening. I realised that my moods were often scarily linked to my interpretation of a day well spent. Taking a whole day to read and relax was okay if I had given myself permission – like on the occasions when I was particularly unwell – but it wasn't okay to fritter a day away that had been earmarked for serious output.

As you were! Tally-ho! Keep up the good work!

Recently I had unearthed a meditation CD and had been listening to it on the days when I needed some repose in the afternoon. I usually fell asleep as soon as I relaxed, so it ended up being a micro-snooze rather than a meditation. It was just enough to revive me somewhat. I worried that needing afternoon naps at this age didn't bode well for my dotage – I would never get out of bed at all. Then I reminded myself of such luminaries as Sir Winston Churchill who had been in the habit of napping during the day, so I was in good company – even if my excuse wasn't quite as grand as having to keep the British Empire running!

My gardening obsession continued to intensify and actually began to impact on my writing obsession – it was very disconcerting! Nonetheless, a bit of writing slithered onto the week's itinerary and on Wednesday I did my weekly painting. The reference I used was a photo I'd taken looking up into the canopy of my dad's oak tree. It was about sixteen years old and a fine shady specimen. Sixteen years earlier Dad had visited the old soldier-settlement farm, near the southwest town of Busselton, that his grandfather had originally established upon immigrating to Australia in around 1912. Dad's grandfather was a keen and consummate gardener and had brought with him some acorns from England to plant in his newly adopted country. These had since grown to lofty heights and sired many a crop of acorns over the decades. The current owners had kindly allowed Dad to collect some and amongst them was the embryo of his own tree: the tree I was about to paint.

I'd heard it said over the years that one would never get to sit in the shade of an oak tree they had planted themselves because of the tree's ponderously slow growth. This proved to be nothing but ill-informed twaddle. Even after eight years Dad's tree had possessed a fine canopy of leaves that threw substantial shade around for sitters and standers alike.

While I was painting, a friend rang to get some insights into setting up her own POD site and I continued to paint while we chatted. But I should have stopped for the duration so as not to compromise the act of being present while painting. I often used to chat on the phone while doing my illustrations because it was convenient, time-wise, to paint and hold a conversation simultaneously. But I rarely did it these days having weaned myself off the habit some time back. It had always felt wrong, in fact, almost blasphemous, not to be giving my full attention to the muse.

I later spoke with the agent and got an update on the latest developments. Since our last conversation, our current potential publisher (number three) had rung her to find out about my suitability as an author. She wanted to know a bit more about me as to my congeniality, and if I would be the sort of person capable of helping in the promotion and selling of my own books. My agent had given the publisher her own assessment of my suitability and also referred her to my blog for further insights. She told me that publishers like it when authors have some sort of profile, which was only natural. But despite the embryonic state of my blog with its low visitor tally and all but non-existent comments, the publisher told the agent that she liked what she saw. But I wondered later if maybe she'd been expecting it to be OCD related rather than painting related – or if she was just being polite. Nonetheless, on face value their discussion had sounded encouraging. She had only skimmed through my book at that stage but was intending to have a more thorough look and get back to the agent on Monday.

Not every moment could be devoted to my creative life. On Friday I nipped to the shops with the intent of updating my wardrobe. It was in sore need of a revamp because I always put off clothes shopping for as long as possible – I'd rather be in the garden or at the easel. I had mixed results but found just enough items to make it worth being subjected to the many unflattering angles of the fitting room mirrors. Hideous lighting must be compulsory in these places as every blob of cellulite casts the sort of shadow one would expect from a small hillock! On the drive home I lashed myself with recriminations for having gone to seed, but then I reminded myself that pining for a fairer figure was vacuous and puerile when one had their basic health. Too many people I knew lately didn't have such good fortune.

Sunday was a very wasteful kind of day – neither relaxing nor doing anything productive. The time-wasting had escalated a lot lately by way of checking my blog and POD site and emails. I liked to see what sort of visitor numbers I was getting but felt a bit embarrassed about it. On the one hand, I felt it was entirely legitimate to be building up an online profile, but on the other, I suspected I was simply getting sucked into this current popularity caper.

After breakfast I'd scuttled back to bed to read but couldn't concentrate for long. Ideas for my book bombarded me from the ether and I felt compelled to jot them down. It was impossible to relax as that appeared to be the most conducive time for creative ideas to pop into my head. Ideas come to me most frequently when winding down before sleep and while showering. A whole anecdote came to me almost verbatim just the other day while washing my hair. Unfortunately, by the time I got out of the shower and remembered to write it down, it didn't sound quite so scintillating. But it was enough to polish up from there.

I was particularly dull-witted and inefficient in the week that followed due to lack of sleep and a tenacious week-long headache. Where was that stick? My kingdom for a stick! If only I could ensure early nights and better sleep then I would be able to meditate efficiently without nodding off. No matter how much I turned the screws, or how often I implemented the sleep challenge, it seemed I was immune to my self-chastisement. My sleep challenge was an utter farce. Anyone would think I was trying to give up a heroin habit rather than a getting-to-bed-too-late habit. What was wrong with me? I continued to marvel at how I'd been capable of such amazing self-discipline in my creative life this year and yet impervious to positive change on other fronts. The contradictions would be quite fascinating if they weren't so annoying.

Many of us find it hard to comprehend why certain people can't get their acts together in ways that we find so easy. Yet when we stop to think about it, we all have our own unique areas of weakness that appear resistant to common sense or discipline that others would roll their eyes at in exasperation. I'd certainly attracted some eye rolling over my sleep issue and they'd been perfectly justified. But because of other people's late habits and everyone eating at different times, getting any sense of routine at night simply felt too hard for me to manage at the moment. I decided to go easier on myself in the face of this failure. With it largely beyond my control at this point in time I would stop chastising myself. I'd have to ride it out and work on it again at a later date when certain other members of the household had either moved out or curbed their socialising in the wee hours.

The agent had been told she'd hear back from the publisher on Tuesday, but so far no word had come through.

Challenge # 17 – 10,000 words in remainder of week

On Wednesday far too much time was spent agonising over what to paint. Nothing was gelling, so I decided to do some writing instead.

I had been faithfully – anally in fact – recording all the times and word counts when I wrote in order to keep tally for the challenges. The conscientious record keeping added to my sense of achievement. It no longer felt right to begin writing without first recording the time and word count. In addition, I felt compelled to take note of the exact time spent on each painting. Once the year of challenges was over I would no longer need to keep it up. But I must confess that my obsessive nature revelled in it. I had taken a mental note of my daily word count when writing my previous book, but I hadn't felt the need to record my progress anywhere.

Things didn't flow so well today. I was looking forward to hearing from the agent so I had to distract myself from the urge to constantly check my emails. I still hadn't heard back regarding publisher number three – the one that had sounded so promising. Prior to this latest development I had barely been thinking of the OCD book but now it was rattling my chain again. At least in pre-internet days, when we relied on more traditional forms of communication, there was only one time of the day to be checking for much anticipated written correspondence. Once the mail had arrived there was no point checking the letterbox again until the next day. It was time to divert myself with a good book.

Along with obsessively checking emails I was becoming increasingly preoccupied with all-consuming thoughts of my blog and POD site and what my next move would be to increase my "profile". Owing to what the latest publisher had said to my agent, I had begun to fixate on the success of my blog – thinking it could make or break whether or not my book would be published. With visitor numbers barely negligible, I was potentially in deep doo-doo!

There were times when I longed for the simpler days. A time when we didn't cloister ourselves unsociably in our own little worlds: constantly plugged-in and checking our communications relentlessly. But even in those simpler days, the seeds of the developments to come were already being sown.

Long before anyone knew what LOL or LMFAO meant, we actually knew how to entertain ourselves with the simple things in life. One really could believe in the saying "The best things in life are free". When I was a child living on our farm, many a hot summer's night would find Mum, Dad and us three kids draped across the bonnet and roof of our car, on our backs staring up at the heavens; the inky sky a grand panorama of glittering stars, and the Milky Way a great cloud of diamond dust. We were miles from anywhere. With skies unsullied by reflected light, it allowed us a clear sparkling view of the cosmos.

The mystery and vastness of space revealed itself in all its glory right there from the top of our Ford Falcon station wagon. Although we were exposed lying out in the open, it was as if the five of us were cocooned in a magical cloak of inky, star studded darkness. I could almost feel myself falling into the fathomless depths and merging with it all.

Dad would tell us what he knew about various stars and moon missions. He'd point out satellites to us and we'd watch their steady trajectory through the sky. Looking for satellites became a ritual and as soon as our backs were pressed to the metal, we would search frantically to be the first to spot one. For a bit of fun, Dad always gave the winner a few cents, which went a long way in the lolly shop at the time.

Our visual masterpiece was admired to the aural accompaniment of a chorus of crickets.

The only artificial light we had to contend with came from the kitchen window which meant that the generator was on. The generator made quite a racket but strangely doesn't feature at all in this halcyon memory. Maybe the crickets drowned out the sound.

As Dad regaled us with facts and figures about the heavens, my attention may have wandered off occasionally if I'd been the first to spot the satellite. I'd get distracted with wondering what sort of lollies to buy with my winnings. Hmmm, milk-bottles or spearmint leaves? I certainly wasn't thinking about the global communication applications that would arise over the next thirty or forty years from what looked like slow moving stars. Little did I know what these fascinating shiny objects were to herald or I would have thought WTF? Or something along those lines, only more wholesome.

When the lolly dilemma had been resolved, I tuned back in to listen avidly to Dad's stories and was once again aware of the glittering cosmos above me and the cool metal under my back – thinking OMG!

On Thursday morning an email came through to say that publisher number three had declined on my book. Gak! I rang the agent to get the blow-by-blow and she seemed genuinely surprised that they hadn't taken it on. But she reiterated that she was finding the market had changed enormously of late and reckoned she wouldn't have had any trouble selling it even quite recently. No doubt, digital productions, online bookstores and the global financial crisis were all playing a role in throwing the traditional publishing industry on its ear.

Thankfully, I felt pretty upbeat today and managed to be philosophical about it all. The agent said she'd already sent it to publisher number four so that took the sting out a little. She remained confident about it, so today's disappointment was nothing compared to if I'd gone solo and had just received an impersonal rejection letter, leaving me wondering what my next move would be. I felt very fortunate having her in my corner. I admit I was still dining out on the thrill of having an agent at all so maybe that too helped take the sting out of things. Getting published would almost feel like a bonus!

So it was straight back onto the old nag for me. I returned to the computer and began typing in earnest. I racked up another 3,500 words over the course of the day.

When I'd gone to bed the night before I'd felt scattered mentally and was thoroughly fed up with my blog obsession and with the POD site – I was wasting so much time glued to the computer screen. In a rare moment of clarity, it suddenly dawned on me that all the time spent on the computer was keeping me away from my writing. Belatedly I remembered my intention of making a tilt at getting this book finished by the end of the year. I'd known it was a wild dream, but if

I kept wasting time the way I was now, I wouldn't even get my first draft finished!

It was as if I'd been sleepwalking these past couple of weeks and had lost sight of the bigger picture. The dream of being able to finish my book by year's end was *so* deeply in the realms of fantasy now, even the fairies at the bottom of the garden wouldn't have believed in it. However, if I could get two to three thousand words done each day I would make quicker progress than I did with the last book at least – particularly now that I was writing in a more linear manner.

Once I realised I'd have to pin myself down to get some focus, I resolved to challenge myself to do 10,000 words this week. A brutal challenge considering it was already Thursday and I'd only done one and a half thousand words so far for the week. However, by 1pm I had done a further 2,400 words so it actually began to feel possible – the game was on! I would aim to get to 10,000 words by Sunday night. I was thrilled at how many words I was getting down, but it was as rough as an Ocker's accent at this stage. There was a long way to go yet before it would be suitable for anyone but me to lay their eyes upon it

For the remainder of the week I wrote at every spare moment and managed to meet my 10,000 word target which I was very pleased about.

Challenge #18 – 10,000 words in a week

On Monday, still full of the heady writing success of the past week, I challenged myself to come up with the same amount this week. I checked my rash of cyber sites but this time in an appropriately moderate manner. I was back to a healthy level of checking and spent mere minutes on it today. I sat to do a proper meditation in the morning rather than just using the tape to snooze along to and almost managed a little stillness. I hoped to make it a more regular habit as there were so many benefits to stilling the mad mind. Meditation is also an excellent practice for encouraging the muse to cavort freely. Most mornings lately I had been making a conscious intention to "go with the flow". When the intention is taken seriously, it's amazing how obvious a difference it makes to the day. Synchronicity flourishes.

As well as funny little coincidences becoming more prevalent, I was feeling rather mellow at times. I was in a lovely languid state; quite joyful in fact when I drove the half hour to Lullfitz Nursery at around midday. As I was about to turn on to the freeway I discerned a perfection to the day in the way the sunshine highlighted the pom-pom heads of dry grass that only weeks before were green and in their springtime prime. Now they were white and sun-bleached and although we were still a month away from summer, it seemed the epitome of a gorgeous, shimmering, summer day. I looked in the rear-mirror as I was about to turn onto the freeway and noticed a little red car behind me that was sporting long black eyelashes. They seemed to make perfect sense on a beautiful day such as this.

Lullfitz nursery is well known locally for their good quality and extensive selection of West Australian native plants. I felt blissful walking amongst all the potted seedlings and saplings. There was such a great choice and all at great prices. I was thrilled to find a little plant that I recognised as the same type that grew on our farm in the wheat-belt. I hadn't seen one since I was a child when we lived there. I bought a few of those as well as a stack of other plants including fabulous strapping kangaroo paws of every hue.

All the while, I was swimming in a soup of alignment and joy.

By mid-afternoon, after unloading the plants and doing a grocery shop, my at-oneness was fast evaporating into tetchiness. But I felt back to sorts after a catnap and began writing.

As the weeks passed I was organically able to incorporate more into my days without having to work so hard at it. And, as I thought about it further, I realised that I'd triumphed over the barrier thing again like I had earlier in the year. I also continued to refrain from checking my computer sites so rabidly. I could once again think – oh I have a spare hour, I will write, whereas a while back I would have to break the barrier afresh and fritter hours away before I could work up the momentum to break the surface. I believe the recent 10,000 word challenge had been the clip over the ear that I'd needed, yet again proving how potent the challenge was for getting things done.

I found myself fantasising about how many words I'd be getting down if I was able to spend full-time hours on my writing. However, in reality I wouldn't be able to keep up the pace. The prolific output only seemed possible when done in sprints, I usually found that after a couple of hours my brain became too mushy to continue and the quality declined if I tried to push through. No marathons for me. Not at this point in time anyway.

Lately I'd been more organised too; keeping up with the domestic basics and still getting a lot of time for writing and painting. At my most organised I would make a start on my writing in the late morning, or around midday, once I'd done the morning jobs. Getting things out of the way first allowed me to begin with a quieter mind rather than feeling that things were hanging over me. On days when there was a lot on the agenda besides the usual everyday stuff, it was thrilling to find I was able to compress serious slabs of work into the tiniest of spaces. The days seemed very Tardis-like, as if there was more time in the day than there was room to hold it. Along with being able to fit in more work, I also seemed able to slip in more smidgeons of rest which in turn allowed the higher output; another example of finding the "genius, power and magic in it".

On Wednesday I went out for a friend's birthday lunch. While chatting and drinking tea I found myself noticing the shade of white in the cup and knew exactly which paints I would mix together to get that colour. I often did this nowadays when out and about sitting with friends over coffee or at someone's house – or even at home in my own company – anywhere at all it seemed. I'd be painting things in my head; every glint of china or shape of leaf became deeply fascinating once I looked at it from a painter's perspective.

Sometimes, when there was a particularly fetching ensemble of china and food laid before me, I couldn't restrain myself and I'd have to take photos before my dining companions could begin to sip or sup. My friends were very accommodating and remained patient and polite at these times. Not so my immediate family as they were the victims of such behaviour far too often for their liking. And who could blame them for being peeved when their cake was going stale and their tea growing cold before their eyes?

I was feeling a bit stymied about what to paint for the Christmas card design I'd been planning to do. In the afternoon I brought out some vintage ornaments with the idea of composing a still life with them, but they didn't look as good as they had in my imagination and I abandoned the idea for the time being.

Adding to the time I could waste checking for comments and statistics on my various online sites, was the inexhaustible supply of videos and memes that found their way into my online orbit. While engaged in my ritual cruise through my sites in the evening, I saw a photo someone had posted of a flooded street in New Jersey supposedly taken in the aftermath of hurricane Sandy. In the photo was a shark swimming in the flooded street just near a wooden porch. I wasn't sure if it was a real image or if it had been photo-shopped. I reckoned it was most likely the latter, but if it *was* real, it allowed one of my worst nightmares to encroach even further into my psyche – being eaten by a shark. At least I always knew I was safe on land, but after the horrors of the Japanese tsunami, I began to worry that our house wasn't high enough above sea level to be safe from deluge should one ever come our way. Amongst the obvious concerns of such a scenario was a less obvious one. What if any sharks caught in the melee saw their chance, nipped in through my window and ate me in my very bed?!

Chapter Eleven

NOVEMBER

The next day I revisited the box of Christmas ornaments and this time teamed up some modern baubles with a green vintage teacup with gold trim. I was pleased with what I thought was an original concept as I hadn't seen any baubles painted with tea cups before (although, I later came across some in blogland). I began taking photos of the set-up with my new camera, but the perspective was warping and the colours were drained of life. I just couldn't get it to look as vital and pretty as it did in real life. Suddenly the penny dropped. It would look better if I painted it from real life! I'd lost sight of the obvious and had succumbed to taking what seemed like the easier option.

It is certainly far more satisfying to paint from life but much more challenging when it comes to dealing with the vagaries of light and fixing the viewing point. However, there was no excuse to take photos when I had the objects right to hand. The camera came in handy though to get some shots of various compositions which helped me see what would work well. I painted for an hour and twenty minutes by which time the painting was over half finished, but I didn't have the mental energy to complete it in one sitting.

I did however have the mental energy to do some writing less than an hour later. Either I'd had time to re-energise myself or there were two different types of energies required for the different types of activities. I wrote for an hour and twenty minutes, tapping out exactly 2,000 words. The first 1,000 had been pumped out in just thirty eight minutes flat! As previously mentioned, having my diary as a guide helped the words add up very quickly, but at times there was still a lot of new, freshly composed content going down – albeit very rough. Being that it was still the first draft, I didn't have to worry about the quality right now. Many of today's words might end up on the cutting room floor yet! There were now over 40,000 words in my manuscript which was very satisfying

At this pace I felt confident that I'd be able to get a good first draft done by the end of the year. I was really enjoying getting the basics down. Being well past the horrors that come in the early stages of a first draft I had settled in for the ride. In the same way my painting skills were improving with regular practice, so too the regular writing sessions were reaping noticeable rewards, both in quantity and, I hoped, in quality.

Later in the day I spent an hour in the garden to continue with the planting. While we were having a few cooler days I wanted to get the last of the thirty plants I'd recently bought into the ground. It wouldn't be long before the high temperatures became relentless so the longer their roots had to settle into the soil the better.

In the evening I had time to relish the sense of fulfilment that came with being able to paint, write and garden all in one day. Having my creative needs met was performing miracles for my mental health. I was so incredibly well mentally these days it was becoming difficult to believe just how *seriously* unwell I had been only very recently.

While in the thick of raising children and struggling with my physical and mental issues, I'd often only had the energy to keep up with the necessary domestic jobs. I never seemed to have much extra energy left over for my creative projects. Now it felt possible to magically fit it all in – including spending lots of nice time with the girls.

The next day I had to really push myself to make a start. I continued with the teacup and baubles for nearly two and a half hours. Much of the time was spent trying to rectify the saucer after realising I had made it look more oval than round. Acrylics are great for such blunders as they are very forgiving when needing to paint over things. I also laboured fruitlessly trying to come up with the fluorescent colours in the red bauble. My dreary mixtures didn't even come close to reality but I resolved to try again in my next session. Despite all this, I thoroughly enjoyed myself. I love the challenge of painting glass and reflective objects. Maybe there is something about shiny, sparkling things that resonates with all of us due to the human race's primal love of bling – which in prehistoric times would have constituted the shiniest shells and stones.

I'd hoped to recover over a spot of lunch but there was no rest to be had, somehow the day sped up and got busier as it went along. I knew I should have gone to bed early but I wanted to get *some* writing done to keep to my challenge. At 9pm I wrote for an hour and then I wrote my diary entry for the day so I wouldn't forget everything.

I felt hot and feverish due to overdoing things, but at least now some of the pressure of reaching the goal of 10,000 words by the end of the week was alleviated. I was hanging out for the weekend to get time to finish the painting and also get some REST!

The year was zooming to its end and I was *still* holding fast to my goals. The spontaneity of seizing the creative moments as they arose was very exciting and enriching. With mixing all my creative enterprises into the thick of raising two teenagers, life felt very full and alive.

I so often found myself drawn into the garden like a feline making for a patch of catnip, spending hours there when it hadn't even been on the day's agenda. I wasn't quite sure how this unforeseen obsession managed to fit in amongst everything else but it did. Gardening had actually been an obsession of mine in the past but not for decades. I had expected a few more years to pass before it resurfaced into my life.

We were having a short cold spell which was great for a better night's sleep. On Saturday morning I luxuriated in bed with a book, but it was hard to relax for long. I got up and pulled some favourite non-fiction titles out of the bookshelves. I wanted to check how others dealt with the structure to move things along when writing narrative and to scrutinise the use of tenses. I had gone from trying to force more creativity into my life to needing to curb it to avoid exhaustion.

I was itching to get onto things so I worked further on my teacup and baubles for nearly two hours then wrote for an hour after lunch and ended just a few hundred words shy of the 10,000 mark; it meant I wouldn't need to pop out many words tomorrow to complete my challenge for the week. While writing today, I got a surprise to find that the things I was transcribing from my diary suddenly felt very recent. This was a good sign that I was getting closer to real time.

I got yet another late night waiting for daughter number one to return. So far I'd had the solace of knowing she would always be back before midnight when she was driving. But tomorrow would be her six month milestone and the curfew would be lifted. I suspected I was in for merry hell considering tonight she only got home at two minutes to midnight. It didn't bode well for future nights if she was already milking them for every possible minute.

I took things easy on Sunday and it was around 4.30pm when I finally emerged from my sloth. I hopped on the computer to knock off the last 300 or so words I needed for the 10,000 word challenge. Until I began writing the phone had been innocently silent for the entire day, and then when it could see I was busy, it rang its head off! I could have happily written for longer but it was time to get started on dinner.

When I finally fell into bed that night my thoughts got up to their usual malarkey of running feral. For some reason I lay there contemplating painting techniques and how it is that many artists feel a strong need to develop their own distinctive style – including me. It's not surprising though as it's hard to stand out from the crowd when there are so many talented artists out there.

Most artists already have an individual style regardless of whether they've taken pains to actively cultivate one or not; much like we all have our own distinctive handwriting style without ever having consciously developed one. But that doesn't mean every artist's style is particularly recognisable when put alongside others unless they have been blessed with *serious* God given talent or have laboured long and hard to evolve something particularly unique. I don't think I'd be alone in thinking that very distinct styles come about through a combination of natural uniqueness plus some considered elaboration of technique. Maybe I'd find out for sure one day! I imagined it took a lot of conscientious effort to create a *really* eye-popping style.

I was yet to see one at all in my acrylic paintings. I certainly aspired to having an identifiable style but didn't feel skilful enough to purposefully develop one. I had been surprised some years back when someone said how they loved my illustration style. Up until then I hadn't known I had one. After many decades I came to recognise that I did have a slightly distinctive illustration style so maybe I had one in acrylics after all? As long as I enjoyed painting and as long as others liked the outcome (hopefully enough to want to buy my work) then I'd be happy with that for now.

Coming across so many varied styles was one of the things I loved about the painters' blogs, there were countless different approaches to similar subjects and it was inspiring to see. It was easy to feel inept when viewing really accomplished work though so it paid not to make comparisons.

Not only do some painters create a very distinctive painting style but they also create a very distinctive persona to go with it. When I was twenty years old I met an artist who was a rock star of the Australian art world. I was waitressing at the time, having recently started a new job at the brand new Sheraton Ayers Rock Hotel in the Northern Territory.

One evening, a week or so after my arrival, I was walking past one of the hotel suites on the ground level with a workmate. The curtains were flung open and all the lights were blazing. Within, we saw a rather flamboyant curly haired man painting a picture of The Olgas (a local landmark) onto a vast board right there in his suite: It appeared he'd transformed his accommodation into a makeshift studio. The next morning the painter and his friend were having breakfast at one of my assigned tables and as I filled their coffee cups we got chatting. I mentioned that I'd seen him painting the night before and he told me that he and his friend were collaborating on a book about the intrepid explorer Ernest Giles. He was creating the artwork, and his friend was composing poetry to accompany the images.

"Oooh, how fascinating!" I said. "What's your name?"

"Brett Whiteley," he said.

I cocked my head a little in order to better trawl through my unworldly, been-nowhere, memory banks and said, "Nup, haven't heard of you!"

I said it with kindness, naturally, as I didn't want to hurt his feelings.

I breezed off to the kitchens to refill the coffee pot and whipped around attending to my customers' gastronomic needs. With every stop at their table, I chatted further to Brett and his poet friend Michael Driscoll, pumping them for information on their project. Upon discovering that I had yet to visit the nearby Olgas they asked if I'd like to accompany them there later in the day to watch the sunset. While there, Brett also wanted to collect some small rocks to use as colour reference for his painting.

The Olgas, also known as Kata Tjuta, are a group of immense domed rock formations that lie around twenty-eight kilometres from the resort – which at the time was accessible by a corrugated dirt road. It is the second major tourist attraction in the vicinity. I thanked them for their kindness and said I'd let them know. Despite their credentials as artist and poet I felt a bit uneasy about accompanying two men on my own when I had only just met them. So I asked my waiter friend – who I'd also only recently met – if he'd come along too.

The four of us drove to The Olgas after work. Brett and Michael sallied forth to siphon off the ambience and, while they nourished their muses, my friend and I soaked up the amazing scenery and the majesty of it all. Permeating the landscape was a timeless, sacred aura that was so tangible you could practically shake its hand. I was giddy with awe and no doubt blabbing to anyone who would listen, about the epic rock formations.

What I really wanted to do was take some photos of The Olgas, but Brett and Michael were in my way. They were collecting and sifting through rocks looking for the exact hue they were after, so I waited for them to move out of the scene. I didn't want my photo being sullied by having people in it. I have since regretted *not* having them in the photo!

At some point in-between oohing and aahing and wishing I could get a clear shot, I suddenly recalled that I'd seen Brett on *60 Minutes* a year or so earlier. It all came back to me; he was into modern art but I also recalled seeing some realistic work he'd done which was more to my taste in those days. I had been impressed with the documentary. I told him the good news that I had heard of him after all.

He invited us all back to his hotel room for drinks where we were able to admire his work-in-progress that dominated the suite – a picture of the Olgas. The red domes were mesmerising and we were very taken with it. We also got to look through one of his books that featured his art work. I admitted to him that I wasn't really a fan of his abstract stuff but was impressed with his more representational work. Being that he was suitably celebrated by those who mattered, he was unperturbed and smiled indulgently at my gormless comments and lacklustre appreciation of his celebrated works.

Thankfully, he must have found my honesty refreshing rather than ignorant, and even said I reminded him of his daughter. He took my address and said he'd send me a copy of their book once it was published, which I was very excited about.

Receiving a copy of their book *Native Rose* never did eventuate, but when I visited Brett Whitely exhibitions in the years that followed, I felt a particular connection to the book and to his Olgas paintings. It was a special thing to have seen one of his paintings as a work-in-progress and to have been invited by the artist himself to view it. I recently looked up one of his works from that era: *The Olgas for Ernest Giles* and saw it had sold in 2007 for $3.48 million dollars!

CHALLENGE #19 – 5,000 words in a week

The following Monday was the beginning of Lola's exam week and because I was feeling under par with fighting off a cold I didn't challenge myself with 10,000 words. I decided to try for 5,000 instead but that soon deteriorated to just getting as much done as possible. Thankfully the cold didn't become full-blown and was entirely gone by Tuesday. I knew I was tempting fate to even think it, but I was thrilled to note that I hadn't properly succumbed to a virus for the whole year so far. This cold was the closest I'd come which was a record for me. Usually I'd be continuously coming down with viruses, sinus and chest infections and bronchitis. My immune system was the best it had been for many a year – if not ever! Again, I believed I had the high-octane creative juices to thank for it.

I caught up on a bit of socialising and also finished the teacup and bauble painting on Tuesday. I had been thrilled on the weekend to get the baubles looking like baubles even without the blast of fluorescent shine I had been vainly trying to capture.

The teacup had a delicate gilt pattern around the top which I had purposefully left painting until last. Because it was so fine and intricate I'd been dreading that I wouldn't be able to do it justice and feared I would ruin the entire painting because of it. This was a distressing thought after all the hours of effort I'd put into it so far, but in the end I managed to portray it without mishap and it actually looked pretty good. Ironically it turned out to be the quickest and easiest part of the still life to paint. I so enjoyed doing the detail on this picture. I was entirely over my obsession with trying to loosen up with every painting. I'd finally come to realise that I enjoyed painting in fine detail just as well.

Usually when I'm working on illustrations I tackle the trickiest bits first so that if I mess up and need to start again, there is less that needs to be redone. Once a mistake is made using watercolour and ink it's near impossible to fix, whereas with acrylics it's possible to go over things so thoroughly that no one would suspect a hideous mess lurked a mere layer below the surface.

I posted the painting on my blog and after dinner managed a spot of writing. It was a productive session but I stopped after half an hour because a favourite TV series was due on at any moment that I didn't want to miss. I rarely watched TV but I'd become addicted to this particular show. Luckily it would only be a short lived series.

During the week I uploaded the Christmas bauble design onto my POD site and ordered some of them to use for my Christmas cards this year. I'd chosen a Christmas theme so early because I wanted to get my cards out on time for a change.

I'd originally begun the week with a plan to do only 5,000 words: that way I could take things a bit easier in between the few social days I had planned. Then I decided not to do a challenge at all because the house was a sty and needed urgent attention. I thought it was time to revisit the challenge structure from earlier in the year whereby I'd have fallow weeks in-between the creative weeks, and this could be one of them. But I just couldn't keep away from it. Also, I found myself unexpectedly sucked into the gardening vortex on more than a few occasions. Not only was the siren song of the garden calling to me, so too the keyboard warbled alluringly and I couldn't keep away from that either. With resistance futile, I revived my 5,000 word challenge and by Saturday morning I had fulfilled it, *and* threw in a few hundred extra words for good measure.

Towards the end of the week I tidied away my paints and got all the Golden Glitter Girl material out to revisit and spent the rest of the week redoing roughs.

Catching up on other things

The next week came and went without much opportunity to do any painting or writing. Social engagements and being on taxi duty were clogging up my diary. Lola's school year was winding up with her final exam at the beginning of the week, followed by a flurry of end of year activities and socialising that called heavily on my time in the form of running her around.

I also caught up on the domestic chores I had intended to do last week. I cleaned out the fridge and broke the back of the paperwork. The pile of ironing on the laundry bench had become such a regular fixture that I almost forgot it was something that needed attending to. My mind was deteriorating into ever deeper layers of mush, so much so that I'd literally forget to do the washing as regularly as usual. All the regular jobs used to be a steady niggle in my brain that would constantly elbow me to be getting on with them, it was impossible *not* to think about them hanging over me. It was very strange to have this internal prompter of a lifetime suddenly become quiet. I'd read recently that poor memory due to menopause is only a temporary thing – and here's hoping it was only due to menopause and not something more sinister. It felt worse than I could remember pregnancy-brain ever being. It was unsettling for someone who used to pride themselves on having a memory like a steel trap. I hoped it wouldn't prove to be a permanent change.

In amongst the appointments and activity of the week, I was able to slip in a little work on my mermaid book. I devoted a couple of hours to it on Thursday and finished it off in the afternoon. "Finished" meant that all the illustrations were now at the detailed "rough" stage rather than the final colour versions – except for the cover which I had done in colour. I hoped to attract a publisher's interest before committing to the immense tracts of time it would take to complete fourteen coloured illustrations. The pencil outlines would serve perfectly well to indicate how the pictures would complement and enhance the words. I cranked up the printer and ran off copies of the cover, roughs, and text and glued them into a mock-up book ready to send to the agent.

Not long before 3.30pm it suddenly occurred to me that I'd better keep my ears pricked for the arrival of the mum of one of Lola's friends. She was due to collect her daughter any minute. I'd noticed earlier that one of our resident bob-tail goannas was reclining by the front door as it was wont to do on occasion. Usually we only lay eyes on it once or twice a year and often in the company of its mate. They're not a common sight in many gardens these days, particularly in gardens that are highly coiffed.

Because Lola's friend's family was relatively new to Australia, I thought her mum may not even know of the existence of these local goannas, and at first sight she might mistake it for a fat-gutted snake. She might not even have the courage to get to the door to ring the doorbell if she saw the goanna first. Sure enough when I did hear her footsteps – ever so belatedly – she was already in quick retreat away from the door while frantically dialling our number from her mobile phone to be rescued. I had been right in suspecting that she hadn't had prior knowledge of their existence, and she was duly shaken upon the discovery. I chastised myself for not heading her off at the pass in time.

Throughout the year I'd been continuing with my efforts to remain in the flow of life which I was more successful at some times more than others. The nature of the creative life seemed to support this state organically. When I was able to exist in this relaxed and flowing way of life, I'd find that not only did synchronicity increase but I'd begin to have the odd premonition-ish dream; rarely about anything of import, but rather, surprisingly mundane things.

I'd dreamt the night before that I was in a school or university type situation where I'd taken out my mobile phone to make a call. There were a few young guys nearby who noticed and they all began marvelling at my retro phone (a Nokia Brick) and said how cool it was. That was pretty much all I could remember about the dream by the following morning. Later that evening I was checking a message on my phone and Lola happened by at that moment and commented archly about my ridiculously old phone. I retaliated by saying how these young guys had thought it was really cool, and then I remembered it was a dream. I laughed at how I could have mistaken a dream for a real happening. Lola said, "Yeh, *only* in your dreams would anyone think *that* was cool!" before flouncing off with her state of the art iPhone in her hot little hand.

Moments later Olivia was about to head out to visit friends. I suddenly remembered her telling me earlier that her phone was dead and she couldn't revive it as she'd left her charger in a friend's car. So I insisted she take mine as I didn't like her out on the streets at night without one. When she returned it to me later in the evening, I noticed that it was on the games settings – a setting I never used. I asked if she'd been playing games on it and she laughed and said no, but when the boys she was visiting had seen it, they all thought it was *really* cool and wanted to play on it. Doo doo, doo doo! (cue spooky music).

I'd always found it strange that my premonition type dreams were usually about such prosaic things. Why couldn't

I dream up the lotto results instead? I never complained though, as I knew someone who'd had some rather accurate premonitions about horrible things happening and it scared the proverbial out of her – as it would me.

It's boggling how quickly technology becomes outdated; my phone was around a decade old and yet next to the latest models it was like comparing Leonardo da Vinci's flying machine with a Stealth Bomber. I always joked about my "retro" phone before anyone else could. It didn't even have a camera but I'd held on to it because I liked its simplicity. I'll be the one laughing when they become collector's items!

On Friday I gave myself up to the gardening gods, and on Saturday I began a painting of a lovely art deco tea strainer I had picked up at an antique shop in July. I placed it on a vintage floral saucer and found a pretty fabric to sit them on. After painting for two hours I wasn't happy with the way it was going. By then it was lunchtime so I had a good excuse to take a break. Afterwards I popped down to the local shops and posted the mermaid manuscript to my agent. It felt good to get it off, but it should have felt *more* momentous. Reworking the manuscript for at least one more try at publication was one of the more significant challenges of the year. After all these years I wanted to be finished with it one way or another. I had anticipated it taking much longer and requiring far more effort to get it to this point but in the end it had been a relatively easy undertaking.

I resumed painting later in the afternoon and finished it off by early evening. I was pretty happy with it in the end and hoped it would be good enough to use for my greeting card range. The weekend concluded with visits to a Sunday market in search of old teacups for Lola's pending birthday party, and then to a garden centre to buy pretty pot plants to dot around our paved area where the tea party would be staged. It was to have an old-fashioned high tea theme. After some afternoon socialising, I spent hours in the garden tizzying it up for the big day.

The next week also passed in a blur. The feeling of urgency to get everything in hand for Lola's birthday party had ratcheted up another notch.

When my OCD had been at its height, birthday parties were occasions I dreaded for months in advance. Having a flock of children in my care always felt like a life or death situation owing to my irrational fear of harming them via contamination. Thankfully at this point I hadn't succumbed to those concerns, but it didn't stop me from worrying that I would succumb to them *on* the day. In the meantime, with the big day still some way off, I was able to simply enjoy spending time with Lola to find party props that fit the high tea theme – we had a lot of fun with it.

Growing up, we had referred to the delightful tradition of drinking tea and eating cakes/biscuits in the mid-afternoon as afternoon tea, and high tea was understood to be the more formal, full-blown, three-tiered-plate affair at refined establishments. Now I was becoming a bit confused, I had seen the term high tea used interchangeably with afternoon tea but I gathered it wasn't strictly correct. Those who are more exacting with their definition of such things would no doubt frown upon this usage. I decided to run with both.

CHALLENGE #20 – 10,000 words in one week (later revised to 5,000)
Big picture challenge – finish first draft by end of year

The following week began with a frenetic morning on very little sleep. I knew I should have been trying to get a rest, but I just kept moving. I took a ream of photos of my tea strainer painting and uploaded them onto my POD site. I forced myself to lie down for a rest but after ten minutes I leapt up again because I felt the day was evaporating. I wanted to get into the garden to get some more plants into the ground. After an hour and a half of weeding, pruning and planting, I came tottering back in filthy and fatigued. I had intended to make a salmon and leek mornay for dinner which usually took me at least an hour to prepare. I got as far as wiping down the kitchen bench before I felt myself hit the wall and I ordered pizza instead.

I seriously needed to take myself in hand with this gardening and creative-frenzy lark. I was still forgetting to do the washing and ironing, going days without it crossing my mind to put a load on. It was very strange and unsettling. Meal preparation had also suffered from the fallout. I continued to cook, but I cut corners where I could. Any spare moment caught looking even *slightly* unsure of itself was recruited on the spot in order to serve the muse.

But suddenly, as if overnight, it felt that we had passed the point of no return and were now on the slippery slope to Christmas. From here on in, every free moment would be needed for knocking jobs off my to-do list. Having a birthday party on the list made it all the longer. So time would be harder to come by now for my writing.

It was only back in September when I first entertained the thought of it being possible to finish my book by the end of the year. Even at the time I knew it crossed the line into fantasy, now it was so ludicrous as to make fantasy look like a documentary. If I didn't get my act together soon I'd be lucky to finish even the first draft! So to avoid that eventuality, I decided to make this week another 10,000 word challenge. I also upped the ante by officially declaring that the first draft must be finished by the end of the year. As well as this, I reminded myself to stick to doing tea party themes for my weekly paintings. I was intending to build up a series of them ready to print as a range of greeting cards in the new year.

On Wednesday, I notched up 2,000 words in-between worming my way into the garden several times over the course of the day. Gardening was simply the most divine way to relax. I read an article recently by someone in their thirties or forties who was embarrassed at their recent discovery that gardening was such a delight. Until now they had always viewed the activity as the preserves of the old and boring. Imagine passing up such fundamental pleasures because of the fear of appearing uncool! My own fascination with plants and nature was written in my DNA, I'd developed a passion for growing pot-plants by the time I was ten years old. I realised at some point that it was a little unusual for one so young but what could I do about it? I loved it like I loved to breathe.

Having overdone things all week, by Thursday morning I felt weak and ill and not great mentally. I decided to relax in bed with a book for the morning as I knew I must stop constantly pushing myself. No sooner had I opened the book than I began to notice loud popping sounds. At first, I assumed it was related to the building work going on next door. I'd almost become immune to the sounds of construction work after two solid years of it. But then it occurred to me that it sounded like fire crackers or fireworks going off. I took a cursory look out the window but couldn't see anything. I thought someone nearby must be messing with firecrackers, which admittedly seemed an odd thing to be doing at all, let alone during the day. A few minutes later, I heard a car pull up to our kerb; I got up and looked out the window thinking it must be the friends Olivia was waiting on to collect her for a beach outing. But the two young people who'd jumped out of the car were hurrying up the street in an oddly urgent kind of way. I looked further along in the direction they were heading and recoiled in absolute shock. Not far up the next street was a house *totally* engulfed in huge flames. It was horrifyingly surreal! By now there were a number of people heading rapidly towards the house on foot. I rang the fire brigade just in case everyone else had assumed that someone else would have already called (which had been my first thought). Thankfully, it had already been reported and within a moment of hanging up the phone, the fire trucks came screaming onto the scene. Several huge trucks and attendant support vehicles, along with the police all arrived in a short space of time.

It took quite a while before the flames were under control. By then the house was unsalvageable with the top floor totally gone. It was such a huge and ferocious fire, we heard later on that neighbouring houses had come close to going up with it. It would have been absolutely terrifying for the next door neighbours. With the flames licking at their own walls they'd had to evacuate. Luckily they ended up just with scorch marks. It had been horrendous initially not knowing if any lives were at risk, but the lack of an ambulance gave us reason to assume it was just the house that was endangered. Thankfully no one had been harmed and it came out later that the fire had been suspiciously lit.

There were so many rubber-neckers – including us of course – but we watched from our balcony. It would have felt strange to go closer and be in the way of the emergency services which had closed off that part of the street. Cars were appearing from everywhere and our quiet street had to contend with bumper to bumper traffic for a while. Streams of drivers had been drawn in by curiosity with the huge plume of smoke plainly visible from the highway.

It made me feel shaken and vulnerable seeing such a thing play out so close by. That someone's home had just burnt to the ground within a hundred metres of our own felt very surreal. We all live under the illusion that our homes are a place of refuge and security, hence the saying, "safe as houses".

All the drama put paid to my restful morning as I felt terribly churned up. Instead, I pottered inefficiently at various jobs and the day was wasted. No writing got done other than my diary update which was something at least.

The next day I had to drop Lola down at Fremantle for a whole day work induction. Because it was peak-hour the usual forty minute drive took closer to an hour. I did a spot of tidying up on my return and it was around 11.00am when I began to write. I luxuriated in the knowledge that I had until the late afternoon to spend on my writing. A while later Lola rang asking if I was still in Fremantle as she needed some lunch money. My heart sank; it hadn't even crossed my mind in the morning to ensure she had money for food.

I'd automatically assumed the company would provide their inductees with refreshments for the day. Olivia's employer had supplied lunch at her induction last year.

I told her I was already home but did she want me to bring something down for her? Because it would take so long to drive back, her lunch break would have been and gone by the time I arrived and it would make for an embarrassing interruption. She said no and hung up immediately before I'd had a chance to embark upon the inevitable fussing and quizzing I was about to subject her to. I tried to ring her back but she had already turned her phone off. I had form in these types of situations so I couldn't blame her, but not being able to resolve what to do sent me into a lather.

She hadn't been able to eat breakfast because of feeling anxious so that was playing on my mind, and while I knew it was unlikely she'd starve to death, I feared she'd be on her last legs by the end of the day. After my initial panicked reaction and expecting to feel sick with guilt about it for the rest of the day, I was able to get more perspective on it. I knew she had a water bottle and that she'd taken some crackers at least, and I would take some food with me for her to tuck into as soon as I collected her at 5.30pm.

If this had happened at the height of my OCD, I would have been beside myself with anguish at my oversight and believed I was the worst mother that ever drew breath. I'd have spent the whole duration catastrophising and freaking out that I'd arrive in Fremantle at the end of the day to take delivery of her dead body. That's if I hadn't instead ignored her directives and humiliated her in front of the others by racing back to deliver something for her to eat – which would have been a very possible scenario.

I forced myself to get back to my writing even though I wasn't expecting to be able to concentrate. But, amazingly, the creative energy dissipated my obsessive thinking and the sick feeling began to subside. It was like taking medication! It would have been unheard of last year to be able to put it into the background. It was exciting to see the reality of how far my health had improved when in a situation that would in the past have sent me spiralling down – and staying down – into utter OCD panic.

It ended up being a productive writing session. I had realised early on in the week that my goal of 10,000 was impossible in the face of such a full week and had knocked it back to 5,000. In the end I did 5,204 which I was happy with.

As I got closer to Fremantle in the afternoon with just my thoughts to keep me company, I became anxious and panicky again. What if she had become weak and dehydrated and what if it had damaged her health irretrievably? How could I live with myself? What was I thinking by not delivering her something when I'd had the chance? My irrational OCD thoughts once again turned things into a life or death situation. But I'd worried for nothing, it turned out that she'd taken stuff with her that I hadn't known about – as well as being provided with morning and afternoon tea which had kept her going.

Saturday was full of jobs and a social outing with Lola. Also I helped Olivia get organised for her trip to Adelaide which she was to embark upon the following day. I spent some time in the evening packing up my painting gear and getting it loaded into the car for our early getaway in the morning.

The next morning Olivia and I got up at 5.30am and left by 6.30am to head to the airport. After a big hug and watching her disappear through the boarding gate I headed off to my next destination which was further afield in the hills. I had booked to do a painting workshop with an artist I had long admired.

I arrived at Greg Baker's house just after 8.30am for a prompt start at 9.00am. I had first seen some of Greg's spectacular work a few years back in a local gallery and had marvelled at his skills and style. I'd rung him earlier in the year to see if he took on students for regular classes, but unfortunately he didn't. He was, however, hatching a plan to run some workshops and said he'd be in contact once he'd organised some dates.

There were about thirteen of us attending the demonstration at Greg's magnificent studio at the back of his house. From the balcony at the front of the house were sweeping views of the Perth coastal plain and across to the ocean. From the elevated vantage point, the city of Perth could be seen as a distant little huddle of skyscrapers adrift in a sea of suburbia that stretched for as far as the eye could see. There were also large tracts of undisturbed native bush in the immediate vicinity of his house.

Before we got started we had time to admire many of Greg's beautiful paintings in various stages of completion that adorned the limestone walls of his studio. Throughout the morning he did demonstrations in oils, pastels and acrylics and did around five paintings – he didn't entirely complete them but almost. It was very insightful to see how he worked. After a lovely lunch sitting and chatting on the balcony, we got our materials out to do our own paintings. Many of us worked from one of Greg's demonstration photos of Rottnest Island waters. He'd already done three versions of it. He had very nice things to say about my painting which I was pleased about and he only made some very small improvements. It was *such* a great day!

It had been freaky how the whole morning had unfolded with the precision of Swiss clockwork, particularly with having two far afield and disparate activities to tie in with each other – the airport drop-off and getting to the workshop on time. Not a single minute had been spent waiting or rushing, so seamless was the timing that top military logisticians would have looked on in envy. It was unprecedented and uncanny.

I believed it was due to the "go with the flow" energy I was tapping into these days. It was very different to how things worked in my previous "non-genius, power and magic" kind of life. Anytime – or should I say *every* time I had more than one thing happening in a week, let alone in one day, I could be sure there would be a clash of the most violent type when it came to timing; usually to the point that one thing would inevitably need to be cancelled or rearranged.

The following week was unrelentingly hectic and stressful beyond words and all the "go with the flow" unicorn stuff disappeared in a puff of pink glitter. It was back to business-as-usual on the clashing front with not even a moment to devote to my painting or writing. The closest I came to anything creative was to do a blog post on Tuesday night about Sunday's painting workshop.

During the week I attended two funerals. My brother stayed for a night as he came up from the country for our cousin's funeral. It goes without saying that it was a *very* sad week and wasn't an easy one to get through. I collected Olivia from the airport on Friday. She'd had a great trip and it was lovely to have her home again.

Chapter Twelve

DECEMBER

Lola's birthday party finally arrived and the weekend was frenetic with getting the last things in place. Earlier in the week the garden had been looking tea-party perfect. The plumbago hedge was a fluffy bouffant of delicate blue flowers, the lawn was green and lush and the standard roses were a froth of white perfection – all petals and perfume. Then an unseasonal storm romped through with gale-force winds and ripped them all to shreds.

There were barely any leaves left on some parts of the hedge, let alone any flowers. Thankfully the rose bushes retained some blooms and worked bravely to squeeze out a few more by the big day.

Lola's party was a roaring success in the end. The garden had scrubbed up well with the aid of floral bunting and paper lanterns strung around the Hills-hoist, and we'd also been able to borrow a mini marquee. The table looked very elegant bedecked in a white cloth and fine china. There were scones with lashings of jam and cream, cucumber sandwiches and lots of other goodies that one would expect to feast upon at a high tea. My mum had kindly made beautifully decorated cupcakes, Kevin's mum had made her lovely Victoria sponge and Olivia had made the scones. It all went to plan and a good time was had by all.

Despite the hectic day, I sailed through mentally, slightly stressed but no OCD to speak of. An amazing outcome considering that parties had always been major triggers for OCD in the past. The only thing that hadn't been quite perfect was not being able to get enough photos of the table once it was laden with food and finery. I had been looking forward to getting reams of photos for art reference.

Olivia and I had ferried all the food onto the table with military precision. Then while the tea was steeping in the pot, I called Lola and her guests to come out to the table to make a start. I didn't want to delay things for too long by embarking on a long-winded photo shoot as it was a hot day and there were cream cakes and ham sandwiches to consider. So I tried to get some quick photos as they made their way outside. I'd anticipated having more time between the food going on the table and the girls taking their seats, but they were upon me before I knew it. So I wasn't able to get as many as I'd have liked before it seemed a little over the top and Lola was giving me a look that said ENOUGH ALREADY! Anyway, I managed to prevail a little longer to get a photo of them all smiling around the table. I was itching to take more – even just of the food, but I knew I had to let it go and retreated back inside; my camera button finger twitching as I went.

Business as usual

For weeks now, life had been unbelievably frenzied and exhausting with one huge day after another, but I felt a significant change mentally once Lola's party was over. I could finally think in a straight line again. There wasn't an immediate end to running around, but I was able to take things a bit easier and decompress with a John Grisham novel and copious cups of tea. His book really hit the spot and I got a holiday from my head for a while.

By Wednesday I hit the keyboard again after not having worked on my book for well over a week. It felt good to be back in the writing groove, and not a moment too soon as there were just under four weeks until the end of the year with Christmas and all the attendant hoo-ha still to contend with in that time.

I spoke to the agent on Thursday to see how things were going. There was still no word from the latest publisher and it was all quiet on *The Golden Glitter Girl* front as well. It wasn't looking good for a nice neat ending to my creative year by getting a yes at the last moment. However, I was so busy and so embroiled in other things it was like water off a duck's back right now.

I spent the afternoon barefoot and gloveless in the garden in the thick of the dirt and leaves like a pig in muck. It was so therapeutic and *so* addictive. I felt as free as I had as a child when I'd mooch around in the bush for hours on our farm examining and enjoying all the wildflowers.

Even though writing was now my top priority, the garden lured me in like a peeved lover, tearing me away from what I should have been doing. I had earmarked the day for pounding out words but it was the garden that triumphed.

So to appease the writing gods, I caught up a little on my diary in which I'd fallen scarily behind. I liked to keep up with it daily when possible because my feeble memory had to struggle to remember what had transpired the previous day. Sometimes I'd have a hard time remembering what I'd done in the morning even when writing my entry in the evening.

I managed a bit of writing on Friday around a busy day of domesticity and got to bed late. I fell asleep with the hope of a nice long sleep-in. On Saturday morning the building work next door was non-existent. Usually, if it wasn't the noise of building work then it was Kevin heading off early on his motorbike. But this morning it was quiet in both those arenas. However, it seemed the god of early morning noises wasn't as happy as I was without the usual diet of 7am banging and clattering. So it had teed up with the neighbour on the *other* side to kindly hold a busy-bee with half a dozen men. We were regaled with interesting loud noises and robust profanities as they manfully got on with lots of heavy-duty jobs just metres from our bedroom window. I got up in defeat.

On Saturday I didn't feel inspired to paint but, being that it was my main goal of the day, I knew I must follow through or it would only get harder to break the barrier, or I might risk stopping altogether. The painting barrier had been the harder one to navigate earlier in the week and in general was always the hardest one to overcome. Probably because when I paint, a certain amount of stamina is required to see it through. It feels like I'm on a ride that I can't get off until the end, and I'm never quite sure how long it will last for. Whereas when it comes to writing, I know I can just commit to an hour, or even half an hour and I'll have achieved something of substance. If I stopped too soon into a painting, it would just make it all the harder to return to it later – and being that I work in acrylics, the paint would dry up by the time I returned.

It was yet again a good illustration to show how quickly a blockage could develop and how essential it was to keep painting regularly. It was also a good reminder that I mustn't ease off in the new year. I could see there was a danger of that happening once the year of challenges was over and the pressure was off.

Demoralising as this revelation was, I had come to find that even painting once a week wasn't quite enough to keep blockages at bay. It called for a certain amount of courage to break through afresh each time, whereas on the occasions I painted for several days in a row, it was so easy to just pick up where I left off – or begin something new. In fact, when I painted more often I found I was *itching* to get back to it. I wouldn't leave it to the end of the day as I had today if I could possibly help it. Part of me would love to paint every day but it still wasn't feasible at the moment.

Over the last few days I'd taken a lot of photos of the beautiful hydrangea I'd had on the table for Lola's party. I chose a photo to work from and *finally* reared up and began painting at around 4.20pm. I decided to give myself till 5pm to force a quick loose style. I went a bit over time and finished at around 5.20pm. Early on it seemed to be coming along nicely only to take a nosedive halfway through. It was turning into a staggering disaster and I wondered if I'd have the confidence to post such a horror on my blog just to prove I'd painted for the week. As I took a photo of it I was surprised to find it didn't look quite so bad through the camera lens, so I tweaked it a tad further and then signed my name. While I still wasn't happy with it – I now felt it wouldn't be beyond the pale to post. Strangely, it actually began to grow on me after a while. Funny how I could go from thinking something was a *staggering* disaster to "meh" within such a short space of time! I still hadn't achieved my long held ideal of a hydrangea painting so I would make another attempt soon.

I finally got a sleep-in on Sunday. The god of peace and quiet must have had a few words with the god of early morning noises – words to the effect of "Shut the eff up!" – and finally there was peace in our end of the street.

I dropped Lola at work for her six hour shift that began at 11.00am. As I crested the hill on the return home, the ocean looked ridiculously inviting. It was an eye-popping tropical aqua colour. The days were brighter than usual lately in a way that is only possible on very hot summer days. There was a crisp clarity to everything and it seemed the light had been ramped up a few notches: as if a floodlight in the ether had just lit up the set. Rather than make the colours appear washed out, it had the opposite effect. The blue of the sky was of an intensity that defied comprehension. The colours in everything I set eyes upon pulsated with a vibrancy that took my breath away.

This type of heightened summer day was equally beautiful but subtly different to the type of days that occurred mostly in spring – when they appeared more effervescent and sparkly than usual. I sometimes wondered if these freakishly beautiful days could simply be the product of my perceptions relating to a certain mood. But I'm sure a meteorologist would soon be able to tell me what makes the difference – probably things to do with barometric pressure and the like. All I know is that days like these make me really appreciate being alive and living in this part of the world.

So many things in life involve breaking through psychological barriers. It wasn't just the creative exploits that I had to be vigilant with. Because I hadn't swum at all last summer due to being so wiped out from the anaemia, and due to the rise in fatal shark attacks occurring along the Western Australian coast, I didn't feel comfortable to just nip down for a swim. Today I felt a yearning to dive into those beautiful waters, but having gone so long between swims I was out of the habit and it seemed like too big an effort. Also, I was determined to get some writing done. I felt I shouldn't distract myself, particularly as I hadn't even had breakfast yet and it was just about lunchtime. But as I mentally put the finishing touches on my excuses, my friend Barbara rang to suggest a quick dip and suddenly it all felt too easy.

It was almost midday by the time we walked down together. We'd missed the sweet spot of the day so we only had a short dip but it was glorious! The brightness and clarity were so palpable it was overwhelming, and the smell of briny air was indescribably divine. At one point I wondered what had possessed me to get in the water in this shark infested era and area. My eyes were on stalks watching out for shadows and fins. In the end it was Barbara who squealed at the sight of a big lump of brown seaweed that appeared out of nowhere in a nearby wave. My shark fears must have got to her too. I swam parallel to her but not as far out. The visibility wasn't very good so I felt more comfortable staying in closer, even though I was practically grazing my knees on the sand as I did breaststroke. We didn't stay long – just long enough to soak up the loveliness, refresh ourselves and have a laugh. We returned for a chinwag on the balcony where we dripped contentedly in our towels and sipped tea.

As always after a dip in the sea, I felt I was living life to the full and that I could take on the world – should it need taking on. There is something primal and amniotic about swimming in the ocean. Our evening beach walks felt similarly invigorating. When air temperatures are luscious and the sea breeze lively, a walk in the shallows is almost as refreshing as a swim.

It was mid-afternoon by the time I got onto my writing.

Christmas preparations

I had a few moments of excitement on Monday morning. I'd just missed getting to the phone in time to answer it but when I played back the message I was excited to hear my agent's voice asking me to call her back. I had noticed some time ago that when she had bad news to impart, she always emailed me. So I thought the fact that she'd rung this time must mean good news. But alas, it didn't. It was a similar story to the previous responses. In the agent's paraphrased words, the publisher thought the story was charming and the writing was very good, but didn't want to take the risk due to my lack of profile. Very frustrating! It was akin to going for a job interview and being knocked back due to lack of experience. How is one supposed to get the experience/profile if not given a chance in the first place? As usual the agent had very kindly teed up the next submission before she contacted me. It was a smaller house this time but one that appeared to focus on exactly my type of book.

It was amazing how high my hopes had risen in the few minutes it had taken for me to return the agent's call. I had let my guard down on this one and felt a bitter flash of disappointment upon hearing of the rejection. But it didn't last long: hearing it was already back in the pipeline was a nice cushion for my nerves to fall upon.

After that little bit of drama, it was once more into the breach as I raced off to meet Olivia at her dental appointment. I wanted to find out about her wisdom teeth situation and to see if she needed an x-ray in order to ascertain whether or not she'd need to have them out. They duly took x-rays and we were told we'd get the results soon. I was dreading it as the girls' dental issues had made me wild with OCD anxiety in the past.

I'd hoped to have swathes of hours to spend on my writing as well as to make a start on writing out Christmas cards. But as is often the case, the little jobs ate into those vast swathes and it was around 2pm before I began on the Christmas cards. A very time consuming business it was too. I usually kept the lists from previous years in a particular box, but the last few lists were inexplicably absent. I realised with a sinking heart that I would need to brave the piles of books and papers in my art room as I suspected that's where I would find them. I scrabbled through so many layers of paperwork I felt I'd been on an archaeological dig. Eventually I found them in the Jurassic period under some coffee table books where they must have been fossilising since the beginning of the year. Then I rang my mother-in-law for updates on various cousins' latest addresses.

I suspect that the Christmas card may be a dying nicety. It's not hard to foresee a time in the not-too-distant future when all yuletide messages will arrive via email, Facebook or

Twitter, or whatever social platforms may supersede them. It is already beginning to happen. Maybe in the future people will pay good money to buy vintage cards to display on their mantelpieces in an endeavour to reclaim the Christmas ambience of their youth.

I feel ambivalent about this scenario as I love the sending and receiving of Christmas cards. It used to be one of my very favourite aspects of the whole festive to-do. Being a correspondence junkie from way back, I used to handwrite letter-length greetings in the cards that I sent to each and every person on my overseas list. It became very time consuming at its zenith. Aside from the sending and receiving of them, I also love to design Christmas cards. I have literally hundreds of Christmas cards squirreled away that I've received over the years; kept on the pretext for being used as art-reference material. It has nothing to do with my borderline hoarding tendencies at all!

Hmmm, I will be well positioned to do a brisk trade in vintage cards when the time comes.

I hadn't managed to get any writing done other than my diary entry, but some inroads were made on the day with having started on the Christmas cards. I was pleased to have made an early start on them this year compared to recent years. Usually, somewhere around the 22nd of December, I was still frantically getting the overseas ones into the post, with the adage "better late than never" running guiltily through my head.

I noticed with surprise on Tuesday that an email had come through from the agent. I'd had a feeling we would hear back quickly from this latest publisher, but this felt *too* quick for comfort. My heart sank as I read it had already been rejected by this latest publisher – number five. The agent also wrote that we'd speak tomorrow afternoon as it was nearly 5pm her time (Sydney being three hours ahead). It seemed like a long time to wait to hear about her next plan of attack.

I felt more gutted than usual by this one. I had certainly been disappointed yesterday, but no sooner had the agent delivered the blow, than she was telling me about the next possibility. So it had only been minutes before my disappointment returned to "waiting in hopeful expectation" mode. But despite how well I was able to bounce back, it was inevitable that each rejection made me feel a bit more doubtful about ultimate success.

I whipped down to the newsagency to buy stamps and post the latest batch of Christmas cards I'd written out. It seemed to take forever to get all the stamps on the envelopes as I was dying to get back to ring and tell Jenny the bad news and to have a little wallow.

When I spoke to Jenny on the phone, I told her that the agent had mentioned how the publisher hadn't found my story dramatic enough. I felt peeved that my honest and exposing account of years of mental anguish wasn't entertaining enough for him. There was a gratuitous misery-with-no-purpose genre out there which I wasn't at all interested in reading – let alone writing. I'd written the book with the sole intention of helping others, not just for cheap entertainment.

It was good to have a whinge and get it off my chest. But it wasn't just for this book that I felt disappointed. If this book didn't work, then I feared none of them would – including the one I was slaving over right now. I felt back to square one: the square where it seemed impossible to break into the game. I was beginning to worry that my agent was about to give up on my book – and I wouldn't blame her.

It is such a bleak feeling when it seems like all creative endeavours are coming to naught. For me, futility and depression come to the fore. The deep and profound drive to create is so powerful it makes me feel as if it's my destiny to devote myself to art and writing. Along with that powerful drive is the equally strong need to share it with others and to be successful. If I could make it pay then it justified me devoting my time to something I felt born to do. When I was younger and working in jobs that had become repetitive and familiar, I felt claustrophobic and enslaved, feeling I was tied into a rut with no escape. I'd never had extra energy at the end of the day to be creative.

With the advent of the internet, it's driven home even more clearly that there are a *lot* of seriously talented people out there creating beautiful books and works of art – more it seems than there could possibly be customers for. Anyone with a computer now has access to order products from these multitudes – even those in the most obscure and far flung reaches of the globe where merchandise is delivered by Yak.

After unloading on my long-suffering sister (we take it in turns to be the "unloader", so I didn't feel *too* bad) I did a bit of trawling on the internet. Thinking I was on the verge of losing my agent, I looked into various other publishing options, both traditional and self-publishing, which only made me feel *more* sorry for myself. But then after thinking it all through, I remembered what I'd been saying to Jenny just the week before. She'd had a disappointment with her current book (I was the "unloadee" this time!) and I was telling her that we mustn't despair as we had to trust that we both have good books in us. It was just a matter or time before one of our books would do well and by then the others would be waiting fully formed in the wings ready to ride on the other one's success.

I began to wonder about entirely reworking my book in the narrative. One of its stumbling blocks was its part-memoir and part self-help style which was proving to be an issue for some publishers. But the thought of revisiting it in any major way while feeling so well mentally really weighed me down – I didn't want to risk picking at a scab which appeared to be healing so nicely. My ambivalence had continued over the year with wondering whether or not I wanted to get it out there at all, so if it didn't happen, maybe it would be for the best and I'd be able to live with it.

The gap widened in my self-pity and I remembered to embrace the philosophy of "letting go and letting God". I had to trust that the Universe – or whoever was in charge – would get the publisher I needed, or maybe not one at all, if he/she/it decided that publishing this book wasn't the best way to go after all. I would stop pouring needy energy into it and get out of the way to allow the cards to fall as they should. I would trust that the best option would come to fruition, and as I was in no position to know what the best option was right now, I divested myself of any thoughts about wishing this or that.

By the end of the evening, I felt fine about it. I actually went to bed feeling quite relaxed and genuinely not minding if it got published or not. It took me a while to get there, but when I did, it felt enormously liberating. I'd come a long way baby! There was no way I could have been so philosophical about something of this nature a few years ago. It was at these times that I could really see the emotional growth I'd sustained over the years from all the adversity – aka hell – I'd been through.

Once I'd entered this flowery, puppies and kittens state of mind, I was able to get some perspective. I could see that I had become more deflated with this latest rejection than previous ones because the agent hadn't had another option to tell me about straight away. It was amazing what a strong cushioning effect it had. However, with each rejection the cushion was becoming discernibly more threadbare.

On Wednesday I spoke to the agent on the phone. After all my worrying that she'd had a gutful of getting rejections and decide to let my book go, she was totally relaxed about it all. I guess for her, it was business as usual. At the beginning of the conversation she said she'd work out her next move later in the day, but by the end of the conversation, she had already decided on her next target. Through speaking to her, I was able to get over feeling miffed about the latest publisher's response and decided to use the feedback for good rather than ill. In the cool light of day I could see that his had been a perfectly valid interpretation.

When she mentioned the name of the next publisher that she had decided to send it to, it clicked that the name had stood out when I'd been surfing the net last night – maybe it was a sign! A sign that I was looking for signs if nothing else ha ha! Anyhow, I was still in complete "let go, let God mode" and by the time I was writing up my diary in the evening I took a while to even remember that I'd been speaking about the book with the agent in the morning, so well had I recovered from it all.

With a two hour writing session in the morning and another hour in the evening, I added a further four thousand words to my manuscript. I was up to the 3rd of December now – so close to real time I could feel the breeze of the minute hand. There was no need for specific word-count challenges any more with the final goal so close to hand.

A profusion of shopping bags full of unsorted and unwrapped Christmas presents were accumulating in my art room. Other random paraphernalia had also accrued throughout the year left unsorted due to spending all my available time on painting, writing and gardening. My art space was so clogged and overflowing it was starting to affect, in fact, continuing to affect, the energy in the room. It would be quite the excavation once I was able to devote myself to it. But I wouldn't be able to get on to clearing the slate of 2012 until I got this first draft licked. I had to finish it before the end of the year which meant getting up to real time by the 31st December to fulfil my challenge.

The remainder of the week was busy in the way only December can be busy, but I managed to sneak in a spot of writing here and there. On Sunday evening I got side-tracked with my painting blog. From the beginning I'd noticed that a lot of other blogs had lists of followers with their profile pictures displayed at the side. I wanted followers too! I had tried to set it up during the initial establishment of the blog, but I wasn't able to work out how to do it and hadn't bothered with it again until now. Anyway, tonight I devoted a little more time to it and in the end it turned out to be easier than breathing. If I'd been savvier at the outset I could have had it set up long ago and I wouldn't have wasted so many opportunities for building up numbers. It was a shame to think there might have been a few amongst my 1,000 plus visitors so far that would have followed me. What self-absorbed narcissism was this you may ask? But having heard that publishers expect to see some sort of profile, I wanted to move things along.

More Christmas preparations and the wrap up!

When I checked my blog in the morning I was excited to see that I had two followers. It was such a relief! When I'd set the widget up it had looked so sad having none, particularly as right underneath was the total page views of over 1,000. Not that two was much more impressive than none but I had to start somewhere!

At around midday I began writing. I was on a mission to get to real time – no matter what! I wrote for Australia, and two and a half hours later I arrived at REAL TIME! Yay! In that time I wrote 3,124 words and now had a manuscript of nearly 79,000 words.

The girls and I went for a lovely walk on the beach before I cooked dinner. The cold sea breeze had made one of my ears ache and by evening it was becoming swollen. Over the last couple of days I'd suspected my outer ear was becoming infected and had intended to see a doctor. However, I had yet to do so. I didn't like to interrupt a day that could be spent writing, but I couldn't put it off any longer and the next day was taken out with visiting the doctor and feeling very poor both mentally and physically.

My OCD flared up terribly – much worse than usual. I'd become irrationally panicky and claustrophobic about the wick the doctor had inserted into my ear to help with the antibiotic drops. My OCD symptoms were far more extreme than a situation like this would normally provoke and I suspected it was due to being so run-down. By the next day I was becoming more neurotic by the minute. The wick was horribly uncomfortable and I was fretting that rather than doing its job, it was busily piercing my eardrum. By late afternoon I could tolerate it no longer. I revisited the startled doctor and insisted he take the wick out. Because it was supposed to stay in for days longer he began to protest but upon seeing my mutinous expression he thought better of it.

I felt a considerable improvement once it was out – both mentally and physically. It was good timing to feel sane again as a friend had dropped over unexpectedly to pay a Christmas visit just as I returned home. Our friend Rick is a graphic designer and he was complimenting me on the Christmas card I'd sent him and his family – the one of the teacup with the baubles. I mentioned that I was thinking of doing a series of cards in the new year and he kindly offered to scan the paintings for me saying I would get better results that way compared to photographing them. His company had recently bought a state-of-the-art piece of equipment that would do a great job of it. It was very kind of him and I certainly intended to take him up on the offer.

I was feeling much more even in the head after the distraction of the visit. But then I spotted the mail that had come earlier, and amongst the Christmas cards was a letter from the dentist. It was Olivia's referral to get her wisdom teeth out.

I'd had a call the other day after her x-rays were taken to say the operation would be necessary. I'd received the news with surprising calm at the time, but now, because I was feeling my own great discomfort of a swollen head, I felt sick about what she'd have to go through. I mentally revisited my own wisdom-tooth operation at forty which had been a bad experience and wondered how I would be able to face seeing her through her own ordeal. Then guilt got in on the act as well when it struck me that it was bad enough for her to have to go through it in the first place, let alone having her prime carer and comforter turning into a jibbering wreck just when she needed me the most.

On Thursday, there was little improvement with the ear, I had a raging headache and my mental state had plummeted alarmingly again, but this time the OCD was triggered by something unrelated to Olivia's operation. Seemingly from nowhere, a wave of hot panic washed over me in the morning as I latched onto something to do with one of the girls. It was caused by an insidious guilt aspect of the disorder that I used to be very susceptible to – whereby I'd suddenly worry about something from the past that I feared had impacted negatively on the girls' current health. Immediately I'd feel that I'd damaged them permanently from something I'd overlooked in their diet a decade ago or maybe a contaminant I imagined they'd been exposed to that had occurred at some point in their lives due to my careless oversight. Interpreting a previously innocuous memory through my disturbed mind was the sort of thing that in the past could plague me for days, weeks or even months. Thankfully, I managed to quell it swiftly by ringing Jenny to help me rationalise it. I *so* didn't want to be heading into that madness again – my brain chemicals had become scarily noxious over the past couple of days.

I knew this horrible little stretch of OCD had been triggered because of feeling so frazzled and poorly. I hadn't been resting enough throughout the whole year and I also suspected that I was in my most hormonal patch at the moment. Unfortunately, knowing what was causing it didn't make it go away.

When in the thick of such an atrocious physical and mental state it was almost impossible for me to imagine getting to the other side. But buried deep down amongst the muck, I knew that I would, so I just had to grit my teeth for the duration. It was a bleak day and I felt sad that my sparkling, glorious year was ending on this ragged, dysfunctional note.

Friday dawned more brightly. I felt much better both physically and mentally. While nowhere near 100%, it seemed I was over the worst of it. For a happy change Olivia and Lola's work times coincided so I was able to get a break from one of the taxi runs. It was only a twenty-five minute round trip but it sapped my energy; not to mention how it cut up the day into smaller pieces because of having to keep one eye on the clock.

The remaining days leading up to Christmas were hectic. In amongst all the driving, shopping, house stuff, visitors dropping in and getting organised for Christmas, I tried to rest as much as possible. Thankfully the mental horrors didn't return and while I still felt worn out, life felt normal and happy again as if my little micro-stint in OCD hell had never happened.

We had a very pleasant Christmas day which began with a swim at the beach as per Christmas day custom. The temperature was already rocketing upwards when we got down there at 9.00am (39.6 degrees Celsius was the day's maximum). Thankfully, the ocean was calm and clear with a light scattering of shark bait (swimmers), but not quite enough for my liking. I was feeling pretty shark-phobic and behaved like a maniac as far as the girls were concerned. I insisted that they stay in close to shore as there had been five shark fatalities in the state this year along with *endless* sightings and beach closures all year. The most recent sighting being at one of the city's most popular swimming beaches. Twelve tiger sharks had been spotted frolicking and feasting on a dolphin carcass just *thirty* metres from shore. It was only a few beaches south of ours!!

Even hardened water babies were thinking twice about going too far out. Kevin, while mocking me for my lack of spine, didn't demur when I said that the girls were not to go snorkelling with him out on the reef. In fact he didn't go himself in the end and there were very few snorkelers out at all despite the perfect conditions. Usually on Christmas day the area is awash with them, breaking in their new goggles and flippers.

The girls soon grew petulant at being herded in closer to shore but I refused to feel guilty about it, which was quite something for me. I felt vindicated for my stand soon afterwards when Kevin and I were gasbagging in the shallows with neighbours from the end of our street who were also staying in close. Both veterans of the morning dip, they would usually snorkel far out with joyous abandon, but today they were also being more circumspect.

We spent a very pleasant day with both families: lunch with Kevin's mum and dad and then visiting my mum and dad, sister and nephew later in the afternoon, all in air-conditioned comfort thank God!

Both girls were rostered to work for the Boxing Day sales. It was another happy occasion where their start times coincided so I could enjoy one less trip out. I felt anxious for Lola's safety as she was to be working in the shoe department where surging masses of crazed women scrabbling for the best deals could prove perilous.

In the evening I watched part of a talk by Eckhart Tolle (spiritual teacher) on the iPad. Due to my little mental glitch last week I felt I needed him. Listening to Eckhart expound upon the philosophy behind his book *The Power of Now* had been my drug of choice during my very dark days of the OCD these past few years. His dulcet tones had literally kept me from a total breakdown. It was so soothing to be watching his stuff again and it was very relaxing viewing him on the iPad while reclining on the bed.

After a dose of Eckhart I felt quite revived and trotted off to the computer to do some writing. It felt good to be ensconced safely among my words again. I wrote until it was time to collect Lola from work at 4pm with the expectation of coming straight home to resume where I left off. But Lola surprised me by wanting to do a spot of shopping for some sale items. She was worn out after her long shift, but must have been fuelled by the smell of Boxing Day bargains. I did another ten minutes of writing when we got back just to finish off the day I was writing about – 19th Dec. Having fallen behind from real-time over the Christmas period, I was very happy to catch up on the writing. Now I felt on track to fulfil my goal of finishing up on the 31st December and I still hoped to slip in one last painting before the end of the year.

Both the girls had a day off on Friday and it was nice to have them both home for a change. I felt free to devote the day to my last painting of the year. I'd wanted to further explore the reference photos I'd taken of the hydrangea and I found one that showed promise. Having photographed it from a distance, it wasn't a nice composition at all due to too much extraneous stuff in the foreground. But the hydrangea itself was at a good angle with good shadows. I cropped it into a square and used the photo for reference directly from the computer as I always do when not painting from life. I painted onto a 15cm x 15cm board and it took me just over two hours to finish it with a lunch break in the middle. I was really thrilled with the finished piece.

As soon as I'd finished the painting I photographed it and posted it on my blog. I was excited to find a lovely comment from an American artist whose blog I had left a comment on the other day. He had also become a follower. I now had a grand total of *six* followers. I was enjoying this new angle, having finally discovered how to follow people and be followed. I had been pleased to see that I was getting consistently higher visitor numbers lately too – in the high teens and twenties.

I'd spent quite a while reading in-between painting. It was good to be getting some rest, even though I knew there were plenty of jobs waiting patiently for my attention. I'd been enjoying not having a lot of social stuff on. Also around Christmas time we go away for our annual beach holiday which unfortunately hadn't panned out this year with the difficulty of co-ordinating the girls' work times. Generally, there was way too much on at this time of year so it was good to lie low for a change.

The next day was busy and went in a flash of banality. After dinner I spent the evening on the internet checking my gaggle of sites. I was excited to see that I had fairly high numbers of visitors today and yesterday. Admittedly, "fairly high" only meant tipping into the high teens! Then I cruised around various other painters' blogs enjoying the wonderful variety and talent. One blog led to another as I clicked onto images that caught my eye in the side-bars. It was a willy-nilly approach but it always unearthed some amazing blogs.

It was like visiting an art gallery from the comfort of my computer chair – dubious though that comfort was.

I was just about to log off when I decided to look at one last site. I clicked onto *Artists helping Artists* and saw a post that sent synchronicitous chills down my spine. The blog creator, Leslie Saeta, was to be hosting a 30 paintings in 30 days challenge beginning on the 2nd January. Immediately, I felt it would make *the* perfect ending to my year of challenges. It was almost a year exactly since I'd first read about the local 30 day painting challenge that had been the catalyst for this whole year of smashing goals. It would make for such a neat circle – the year ending as it began – pondering a 30 day painting challenge. It seemed like such a portentous thing to come up just as my year of challenges was drawing to a close.

The more I thought about it the more perfect it seemed. After all, I wanted to get straight on to my high tea themed paintings in order to get my card series up and running before the high tea craze came to a sticky-fingered end. I could use the challenge to speed things up and create the extra paintings I needed for the range. I'd been a bit concerned that now my official challenge year was all but over, I might lose the impetus to keep going – which I really didn't want to happen. Thirdly it would be a good way to get more exposure and be part of an online group activity.

There was just one big fat fly in the ointment. I was drop-dead exhausted! With the end in sight for my year of challenges I had already begun to smell freedom in the air. I was desperate for some R&R. I'd also been planning to do some serious spring cleaning once I'd rested up a bit as well as getting stuck into the second draft of my manuscript. But the timing of this challenge was so immaculate, *so* flawless, it felt like a nudge from the Universe, so surely I must do it! The optimistic part of my brain won over as I convinced myself it would still be possible to fit in the other things around it and I'd surely get on top of my sleep problems soon which would make things easier still.

In the next few days I planned to write up my new year's resolutions. As this remarkable year drew to a close I could feel my old optimism returning and I felt re-inspired to write a list of resolutions after years of feeling it was a fruitless enterprise. Nowadays I felt anything could be possible.

I had a restless night and found myself lying awake for a while in the wee hours worrying about my commitment to the 30 day challenge. Every time I thought about it I felt awash with exhaustion. Also I felt a buzzing sensation in my mental space as if it was being overcrowded and drowned out. I realised then that I really hadn't been listening to my body at all when I made the decision the night before.

In the last few weeks I had been *so* hanging out for the end of the year. I was ready to finish with the challenges so I could get some downtime before starting the second draft of my book and the series of greeting cards. I had been pushing myself all year and here I was intending to keep it going and with even more pressure! It was madness! I now had a good rhythm going with my weekly painting and high writing output so I should be pleased to continue with that for now. The thought of having to put off starting the second draft for another month had also felt like too big a sacrifice; this made me realise that writing was still winning by a nose when it came to prioritising my various pursuits. Besides, why start the new year off on the back foot when it was looking like being a challenging one in other ways? I had no idea how much free time I would have with it being Lola's last year of high school – not an easy year at the best of times. Not to mention the unknown quantity of how my mental health would hold up in the face of Olivia's pending operation later in the year.

After considerable hemming and hawing, I decided I just didn't have any creative juice left in the tank. I'd be foolish to keep pushing when I'd only just been holding things together as it was to get to the end of December.

Once I'd decided definitely not to do the challenge I felt a big weight lift from me. It was obvious now why I'd been overwhelmed with a wave of weariness every time I'd thought about it. It had simply been my gut trying to tell me in no uncertain terms that it wasn't the right thing to do. Even knowing I'd made the right decision, I still felt a wistful longing to do it: the mind was willing but the body had had the last word.

I got up and had a quick swim in the ocean to liven myself up. It was already in the high 30sC by the feel of it. The overnight minimum had only dropped to 27C! I had the quickest of dips and didn't go out beyond the depth of my thighs. Then I wasted much of the day mooching on painters' blogs as well as checking my own.

I dropped Lola at work at midday. I could barely keep my eyes open in the afternoon, so I slunk off to doze for an hour or so before collecting her at 5pm at the end of her shift. On my return I pounded out a couple of thousand words. No wonder my forearms and hands were aching! I completed up to the end of today.

That night we threw guilt to the wind and had the air-conditioner on all night – not that it was particularly refreshing. After so many days of high temperatures and no respite even overnight, the air-conditioner had lost its teeth. The brickwork was storing heat like an oven about to cook a pizza. I'd had a particularly restless sleep where I kept half waking through the night. In my light dream state I tried repeatedly to make sense of how the game *Rock, Paper, Scissors, Carrot* worked. I'd been able to get as far as scissors cut carrot but I couldn't for the life of me work out how carrot could possibly triumph over the others. It was a relief to wake up and realise the ridiculous game didn't even exist – and for good reason – a *carrot?!*

On the last day of the year, I got up feeling like a squashed banana. I dragged my mushy carcass around the house in a listless stupor doing nothing and achieving less than nothing. I trawled the internet for a while looking lethargically at other artist's blogs, then by midday I perked up infinitesimally and made a start on sorting out and culling my clothes. My walk-in-robe looked much like Lola's description of the fitting rooms during the Boxing Day sales. There was a slight improvement in my psyche after achieving a little more than nothing. The day slithered along in a heat haze with all of us walking around like the living dead.

Olivia headed out mid-afternoon for an early start on her New Year's Eve carousing where she would be sleeping the night at the house of the friend hosting the party. Lola was collected nearly an hour late for her sleepover party. While we were waiting for her lift to arrive I was getting edgy as the sun was going down at a gallop and I didn't want to miss the sunset. Yesterday Kevin and I had made genteel plans to go down to the beach to watch the sunset with a glass of sparkling Shiraz and some nibbles to see the old year out. We had been rather excited at the prospect of having a nice quiet New Year's Eve with the house to ourselves. Today, being mired in sloth and apathy, I was happy to settle with just getting down there to have a paddle in the waves. It was all I could do to get Kevin to come down at all.

It was hot and oppressive walking the short distance, and it was the hottest I'd ever known it to be right at the water's edge. Usually, on even the most sizzling days there is a lovely coolness by dusk when within metres of the ocean. Even with my feet in the water it was still stretching things to call it cool.

The idea of taking my camera along had flitted through my mind at some point, but we were in a rush and I thought I should just enjoy the moment without always trying to capture it. As soon as we arrived I realised I'd made a mistake. There was a stillness and beauty to the evening that was utterly surreal.

We were the only ones on the beach itself. There were a few small clusters of people who had actually put the effort into doing what we had originally planned to do. They were sitting on the grass and limestone walls with hampers and Eskies full of wine and food. The sun was already half over the horizon by the time we got our toes into the water. I spent the first few minutes bleating and berating myself for not bringing my camera and pining for the perfect shot I could have got of the last moments of 2012 daylight. Then I just let it go and consciously focused on the moment. I wasn't sure if it was due to the particular colours from the sunset or if I was just more present and observant than usual, but the colours in the water were scintillating!

There was about a metre and a half swell with nice volleys of waves coming through washing over my feet and up to my knees. I was mesmerised by the flickering colours in the water which sparkled and glittered with myriad hues from the lightest aqua/green through to deep emerald with shots of pink and orange reflecting the sun. It was a moving sea of jewels. I tried to commit the colours and patterns to memory. I had a fleeting bout of optimism that I would go straight home and paint the scene from memory.

As soon as we left the coolish wash of the waves we were again pummelled by the oppressive heat as we headed home for our less than auspicious fare of leftovers – tasty though they were. We zoned out in front of the TV, and an hour or so later I somehow disentangled myself from the sofa to write about this final day of the year. I finished at 9.15pm on 85,299 words, thereby fulfilling my challenge to complete the first draft of my book by year's end. (Cue fireworks and popping champagne corks) Yay!

I could hardly believe that twelve months had passed since I first began my year of challenges. 2012 had been an incredibly empowering year – my annus mirabilis. Never before had I had such a productive and creative phase. When it came to self-discipline, I had pushed myself to places I'd never been before – and it was exhilarating!

Throughout the year, I sometimes found myself wondering if I had possibly tripped into a parallel universe and merged with an alternate self that was living the life I had always dreamed of. A parallel universe where the best and most wonderful version of me existed: the one who embodied the highest potential that could possibly be wrung from my genes. The *me* who was more superior to all the other me's in every other parallel universe in the … um, universe. And the one who occasionally had a funny little thought visit her – that there might just be a parallel universe out there where her *worst* case potential was living – just skimming the surface of life and falling apart at the seams. She would shudder, and then laugh at the absurdity of the thought, little knowing that she was imagining *me,* living in my universe prior to 2012 – before von Goethe's genius, power and magic came upon me; before I grabbed the muse by the throat.

AND THEN WHAT HAPPENED?

Being that this book is about my *year* of challenges, I'd initially planned to end it with the close of the year; but it felt incomplete to leave things there. I wanted to show that my year of challenges had wrought ongoing benefits to my life, that all the gains I had made didn't turn out to be some short-lived freak of nature.

…

After an amazing year of getting my "resolve muscles" buffed and into shape, I boldly wrote out some New Year's resolutions for the first time in years. I resolved to meditate daily, juice twice weekly and get to bed by 10pm every night as well as a variety of other objectives. Despite my epic year of knocking off goals and fulfilling challenges, it didn't seem to translate into making me New Year's resolution fit. In fact I'd been right all along: the resolution fairy was indeed dead. As custom dictated, most of the resolutions went down the toilet by lunchtime January 1, and by 10.30pm when I had yet to retire for the evening, my pledge for "early nights" also disappeared down the "S" bend.

Thankfully, the resolutions that hit the porcelain only hours into the glossy New Year didn't involve anything arty.

In general, I continued where I left off when it came to all things creative and garden related. But I did make a few big-picture resolutions which included finishing *Grabbing the Muse by the Throat* by March (even I raised an eyebrow while writing that one!) and getting a range of high tea designs finished by February. These didn't come to fruition within my overly optimistic time frames, but did mature belatedly.

January began with my annual burst of enthusiasm to clear away the detritus of the saggy old year to make way for the fresh minty new one. A spot of spring cleaning always feels like the perfect way to cleanse my soul after the madness of the festive season.

My blog had begun to take off after Christmas which was around the time I acquired the first of my regular commenters. I was thrilled to pieces every time I got a new blog follower or a comment.

During the holidays I managed to get some much needed R&R in amongst running Lola around and the usual summer catch-ups with friends. One social occasion stands out in particular for two reasons, one being that it provided great reference photos for a painting and the second reason for what unfolded later on. Friends had joined the girls and me for afternoon tea on our balcony. I'd set the table with my pretty china on a snowy white cloth while Olivia made her signature scones. We enjoyed our elegant fare and luxuriated in the briny sea breeze wafting in from the west. Little could we imagine then, that the balcony would later play host to something a little more dramatic than the taking of tea.

By the time our guests left at around 5pm I felt as limp as the leftover cucumber sandwiches. I decided to leave the hand-washing of the tea-ware until the morning as the computer was calling my name. It was Kevin's turn to host his weekly motorbike night down in the garage and a few of his mates were over. It varied each bike night as to how many came along and occasionally someone new would appear on the scene. I had left them to it and wasn't aware of who was in attendance this particular evening.

At one point I noticed it had gone quiet downstairs and assumed they'd all gone home. Sometime after 11pm I sent an email and checked my blog before finally dragging myself away from the computer. I walked around the corner into the kitchen and was startled to find a man just a few feet away from me. Despite my initial surprise, I assumed it was one of Kevin's visitors that I hadn't met before who'd come up to get a drink. He looked a bit lost as he appeared to be searching near the phone rather than in a cupboard for a glass.

Having made this initial assumption my first response at being startled was either "Oh!" – or, "Hello!" followed by, "Who are you?" My voice had begun in a normal tone but ended on a note of hysteria as it dawned on me by the end of the sentence that this was an intruder. A bolt of terror went through me as I suddenly understood the danger I was in. There was a moment where it seemed the man was making a decision as to what his next move would be; one of the options I feared being to lunge in my direction. So I began to run while shouting out for Kevin who I hoped was still downstairs. The intruder moved fast too, but thankfully towards the balcony door which was in the opposite direction to me.

I raced down the stairs, and halfway down, I heard a great thump outside. I realised the man had jumped off the balcony. I burst through the door into the garage yelling for Kevin. He was sitting reading the paper with the radio on and he looked up blankly having not heard a thing over the noise of the music. It took a moment or so for what I was telling him to sink in – that a man had just been in our house, had jumped off the balcony and was making a run for it. "Quick, get him!" I said.

Kevin leapt up and raced down to the street and disappeared into the night. I wondered instantly what on Earth I had been thinking of to encourage him to chase the guy, not that he needed encouragement, but what if he did catch him and the guy had a knife? I raced to the end of the driveway and was relieved to see a car receding down the street, the tail lights revealing Kevin's silhouette in hot but fruitless pursuit. I bolted back upstairs to check on the girls.

Even while I'd been fleeing down the stairs moments earlier it struck me with horror that the intruder may have already been up to the other end of the house where the girls were before I had happened upon him. It brought to mind that earlier in the week I'd found myself imagining in great detail the action I would take if I caught an intruder who had attacked my daughters. I prayed it hadn't been a premonition. I think that had played a role in me urging Kevin to go after him.

I called out for the girls as I whizzed down the passage and was relieved to find they hadn't had a clue until then as to what had just unfolded. They were both horrified. Olivia said, "I did hear you screeching and just thought it seemed a little worse than your average spider shriek." We were all hot-footing it back down the passage to check on Kevin when Olivia suddenly grabbed me; whispering urgently, "Mum I think one of them is still in the house!" She thought she could see the curtains moving in my bedroom as if someone was hiding behind them. A collective thrill of terror shot up our spines as we gathered speed. We whipped down the stairs to find Kevin busily reciting the getaway car's license number until he could find something to write it down on.

On hearing our new fears he grabbed an axe-handle and went in search of any further intruders with us hard on his heels and with eyes swivelling in all directions. Thankfully it turned out that it had just been the wind blowing the curtains. After a thorough and empty-handed search of the house we rang the police.

Kevin had seen the intruder jump into the passenger side of a waiting vehicle. The license number revealed they were driving a stolen car and we had been just one of a number of houses on their rampage that night. We were one of the "lucky" ones, as I had disturbed the guy before he could find any keys or valuables.

The police arrived straight away and took statements from us. I had felt very embarrassed at the clutter that confronted them in the kitchen having earlier decided to leave the mess of teacups until the morning. If it had been any other sort of mess I could have blamed it on the intruder, but I didn't think the police would believe he'd stopped for tea and cake before looking for valuables.

Needless to say we were all shaken by the incident. In fact, once the drama had died down and we finally got to bed, I realised that I felt quite traumatised. I was very skittish through the night, every noise sounded like someone creeping around the house.

About fifteen years ago I'd had an actual phobia about our house being broken into while we were in it; it was amongst my very worst nightmares. I'd managed to overcome it eventually, but now I feared it would return.

Thankfully, and amazingly, it didn't at a phobic level, but it took some weeks to stop getting up to nervously check out every strange noise. A friend in my wider circle had been through a similar thing about a month beforehand and we relished comparing war stories. I had already begun listening to Eckhart Tolle on the iPad a lot in the lead up to Olivia's operation and it got an extra hammering after our unwelcome visitor. It was great for helping me get to sleep.

We had planned to get a ream of long neglected jobs done around the place in the new year. Since the break-in, the most immediate and necessary was to fit security screens to doors and windows.

I had been following the art-bloggers who had taken on the January challenge of 30 paintings in 30 days and felt disappointed not to be in on the action. But I still didn't regret my decision as it had been the right call at the time. However, around three quarters of the way through I did begin to wonder if I'd made a mistake. I was spending *so* much time cruising through the various participating blogs that I could have been using that time to paint every day instead.

Along with the rest of the publishing industry my agent had been on holiday over the Christmas/New Year period. I patiently waited till near the end of January before I contacted her to see what the outcome had been with my mermaid story. When I spoke to her on the phone she told me it had been rejected, and there was still no word on the OCD book. I was naturally a bit disappointed about the mermaid story's rejection, but was too busy with other things to feel a great deal about it right now.

Things may have been disappointing on the publishing side of things, but I was beginning to build up my blog following. By the end of the month it was up to the giddy heights of eighteen followers! Not enough to fill a stadium but just enough to stop the eerie whistling sound of tumbleweeds blowing across my screen.

The very morning that Lola returned to school on the 4th February, I reacquainted myself with my manuscript *Grabbing the Muse by the Throat* – for brevity and ease I will from now on refer to it as my "current book".

I'd been waiting for the frantic pace of the holidays to be over before returning to my manuscript. The whole week was spent reading and tweaking to check the bones were healthy before I could begin to make a start on a proper second draft. By the end of the first week of February I felt it had potential. I no longer found it necessary to record how many hours I was spending on it as I no longer needed the motivation. Every possible spare moment was being spent on writing.

I had an email from the agent on the 7th Feb to say the latest publisher – number six – was keen and it would be going to an acquisition meeting about a week hence. It had already been rejected by a few of the big boys so getting as far as an acquisition meeting with a big name publisher sounded very exciting. It was only the second time it had got this far with any publishing house.

The publisher who would be presenting it at her company's acquisition meeting felt it had legs. She suspected that it might not be easy talking the others into it but was nonetheless hopeful that it could be done. So we just had to wait and see. I couldn't help but get my hopes up as it sounded much more positive than what we'd been hearing lately.

February galloped along at a cracking pace even as we lugged ourselves through the horrendously hot summer weather. I was still averaging a painting a week amongst writing at every opportunity. Momentum was gathering for getting significant jobs done around the house and yard. This ramped up my stress levels due to the time-guzzling nature of having to make phone calls and organise quotes when all I wanted to be doing was write and paint. I had cut back on socialising since the holidays so at least that had freed up a lot of time. In the middle of the month Kevin was away for a couple of nights which made me realise I still had some vestiges of uneasiness due to the home intrusion. I felt a return of disquiet with him away.

Two weeks after we'd last spoken, I rang my agent to see if she'd had any further news from the publisher. The acquisition meeting had been scheduled for the previous week but still no news had been forthcoming. I didn't feel too demoralised and was able to remain patient as I was so happily ensconced in the creative flow. I had a smattering of social events to attend as the month drew to its close and the writing continued unabated.

By mid-March I had finished the second draft of my manuscript. I hoped to pare things back further in the third draft and flesh-out what remained. It was also around this time that the new security screens were fitted and I felt much happier at being able to leave windows and doors open for ventilation without worrying about what else besides a nice breeze might blow in.

We had recently visited the orthodontist for a second opinion about the necessity of Olivia's wisdom teeth operation. It was a formality really as we knew it was inevitable. I'd held off booking a surgeon until the visit to the orthodontist and now it all felt very real – and terrifying. We booked it in for the 24th June. I was having the occasional 3am horrors where I'd lie awake worrying about it. I'd often listen to Eckhart in the middle of the night to quell the fear and get back to sleep. The dread of the operation hung over me all the time at some level but I could go for long stretches where I didn't think about it *too* much. Everyone else I knew seemed to take these sorts of things in their stride. Why couldn't I?

Mentally speaking, 2013 wasn't shaping up at all like the free and easy year I'd had in 2012. Life began to feel extra stressful around this time. The list of jobs to do around the house lengthened alarmingly when we heard that relatives from the UK would be coming to stay. Originally we thought they may come as soon as April but they ended up booking for August. We weren't alarmed about the visit itself of course, that was very exciting; it was the self-imposed list of jobs we felt must be done before they came. Also, I had committed to taking Lola to Singapore at the end of November to celebrate the end of her school years. Of course, I knew it was a serious luxury having an overseas jaunt to look forward to, but at the moment it just felt like another thing to think about, worry about, and organise.

I had wanted time to consolidate all my creative gains from last year, but now it suddenly seemed the entire year was planned out ahead in great detail. I never liked to feel that a whole week was too booked up let alone a whole year! It felt claustrophobic. Despite feeling overwhelmed, I somehow managed to remain productive.

For quite some time now I had been planning to create a range of greeting cards with a high tea theme. I'd been slowly amassing paintings for the collection and was hoping to get them printed up sooner rather than later.

At the beginning of last year, I had envisaged organising my own print run once I'd created enough paintings that lent themselves to greeting card images. The idea being to try selling them to local card shops and other outlets. But I dispensed with the idea once I discovered the POD option. I thought it would be easier, take less investment and prove to be a way to make an income. Ever since launching the POD site, I had continued to upload photos of each new painting in the hope that someone would buy a copy in card or print form. Despite getting considerable traffic to the site, so far I hadn't sold a thing! So for my high tea range I intended to revive my original idea of a real-life print run.

Wanting to get my illustrations and paintings out there in the form of greeting cards wasn't a fresh idea by any means, it was a perennial idea that continued to pop up intermittently over the years; ever since my initial foray at nineteen with the hand-painted frog range. My main dream was to sell designs to an established greeting card publisher; that way I could just concentrate on designing rather than on sales and distribution. But it was exceedingly difficult to get work accepted. Many companies encouraged freelance submissions but it made for an unlikely proposition when they already had their own designers on staff. With one exception *ever*, my designs were always rejected.

After each round of rejections I'd feel terribly disappointed and frustrated. Because I felt a blistering need to get my work out there, I'd turn yet again to my well-worn idea of "sticking it to the man" by printing them myself. In a frenzy of swashbuckling self-enterprise I'd phone printers for quotes, source envelopes and then do my sums. With the ongoing advances in hi-tech everything, I always thought the costs would have inevitably dropped since my last foray – surely!

I'd get to a certain point with the planning and costing only to scupper things at the last minute because my final take on it would be that it simply wasn't viable. It always seemed just that bit *too* expensive for the risk I'd need to take in being able to sell them all and get my money back. The biggest stumbling block being distribution as it would involve a *lot* of legwork to try to get them into various outlets: it would be hard to make much profit once I factored in my time and the cost of petrol. Even then, would I have any luck with finding retail outlets that were willing to take them on?

I'd go through this cycle every few years, usually after dreaming up a fresh idea for a new range of designs. With each burst of enthusiasm I'd come to the same depressing conclusion *every* time – too difficult to distribute and too time consuming for the returns. I couldn't quite make the leap of faith. Every time I resurrected the idea I was determined to follow through with it *this* time. Owing to my fear and loathing of all things businessy, I would fantasise about having someone who could handle the business and distribution aspect for me, as that side of things brought on brain fog just thinking about it. It was one of the biggest reasons why I always ended up deciding it was just too hard.

More recently I had found a company in the UK that took work similar to my style which had given me fresh hope. I sent in half a dozen or so submissions and a few made it to their shortlist but they always fell down at the last hurdle.

After every rejection I'd ever had over the years, I'd take it to heart and slink off to lick my wounds, allowing many months and often even years to pass before once again girding my loins ready to try to get the next idea out there. In the meantime I would trot out the one or two designs I'd done all year to show people, saying wistfully, "It's just *so* hard to get anything out there!" There came a point when I realised I was being far too precious in the face of my disappointments. When I finally had the breakthrough with my series of children's books in 2005, it was because I had made a commitment to put in *whatever* effort it took to make it happen and not worry about what returns I'd make from it until after the work was done. With hindsight I saw that I had never really pushed long or hard enough prior to my books and had given up too easily. But it seemed I had reverted to this behaviour in the years since my books had been published.

With this long history of "failure to launch" weighing heavily on me, I had begun to think that publishing my own greeting cards could never happen no matter how determined I became. Somehow the kindling always went out before the fire could take hold.

But *this* time, after the POD disappointment, I was determined to follow through. If I couldn't follow through now with my new challenge-fit psyche, then I never would. In the absence of anyone having magically come forth over the years to deal with the business side of things for me, it was time for me to just rear up and do it myself. No more moaning about being clueless, or whining that I just wanted to be able to create while someone else handled the nasty distribution and admin stuff.

I made an arrangement to see our friend Rick at his design studio the following week to take him up on his pre-Christmas offer to scan my paintings. I was keen to find out if scanning was the best way to reproduce the images rather than using professional photographs – or even my own photographs – which was how I'd initially intended to go about it. Rick had recently bought a state of the art machine that was so sophisticated it did everything but make the coffee.

The reproductions looked *very* good and I was keen to compare them to the cards I'd had printed from my photos on my POD site. When I got home and was able to compare the scans to the photos it was very clear that the scans were the superior of the two.

On one of my regular weekly painting days I set up the same props that I'd used for a painting I did about a year ago. I thought it would be a good way to see if I'd made much progress with my still lifes over the course of a year. I set up a white and lime green stripy cup with a cut lemon and placed the original painting nearby to see if I could improve upon it. I didn't find it any easier to paint the subject matter the second time around, but the outcome was far more accomplished than the first. In the first incarnation the white stripes were exactly that, white! In the second I had learnt that white is rarely what it seems due to shadows and reflections. I had suspected my painting ability was improving since the beginning of last year but it was such a thrill to see real evidence of it. I was actually making progress with my weekly painting habit! It was very motivating indeed.

It was becoming increasingly possible to write on the days that I also painted. At this stage I had a very steady output of both writing and painting and was having no problems getting to either. Occasionally there was a slight mist of inertia to drift through but not enough to stop me going ahead with my work. I no longer got the blank canvas horrors. Once I was sitting in front of my easel I knew I was out of danger, it meant I'd already broken the back of any inertia that may have arisen. If it *was* going to arise, it would happen before getting as far as choosing my subject matter. Once I'd got to that point I was safe.

Eager for news, and with a seemly amount of time having passed since I last contacted her, I rang the agent on the 19th March. In our last exchange she had yet to hear back from the publisher about the acquisition meeting. When I spoke to her now I learned that she had since heard back and it was a "no".

I hadn't been too surprised to hear it had been rejected, having assumed I would have heard something sooner if it had been successful. So now we were waiting to hear back from the latest one – number seven – which she had sent through after the last time I'd rung her. She said she'd chase them up and get back to me soon, she also said she would only give my book another month of her time. I said that was fine and that I totally understood.

I was surprised to note that I really *was* fine with it and barely felt disappointed at all. I guess I'd had a skin-full of the endless lifting of hopes and having them dashed. The intensive saturation with Eckhart's talks no doubt also had some bearing on my new found equanimity. After the call it was straight back on my steed to slog out another hour or two's worth of words.

Afterwards when I was telling Jenny about the latest publishing developments – or lack of – I actually began to feel quite excited about trying the self-publishing route. We'd been doing a lot of online research about it lately and while we were very aware of the pitfalls, we were also finding the idea of POD publishing quite exciting. It was heartening to feel there might be a viable alternative out there should things not eventuate through my agent.

Despite the busyness and underlying stress, I was remaining highly productive and thrilled to be very much in the thick of life and living it to the full. I was achieving a high creative output while still helping to facilitate the lives of the rest of the family – not to mention all the social stuff too. The forced structure of last year had definitely paid off. I was now able to live the creative life organically without having to push myself at all.

I still took time to read, and in fact actively needed to do so to force myself to relax. But that too had shifted on its axis somewhat. Even when ensconced in a *really* good book I always felt a little edgy. I was constantly itching to get back to my own writing or painting. I had certainly let a genie out of the challenge bottle when I began rubbing it last year, but I had no intention of tracking it down to induce it back in!

On the 22nd March the agent sent through an email to say my book had been rejected yet again. I felt fine with this rejection and was even a bit pleased about it. Since speaking to her the other day I'd had a tangible shift into thinking I might rather have it back in my own control and try it as an e-book or with a POD publisher. Even while the agent had been pitching to one publisher after another, I was never entirely able to relinquish the uneasiness I felt about the potential publicity should we be successful. If I had it back in my own control, it would be up to me as to how much or how little I'd need to put myself out there to publicise it.

However, I was getting ahead of myself. The agent was just about to embark upon an overseas trip and said she would try it with one last publisher when she returned. I felt ambivalent about continuing to pitch the book at all, but at this late juncture I thought it best to leave fate to deal with it. The book's track record didn't lead me to think there was much likelihood of it being snapped up now.

I hadn't been able to fight the viruses off as effectively this year. No doubt this was due to being less diligent with my health-kick this year as well as having a lot more things on the stress landscape. The main stressor being Olivia's pending wisdom teeth operation which constantly simmered under the surface. I also felt overwhelmed with my huge to-do list that had taken on such a life of its own it practically had a gender.

Ever since the horrible OCD episode I'd had in December, I had continued to listen to Eckhart Tolle on the iPad most nights. Rather than only listening during difficult times, I found the daily dose of Eckhart was the mental equivalent of taking daily vitamins, worth taking even when healthy. Right now it was coming into its own and stopped me from drowning in stress.

I began researching card display stands online but many avenues of enquiry led to dead-ends due to expense and availability in the sizes and style I was after. After a few weeks when all leads appeared exhausted I finally sourced the perfect counter top stands in an industrial estate not too far away. Choosing a business name for the card publishing company I was setting up, and dealing with the attendant paperwork and bank account was all coming together fairly smoothly. Even though I'd embarked on it with trepidation, I knew I could do it. Since having created my blog without help I realised that I was much more capable than I'd given myself credit for and it gave me the confidence to forge ahead in an arena I felt very uncomfortable in. I was coming to see that anything was surmountable if I just worked steadfastly in the general direction of the goal – one doable bit at a time.

Years ago I'd had similar insecurities with my writing skills and always needed Kevin to check cover letters for me before having the confidence to send submissions off. One day, for some reason now forgotten, I decided that I *could* do it by myself – and I did.

My blog followers and commenters continued to build up slowly but surely. I was enjoying it all enormously. My blog buddies were becoming a stalwart creative support network. There was such a great sense of community and I loved too that they hailed from all around the world. It was fun to get a glimpse into their local environs and day-to-day lives by way of their posts. There was a lot to be gleaned through landscapes and still lifes, photos and chitchat. Who could have guessed at the unexpected joys to be had by comparing climates? My northern hemisphere counterparts froze their bits off while I complained about heat waves. Photos of snow draped trees bedecked with red cardinals looked magical to my eyes and vied with my own posts of gum trees sporting raucous parrots and galahs escaping the heat.

I had naively imagined that via movies, TV shows, documentaries and, in particular, reality TV shows, that I had a pretty good grasp on what it must be like in America – even though I'd never been there. So I was both surprised and enchanted to discover that another level of insight altogether could come through getting to know people online through their blogs. Even the countries I had already visited as a tourist offered up new levels of understanding and appreciation of what it must be like to live there. Giving overseas blog visitors an insight into my own locality and the whole exchange of cultures was almost as much fun as the art itself. It was a bit like having penfriends of old only now it was more visual and immediate.

Getting to know people I'd never met in person reminded me so much of my treasured correspondences with various penfriends I'd had as a child, the most enduring being a girl called Lisa who lived on a farm in Wisconsin. The details are a little sketchy now but at some point my sister came up with the novel idea to advertise for a penfriend in an American newspaper. She can't remember why she chose Wisconsin but suspects it was the name that appealed to her. She was deluged with responses and couldn't possibly take them all on. One of the replies came from a girl (Lisa) who was the same age as me so I began writing to her. Quite a lot of kids had penfriends in my era. The local newspapers had weekly columns especially for them.

At the time, we lived on a wheat farm about 354 kilometres (220 miles) from Perth. The closest one-horse town was around 45 kilometres (28 miles) away and we looked forward to the mail deliveries that the "local" post office delivered to our door twice a week. Every now and then amongst the other mail would be a letter from my pen friend Lisa. It was always such a thrill to hear from someone who lived so far away in an exotic location. The world still felt like a *very* big place in the 70s and 80s.

I was still writing at every opportunity and by the 3rd April I had around 90,000 words in my manuscript. The volume of words was daunting considering I hadn't even begun on part two. The more words I had, the longer each draft would take. It took an almighty effort to hone and edit. In my experience it required many, many sweeps through each and every sentence. Luckily I enjoyed the process overall but it didn't mean every minute of the process was easy or enjoyable.

It was around this time that I had a slump in my mental state, the worst in a very long time. It didn't immobilise me but it made for a very miserable backdrop to everything I did.

As the hot, humid weather continued I noticed how wondrously lush and tropical our hibiscuses were looking – they'd never looked this vital and vivacious in previous summers – to me it was proof of how humid things had become. Our sea breezes used to be cool and refreshing but this year they felt humid and disappointingly unrefreshing.

I'd been too precipitous with putting in some new plants a couple of weeks previously and promptly lost a few as the insanely hot weather continued, driving us all crazy in the process. By the end of the first week of April we were still getting temperatures in the high 30s. We feared we may have seen the last of our old-fashioned summers.

It was stressful knowing our planet had become so unpredictable weather-wise in the last decade or so. Not that it was always to the fore of my thinking, but I believe the capricious nature of it eroded a primal sense of security at some level of consciousness. Even if we decided to move to a more congenial climate it could turn around and bite us in unexpected ways, because it seemed no place on the planet had a predictable climate anymore. I couldn't understand how some people thrived in very hot weather, I didn't mind a bit of it but this was getting ridiculous.

After doing another painting or two to finish off my high tea series, my weekly painting habit began to slide as I became side-tracked with all the attendant jobs associated with getting the cards up and running. Sourcing the envelopes and other accoutrements took up a lot of time on the computer and phone. It was difficult to track down some of the items at affordable prices within Australia. Getting the right prices was essential or the whole enterprise simply wouldn't be viable. Along with all that, I was constantly writing and also brainstorming for ideas to name the various card lines I wanted to create.

In mid-April my recently dodgy mental health took a further nosedive and triggered into the worst state of OCD I'd endured since 2010. It took me over two weeks to get to the other side of it again. It was a terrible time but short-lived considering the severity of it. I was a seasoned veteran now and had some great mental tools at my disposal. While I worked on improving my mental state I began working on the mermaid manuscript again and intensified my exposure to Eckhart Tolle.

By mid-May our research on self-publishing was escalating. Jenny had gone further into it still, researching every possible angle as she had a book right ready to go. I now found myself *actively* hoping that my agent wouldn't have any luck with the eighth and final publishing pitch. The thought of a self-publishing adventure was very exciting. I was well and truly over the endless ups and downs of knock backs and the interminable waiting for responses.

Halfway through May, I took my card samples to show a stallholder who sold vintage tea-ware at various markets around the city – she was the first target of my market research. I hoped she would be interested in selling my cards alongside her wares. She was very enthusiastic and said she'd be happy to take the cards on if I decided to go ahead with them. I was very pleased that my first foray into market research had been so positive.

Towards the end of May, Kevin and I took Olivia to see the surgeon who would be performing her operation the following month. I'd been dreading it terribly but thankfully he was a lovely man who possessed a faultless bedside manner. We left feeling we were in good hands and the stress abated somewhat for a while afterwards. Olivia had been pretty relaxed about it all along – I had mostly been able to keep my untoward levels of stress about it to myself.

I'd been designing a cartoon illustration for each of the ranges to feature on the back of every card within my very modest collection. In the end I decided to print twelve designs. Along with the tea-ware subjects, I had done a painting of a friend's cat that just cried out to be a card, as did the painting of the macaw I'd done some time ago. The animal range would be called Growls and Whistles. I only had two paintings for that series but I hoped more would be added should a second print run ever eventuate. There were also a couple of flower paintings I wanted to include which went into the Petalicious range; again a very lean collection with only two contenders so far. The rest featured either china or edibles for the original High Tea Toity range.

I got everything off to Rick and felt relieved to finally have them finished and out of my psyche. Creating the cartoon illustrations had been a lot of fun, but I hadn't been able to stop tinkering with them – trying to make them perfect. This had then invoked the dreaded "barrier" and I'd really had to push through it to be able to finish them off. Maybe it was because of my bad track record with greeting cards in the past that the part of me that didn't believe I could actually go ahead with it was trying to sabotage the other part of me to prove itself right.

Rick had been waiting for the final artwork – front and back – of the twelve designs before creating samples for me to hawk around for some heavy-duty market research. He wanted them to be as close as possible to what the finished product would look like. If enough people showed interest then I would go ahead with a print run. I really hoped this would be the case as I felt I'd gone too far to turn back now, but of course I didn't want to throw my money away either. In amongst all this action I was running Lola to and from her exams and spending time online with blog posts and other suchlike bloggery.

At the end of May I heard from the agent. After returning from her overseas trip she'd sent the manuscript off to publisher number eight and it had been rejected. The problem for this publisher was that it fell somewhere between memoir and self-help, and they weren't confident it would appeal to either audience. It was a recurring theme it seemed.

As had been discussed in our last conversation, the agent would not be sending it to any fresh prospects. She believed she'd given it her best shot and it would be pointless to keep trying. I quite agreed with her.

Some time back, when the OCD book first began to stagger shakily towards its death bed, she reassured me that she would still look at my current book when it was finished regardless of how the OCD book fared. So I expected to retain a loose connection in the interim and was surprised when she now said that we'd be parting ways. She had decided it was proving too difficult to represent new writers in this current publishing climate. I said that I totally understood her decision and that I had been thrilled just to have an agent represent me – particularly one of her ilk – even though we didn't get our happy ending. It had been a rarefied experience for me to get a glimpse into the publishing world. She had been especially kind and supportive throughout our year together and I was very grateful for all her efforts. Trying the book with eight publishers had been a solid effort on her part. So I thanked her for her troubles, we wished each other well and that was the end of that.

Surprisingly, I didn't feel at all disappointed. In fact, I actually felt excited to be set free. Having recently discovered that I'd prefer to self-publish *both* books, it was actually the best outcome. It was amazing how my outlook had changed completely in the last month or so.

The fact that eight publishers didn't feel convinced enough to invest in my book didn't mean I'd lost faith in it entirely. I still felt reasonably confident that many OCD sufferers would relate to my story, and I doubted they'd notice or care if it straddled two genres. I'd certainly read others that were of a similar format to my own. Now that the self-publishing POD format looked like a viable alternative to mainstream publishing it might prove to be quite the jolly escapade. The worst thing that could happen was that I'd be out of pocket somewhat.

Authors are expected to do their own promotional work these days anyway, so they might as well get a bigger share of the pie for their efforts. That's if there turned out to be any pie to share of course!

I'd spent a fair bit of time recently reading through Jenny's manuscript and being a sounding board for the final convulsions of her self-publishing venture. She had gone deeper into the nitty-gritty details of the POD self-publishing option and was poised ready to go ahead – her book would be the guinea pig for both of us. Even though my OCD book was back in my hands it was still a way off from being ready to self-publish. I wanted to reread it again as it would no doubt need some further tweaking. I was also keen to get a professional in the mental health field to cast a final eye over it for me so I could sign off on some of my concerns. There was far too much going on at the moment to give it priority.

At the end of May Rick dropped over the final mock-ups on his way home from work. They looked fantastic! He'd done such a great job with them. I continued to write regularly but the painting sessions had dwindled down to a two-weekly affair. I'd been struggling with low-level bronchitis for a while and it was proving difficult to overcome.

In recent months I'd had a few people say something rather astounding to me. These were either people who didn't know me well or people who did know me well but obviously had very short memories. They'd look at my paintings and sigh longingly about how they wished they could get to their own creative projects, but were experiencing a huge barrier to making a start. Oh how familiar it sounded to the old me and I'd think, "I hear ya sista!" But then they'd surprise me by going on to say – in a tone that intimated they thought

I couldn't possibly understand what they were talking about – "But you're lucky, you're the type who just gets on with things!"

After rearranging my stupefied expression I would tell them that it wasn't long ago at all that I was *exactly* like them and it was *only* because of the challenge format that I was able to kick-arse now. Even eighteen months on I still felt like a fraud to be labelled in such an alien yet flattering way.

At the beginning of June I began taking my anatomically correct card samples to various outlets in the hope of getting at least a few commitments prior to taking the final plunge. After the very first enquiry being so positive with the stall-holder, the next few were not. The retailers in question thought the cards themselves were lovely but felt there wouldn't be enough profit in them to make it worth their while. I couldn't bring my wholesale price down as it was already at a bare minimum to cover my costs and time. I had factored on the retailers being happy to add on a 100% mark-up which would still leave the retail price quite respectable to customers. I was surprised to discover that many of the shops in the big shopping malls expected even higher mark-ups which would tip my cards' retail price into the unreasonable bracket. It was a harsh market out there, particularly when I was up against the rash of card companies that printed their wares off-shore in the hundreds of thousands bringing their unit price down to a pittance. I felt despondent thinking that my cards might not be viable after all, but I wasn't ready to give up yet.

By the end of the first week of June I'd finished my editing notes for Jenny's book – for what they were worth. On the gardening front I was feeling demoralised with the understorey due to the continuing necessity to water by hand despite it being winter. There had been a lot of last minute casualties. They'd limped through the endless brutality of summer only to expire just when it was getting cooler. Probably because I'd initially left the winter watering schedule in the hands of Mother Nature and by the time I realised she had been slacking on the job, it was too late for them.

Early in June, nearly a year after creating my POD site, I dismantled it. I'd had a lot of viewers but not a single sale in all that time. I'd been thinking of shutting it down for a while now and the final straw came one morning when I had a closer look at a batch of cards I'd recently ordered from them. I decided the quality of the photos I had uploaded just wasn't good enough and I only had myself to blame. Their reproductions could only be as good as the raw material that I supplied. I'd initially thought my images printed up fine, but now that I'd seen what Rick's scanner could do for my artwork, my camera was facing unemployment – for this type of work at least. My camera couldn't almost make coffee either!

Another nail in the coffin of my POD site was awakening to the fact that while it was great to have access to a worldwide market by being online, it also meant I had worldwide competition. Doing a real print run and selling them locally might prove to be the better option after all, but at least I had given the online option a go. Overall, I had really enjoyed the ride. Hopefully, having a worldwide audience would be much more beneficial when it came to trying to sell books.

I continued to potter along with the market research for my cards. After the few early disappointments, I began to get a feel for which places were likely to find my wholesale prices viable. Almost without exception the reactions to the cards themselves were very enthusiastic which encouraged me to persist. I ended up with five outlets saying they would put an order in once I'd done the print run. I couldn't ask them to sign in blood so I had to be content to go ahead on the strength of their enthusiasm.

By the 14th I had crunched the numbers and decided I was willing to risk a few thousand dollars on the venture – but it made me nervous. I opted to go ahead with a print run of 6,000. This would give me 500 each of twelve different designs. I would have preferred to start with lower numbers but the price per unit was so much lower when I ordered higher amounts. At around 2.45pm that afternoon I rang Rick to ask him to go ahead. I'd felt terrified up until then, as if I was about to leap out of a plane with a dodgy parachute, but once I'd rung Rick and committed to it I felt a calmness wash over me. Being that it was such a significant moment in my creative life I was surprised I didn't hear the swell of violins and the popping of champagne corks. After so many years of threatening to print my own cards, the kindling had *finally* taken and burst into flames – nay, into fireworks, verily!

I was so thrilled to be following through on my dream at long last, and now that I was, it all seemed so much easier than I'd ever imagined. It was a great surprise to find the aspects that had been my stumbling blocks in the past turned out to be quite fun and satisfying in the end, albeit every bit as time consuming as I'd suspected. I was actually enjoying the business side of things – who would have thunk it? I was also enjoying the cold-calling and running around. Again, who would have thought such a thing? Ah, living in uncommon hours!

By mid-June Rick had dropped over the colour proofs from the printer for me to sign off on. They looked great! The next day I drove to Rick's office and accompanied him to the printer's to see the offset proofs before the print run went ahead. It was very interesting and exciting to go behind the scenes of a huge printing company. Their inner city premises were situated in a slick and cavernous warehouse where numerous shiny printing presses clattered and whirred with state of the art efficiency.

It was fascinating to see how they arrived at the final colour settings on the machines. I too was asked to cast my eye over the samples to decide on the best set-up but I felt like an imposter next to Rick and the printer who did this sort of thing every day. Seeing the press chug out great swathes of card was a sight to behold – it was exhilarating and scary all at once.

False starts

If I hadn't been struggling so desperately with poor mental health for so long, I think it very likely that I would have taken the plunge to print my own greeting cards *years* earlier. When my children's books were published in 2005 I had thought my grand career was finally beginning. Soon after my books had launched I'd come up with an idea for a range of greeting cards that I believed were pretty original and potentially very saleable. I had intended to run with the idea, but it wasn't long after that that I began to decline so disastrously on the mental front.

This particular idea had rattled around in my head from then on and over the years I'd jotted down a few ideas and done a few sketches, but being in the thick of my mental maladies and deep in the embrace of "the barrier" I hadn't gotten any further with it. A couple of years later I was in a gift shop on the east coast, when to my horror, I happened upon a spinner-rack full of cards so similar to the ones in my head, I was sure the artist must have been eavesdropping on my dreams and tapping my phone calls. What made it all the more galling was that she'd done it far more imaginatively than the version I'd had rattling around in my brain. They have since gone from strength to strength around the country and I'm now a big fan of her beautiful work.

It proved to me yet again that we must run with an idea when it is given to us. I'd had similar things happen before but none so comprehensively. I'd have a great idea that was truly original to me, only to see it some time later out in the wider world. Did it prove the theory (I doubt it was my own) that ideas and great inventions are out there in the ether being beamed throughout the cosmos, passing through every atom and particle in the universe – including our minds – just waiting for someone to take them on board? It would certainly explain how multiple independent discoveries in science occur with frequent regularity.

Most of us wouldn't recognise these innovative, inventive ideas even if they bit us right in our brain's nether regions. We just don't have the right kind of grey matter to understand them. But the person savvy enough in the right field of expertise might see the idea so clearly they'd be jumping up to clear a space on their mantelpiece for the Nobel Prize to come.

There are recorded incidents of theories being concocted and scientific breakthroughs being worked on simultaneously by various people around the world; each ignorant of the other's existence until one breaks through – to the shock and dismay of the runner up.

Imagine discovering that the muse has been two timing you!

People often ask where creative ideas come from and I think the above goes some way towards answering it, although in my case of course it's on a more prosaic level. I find there are times when ideas simply waft into my consciousness unbidden. Other times they come when I'm actively brainstorming an idea or already working on something, but it calls for a relaxed state of mind to allow space for the ideas to come through. Often things come to me in the shower or when quietening my mind before sleep. I regularly have to jump out of bed to write things down, particularly when I've just embarked on a new project. When this first began to happen, I felt sure I would remember the idea if I left it till morning, but of course it was nowhere to be found by then. Even now I am still tempted to leave writing an idea down until later as it seems ridiculous that I could forget such a great concept, but I no longer take the chance.

Maybe the Universe doesn't appreciate a cavalier attitude and expects you to take the gift seriously, if not, poof! It's gone to the next in line. Now if I get a great idea, I don't ask questions I just write it down immediately and am grateful that it was *my* head it jumped into.

Instead of reading to relax in my spare moments, I'd again fallen into bad habits of spending too long checking blogs and emails. The anxiety was increasing with Olivia's operation only days away so I upped the ante with preventative doses of Eckhart. Being so busy also helped enormously.

Rick dropped the boxes of freshly printed cards over on Saturday 22nd June. It took me a few days to get up the courage to open the boxes and have a good look at them. I don't know why as I'd already seen the colours. They didn't disappoint.

The day of Olivia's long dreaded operation arrived on the 24th June. I'd had a very torturous night on the eve of it but the procedure went as it should and it was a big relief to know she'd come through the operation alive. I know every parent feels concern when their child has to face such things, but anything at all to do with the girls' physical wellbeing makes me worry to levels that are far beyond normal – or healthy.

While my anxiety lessened somewhat after Olivia's safe return from hospital I still had her recovery to face. The operation itself was only the beginning of what I'd been stressing about for the past six months: the necessary administering of medication was also a huge contributing factor to my levels of dread. To my OCD addled mind, being responsible for overseeing medication for others always felt like a life or death situation because of fearing I'd inadvertently overdose them on something.

I managed to help Olivia with the antibiotics and anti-inflammatories without doing her a mischief – or without making more than half a dozen phone calls to the hospital and pharmacy to double-check instructions (and that was day one!). For the first few days afterwards, preparing and timing her medications and preparing soft food was almost a full-time occupation, but I soon relaxed as she was recovering well and didn't seem to be in too much pain. Thankfully she took it all in her stride and my ridiculous stress levels hadn't rubbed off on her. Thank God it was over!

Greeting card venture comes to fruition

In late June I made my first delivery of greeting cards to a bookshop in a large shopping centre ten minutes away. My greeting card business was off and running and it was *very* exciting!

I barely had time to catch my breath after Olivia's operation as it was full steam ahead with the cards as well as furniture shopping and sorting out a host of other jobs around the house and yard. I'd only had a chance to do an hour or two of writing in all of June and only did two paintings in the same time. The frequency of my painting sessions had dropped off very sharply once my cards took centre stage.

A lot of time was spent prettying up the garden ready for our overseas visitors and I enjoyed myself enormously in the process. It helped to keep my stress manageable which to my disappointment had barely abated despite Olivia's operation coming and going. I feared that Lola would have to go through the same operation but hoped it was still a few years away yet. I even entertained the hope that it wouldn't be necessary at all. A lot of the stress was from having so much on and also due to the self-imposed pressure of wanting everything perfect for when our visitors arrived. From experience, I found that once stress snowballed to a certain level – even when the stressors were removed – it took a while for the momentum to slow, and even longer for it to stop and melt. I had the stress tolerance of a dodgy knee.

The first week of July found me very busy with my cards and other jobs around the house. It took considerable time to fold and package the cards and deliver them to the various retailers that had previously expressed interest. We were also getting a retaining wall rebuilt at the front of the house. Against this busy backdrop, I still had the last vestiges of bronchitis to contend with which no doubt was lingering due to the continual stress.

Two weeks after Olivia's operation I took Lola for her routine visit to the dentist. To my dismay it was discovered that she did indeed need to have her wisdom teeth out and we were advised it should be done sooner rather than later! Wah! I hadn't expected to have to face hers so soon. Then it occurred to me I would probably deal with it quite well if it was *very* soon – having just gone through Olivia's operation. But unfortunately, due to our full calendar of events for the remainder of the year, next January would be the earliest opportunity. Plenty of time to incubate another nice long stretch of escalating anxiety (sigh).

Even if I'd been able to take the news about Lola's operation with sangfroid there was still no breathing space amongst the stress. It came at me from every direction. Olivia was hatching a plan to head off with a group of friends on an outback road-trip, and just thinking about it was keeping my nails short. A day or so into their adventure and after one or two reassuring phone calls to say they were still alive, I managed to get on with life again and knock more jobs off my list without fretting about Olivia all day. I could relax again – until the next thing!

The continuing onslaught of anxiety following what should have been the relief of Olivia's operation being safely over with reminded me that I still had a *big* life lesson to learn. Once and for all, I wanted to be able to stop saying about *every. single. thing,* "Once this is over *then* I can relax." Against all known evidence, I find myself believing that once

I get through something difficult then life will be a blissful stress-free zone for the rest of my days. But life never has worked like that, never will work like that, and with there never being any indication in my life to suggest it could possibly ever work like that, I'm bleeped if I can understand why I still subscribe to it! Why do we all have this perpetual state of delusion going on? There would always be something to worry about if I allowed it. I had to learn to roll with the punches of life, go with the flow and live the tenets of The Serenity Prayer. Life would be a doddle if I could do that!

I was vicariously enjoying Jenny's journey of self-publishing and by mid-July she was excitedly showing me the recently arrived proof copy of *The Lost Art of Room Travel*. She had been inspired to write it after reading a book titled *A Journey Around My Room* by Xavier de Maistre, an 18th century author. Being semi-housebound due to chronic illness, she had decided to try something similar and wrote an entertaining tale describing her journey around her study.

Her experience had shown us that it was possible to create a good quality product and make it available to the whole world with a click of a button. Now the trick was to market it.

I'd gone weeks without doing a painting so in the fallow interim I'd had to scrape the barrel of my lean body of work to date in order to have something to post. I also included a few photos relating to other things going on in my life just to keep the blog looking lively. The cards had taken over entirely from painting and writing. It was *very* time consuming trying to get them out there, just as I thought it would be, but I was enjoying it all.

Everything was put on hold for a week or so around the end of July while I made a full cavalry charge on getting everything perfect for the arrival of our visitors. The house was in a state of shock from all the attention and my body was in a state of shock from all the exertion.

I'd only done one painting in July and not even a single sentence was penned in that month. Nothing creative was on the radar *at all* for the first few weeks of August what with keeping things free to kick up our heels with the rellies. My OCD book had been simmering away on the back burner while I got my cards up and running and I intended to get back to it once our visitors had left.

Our overseas visitors arrived at the beginning of August. They consisted of a squadron of Kevin's first and second cousins and an aunty from the UK – numbering seven – who we spread between both our house and Kevin's parents' house in order to accommodate them all. It was a wonderful interlude spending time with relatives from far afield and getting to know them better. They left a couple of weeks later. Both they and we had thoroughly enjoyed the visit.

Ironically, after raining most days while our visitors were here, the very day they left, the skies cleared, the birds sang and it was God's own country once again. I made the most of the sunny, crisp weather while on walks with the girls and various friends. There was an otherworldly clarity to the light and a sweetness to the air. The ocean was like a sparkly millpond and, in the shallows, the reef could be seen as if viewing through glass. Mother Nature's smugness for a job well done was practically tangible as she sprinkled the last particles of magic into place for the imminent arrival of spring. I got some great photos for painting reference. I made the most of the glorious weather and caught up with a lot of friends over August. It seemed like ages since I'd been in touch with everyone.

The very day after our visitors left, I had begun reading through my OCD manuscript in order to re-familiarise myself with it, having not looked at it since sending it to the agent over a year ago. I felt the need to tweak it as I went along and the further in I got the more ambivalent I became. The writing didn't seem particularly scintillating and I wondered yet again if my words would really be capable of helping others. I hoped I just felt this way because of feeling physically depleted. My state of mind and health always made a big impact on how I felt about my work.

I continued to tinker with my OCD manuscript and found myself rewriting far more than I'd been expecting to. My ambivalence persisted and I felt a bit disappointed with the book overall. When I'd first sent it to the agent I thought I'd had it very tightly honed. But now I thought some of the writing needed considerable improvement – for clarity as much as anything. I continued to hope that my perceptions of the quality of writing were being affected by tiredness, but I suspected that I was actually seeing it more clearly than ever before due to the twelve month absence from reading it. I was no longer so familiar with every word and so could be more objective about the quality of the writing. It struck me now that the agent had probably taken it on because of its overall potential, but with the expectation that further work would be required should a publisher take it on.

Each time I worked on it, I found myself wondering yet again if I really wanted to bare my soul in such a way. I'd moved on so much from that time that it hardly seemed like it was even my life I was writing about. This was a great sign of how much I'd improved since the dark years, but it was unsettling having to relive it all again. I feared that I was risking my hard-won mental wellbeing. It wasn't just the resurfacing of unpleasant memories as I reread and tweaked, I also felt exhausted and depressed just thinking of what lay ahead. It was an all-consuming job to get a book ready to the point of publishing. All along I had genuinely felt it would be worth the difficulties to get it out there if it helped just one person get well again. But it wouldn't be worth it if it sent me back to whence I came. Particularly when I was now thinking it might not be good enough to help anyone anyway. I felt I owed it to my family to stay well as they would inevitably be affected if I went under again.

When the agent had signed off on the OCD book and it was once again back in my own hands, I originally thought that all it would need was a quick once-over tweak. I'd self-publish it and voila! I'd have the perfect ending to this current book – which I hoped to get finished and published by the end of the year. But with the recent turmoil I felt about it and after yet another tussle with my mental health, I decided not to go ahead with it – *ever*! I just couldn't sign off on a few particular aspects that had been worrying me. Maybe later I would be able to move through it, but it was definitely off my agenda right now.

I now had two whole manuscripts festering in a bottom cyber draw. It was *very* confronting and undermining to my longed-for writing career. What if it became a pattern to work tirelessly and passionately on a book for two or more years only to always lose my nerve at the last minute?

I remembered seeing a documentary about an author who casually mentioned, without so much as a facial tic, how their first few books suffered the bottom drawer fate and indeed still resided there. I hadn't been able to get my head around how so much time and passion could be invested in something only to come to nothing. When I'd first heard of such things occurring it was particularly incomprehensible to me as I was still in the passionate and all encompassing throes of writing my very first book of non-fiction. Here I was joining the club, so *now* I could get my head around it. But it didn't seem to hurt so much when already working on the next book.

I wondered if I would pillage and plunder passages from my OCD book to use in this one. I'd done a bit of that Viking stuff with my first book, but that wasn't so much in a bottom drawer as in the morgue. It had no chance of revival. Despite having washed my hands of it for now, there was still a flicker of hope for the OCD book so I didn't want to pull it apart too precipitously. I did however, spy one little passage that could easily go unmissed, in fact it would be actively better without it, but would I be able to fit it neatly in to this one?

In late August, I got a request to restock my cards for an existing stockist which was a very validating experience. Selling well enough to warrant a second order meant I was over a significant hurdle.

Once again I had to wean myself off the obsessive computer checking. It had become a never ending cycle. But before I was rehabilitated and while still on one of my long-winded, eyes hanging out of my head, blog visiting benders, I happened upon the information that Leslie Saeta was again to be hosting a 30 paintings in 30 days challenge. This time my gut instinct knew immediately it was the right thing to do. The timing was particularly perfect. Now that a triumphant publishing outcome for my OCD book wasn't about to rock the world, I had been wondering on what note to end this book. Now I'd get the neat circle, 30-day-challenge, ending that had looked so flawless in January.

This 30 day challenge would be the litmus test of how much I had grown since first embarking on the challenge format in 2012. At that time a 10 day challenge with a weekend off in the middle had almost finished me off. What a lily-livered creative weakling I had been back then! I'd since done some hardening up.

I'd only seen the 30 day painting challenge first mentioned a couple of days before it was due to start, so I didn't have time to prepare anything in advance which made it extra daunting. Some bloggers were posting about their well thought out preparations in the form of primed canvasses and boards and subject choices. I would be flying by the seat of my pants. But underneath the terror I felt quietly confident that it would be well within my capabilities. I'd begun to notice how popular the challenge format was becoming in the wider world these days. Everywhere online were writing challenges, sketching challenges – not to mention cooking, photographic and even fingernail-art challenges – it was great to see.

...

I'm very happy to announce that I completed the challenge to the letter! I thoroughly enjoyed myself in the process despite coming out the other side rickety with exhaustion and looking like road-kill. Within the challenge I also achieved various other goals. I created more paintings to be used for greeting cards and I worked on producing a signature style for painting quick local beach scenes. I even managed to loosen up on some of the paintings. A wonderful aspect of the whole thing was the online camaraderie and support out there in blogland – it was *fantastic*!

Words don't come close to describing the satisfaction and empowerment I felt at discovering I was capable of painting 30 paintings in 30 days! It was something I had considered laughably impossible just a short time ago. For most of my adult life I had carried Goethe's little saying around in my head like a talisman, but it had never prepared me for the utter exhilaration that came with actually living it. I'd had many amazing moments since beginning this journey at the start of 2012 and completing the 30 day challenge was right up there with the best of them. I felt like the atoms of my very being had been rearranged, making life seem dazzling and rarefied.

Should you be interested dear reader, you will find a day by day account of my challenge in all its technicolour splendour by visiting www.wendybarrettpainting.blogspot.com and checking out the posts during September 2013.

I am yet to find out if all my efforts over the past eighteen months and more will result in being able to make a living from my creative talents. But even if they don't, I will be able to stand my ground and look my eighty year old self in the eye knowing that I gave it my all.

When I first embarked on this journey of creative self-realisation, my skills at harnessing motivation and flow were of such a primitive nature that it forced me to grab the muse by the throat. But through discipline and diligence the muse and I have grown better acquainted. Our relationship is now more civil and refined, and instead, I will send her an invitation to join me over a nice cup of tea. I make a start on my work while I wait to hear back, and she always comes – eventually.

The End

Post Script 2015

Publication for this book had been looking likely for mid-2014 until a trip to the UK and then the decline of my father's health called a halt to things for a while. Since then I've undertaken a second 30 day challenge and the successes of 2012 continue to reverberate throughout my life.

ACKNOWLEDGEMENTS

My heartfelt appreciation goes to my family and friends who have encouraged me throughout the process of writing this book. In particular, thanks go to the following people who very kindly – and bravely – read through some of my earlier drafts in order to offer insights and feedback: my husband Kevin, daughters Olivia and Lola, my mum and dad and sister Jenny, Barbara Foo, Barbara Gasson, Corinne, Yanik Kerr Nichols, Brett Kibblewhite, Heather Leane, Brunette Lenkic, Anita Logan, and April Powell-Willingham. Everyone's feedback proved essential to moving forward with improvements.

It has been a wonderful thing to have my husband Kevin's support in pursuing my creative dreams and it is greatly appreciated. My sister Jenny has been there for me at every turn throughout the book's journey. She showed great patience and diligence when reading through numerous drafts in their entirety as well as many passages and sentences in-between. Her feedback has been invaluable. My daughter Olivia has been a great sounding board for various and eclectic aspects of the book. Her wealth of insight and knowledge belie her tender years. Both of my beautiful daughters Olivia and Lola have been my muses throughout their lives and I expect that will continue for as long as I draw breath.

Last but not least my thanks go to the inscrutable Muse. I feel blessed to have her in my life.